A Living Wage
for the Forgotten Man

A Living Wage for the Forgotten Man

The Quest for Fair Labor Standards 1933–1941

George E. Paulsen

Selinsgrove: Susquehanna University Press
London: Associated University Presses

HD
8072
. P312
1996

Associated University Presses
440 Forsgate Drive
Cranbury, NJ 08512

Associated University Presses
16 Barter Street
London WC1A 2AH, England

Associated University Presses
P.O. Box 338, Port Credit
Mississauga, Ontario
Canada L5G 4L8

The paper used in this publication meets the requirements
of the American National Standard for Permanence of Paper
for Printed Library Materials Z39.48–1984.

Library of Congress Cataloging-in-Publication Data

Paulsen, George E., 1923–
    A living wage for the forgotten man : the quest for fair labor
standards, 1933–1941 / George E. Paulsen.
        p. cm.
    Includes bibliographical references and index.
    ISBN 0-945636-91-1 (alk. paper)
    1. Labor policy—United states—History—20th century. 2. United
States. Fair Labor Standards Act of 1938. 3. Wages—Law and
legislation—United States—History—20th century. 4. Hours of
labor—Law and legislation—United States—History—20th century
5. Full employment policies—United States—History—20th century.
6. New Deal, 1933–1939. I. Title.
HD8072.P312   1996
331.2′0973—dc20   96-17806
                                                              CIP

PRINTED IN THE UNITED STATES OF AMERICA

Contents

Preface

PRESIDENT Franklin D. Roosevelt called the Fair Labor Standards Act of 1938 (FLSA) the second most important New Deal reform after the Social Security Act. Yet despite the importance of the economic and social consequences of national regulation of wages, hours, and child labor, historians have paid little attention to the law. Since Congress passed it when the New Deal reform impulse was in decline, they refer to it as something of a last gasp of humanitarian reform before Roosevelt turned his attention to pressing world problems. Nevertheless, permanent peacetime regulation to eliminate "sweatshop" working conditions, limit the workweek, fix minimum wages, ban child labor, and promote purchasing-power recovery was an unprecedented violation of laissez-faire dogma and free enterprise in the nation's market place.

The FLSA should be seen as the Roosevelt administration's second attempt to promote recovery by raising wages and reducing hours. After the demise of the National Recovery Administration (NRA), the president abandoned further experimentation in government-sponsored industrial cooperation and sought to promote recovery by regulating wages and hours in order to improve the incomes of millions of industrial workers. Since mass production required mass consumption, he believed a reduction of the workweek and a ban on child labor would create jobs and reduce unemployment; raising minimum wages would stimulate consumption and improve the living standards of millions of poor workers. Although the "living-wage" concept was not originated by New Deal reformers in 1937, Roosevelt's proposal for national regulation of "fair labor standards" set off a debate over wage and hour fixing that continues to this day.

Shortly after Congress passed the FLSA, several short articles appeared covering its enactment, and *Law and Contemporary Problems* published a series of studies on its passage and provisions. Ten years later, Irving I. Paster's dissertation, "National Minimum Wage Regulation in the United States," presented a more detailed study of the FLSA and its amendment through 1948. James M. Burns in *Congress on Trial* (1949), and James T. Patterson in *Congressional Conservatism and the New Deal* (1967), briefly surveyed the congressional struggle.

7

In "Fair Labor Standards Act of 1938: Maximum Struggle for a Minimum Wage," Jonathan Grossman reviewed the struggle over the law in a short article on its fortieth anniversary. Since these studies were published, additional archival material has become available that makes possible a much better understanding of the controversial economic, social, and constitutional issues raised by the proposal for living wages.

The movement for national regulation of wages and hours began in the last year of the Hoover administration, when the American Federation of Labor (AFL) asked Congress to establish a 30-hour workweek in order to promote employment. The federation claimed that the shorter workweek would create jobs and improve living standards for as many as seven million unemployed workers. Clearly, multitudes of unemployed and poverty-stricken "forgotten men" wandering in the industrial wilderness, ill-fed, ill-housed, and ill-clothed could do little to improve purchasing power. Although Roosevelt was not committed to a 30-hour week, during his 1932 campaign he promised to help the forgotten men at the bottom of the economic pyramid and recognized their need for living wages. Nevertheless, the AFL's demand for a 30-hour week was seen as a "share the work" panacea that would do little to eliminate sweatshop standards, provide living wages, improve purchasing power, or stimulate recovery. Any law reducing the workweek would have to include provisions for minimum wages in order to maintain purchasing power and living standards.

The living-wage concept as a remedy for sweatshop labor standards and poverty became popular in America after the turn of the century. It originated in the Middle Ages, when Church fathers admonished masters to pay their workers a "just wage." In the late nineteenth century sweatshop standards in British factories stimulated a movement to require employers to pay "fair wages." Since compensation sought to provide a subsistence standard of living for a family, fair wages became known as living wages. In America prior to World War I, a number of states passed laws requiring employers to pay women and children living wages sufficient to sustain their health and well-being. But in the 1920s the Supreme Court temporarily checked the living wage movement by voiding these laws for violating "freedom of contract." Although the depression stimulated a revival of interest in state regulation of living wages, the Court's ban remained a major obstacle to either state or national regulation. Even if the constitutional prohibition could be overcome, state laws did not cover men, and there was no certainty that all states would pass any type of wage law.

Although states could exercise their "police power" to protect workers, legal scholars doubted whether Congress could use its commerce power to regulate labor standards in localities. The Supreme Court had upheld a national hours law for railroad workers, since they were clearly engaged in activities in interstate commerce. But when Congress used its commerce power to ban child labor, the Court voided the law as a violation of state power. Nevertheless, by the early 1930s a number of legal scholars thought Congress might pass a labor-standards law based upon its right to remove impediments to commerce caused by labor disputes in the states. There were doubts, however, about the willingness of Court's conservative majority to accept national regulation of local labor standards.

National wage and hour regulation would mean massive intervention in the nation's free-enterprise system. Many neoclassical economists believed regulation would curtail production, disrupt the economy, increase unemployment, and actually delay, rather than promote, recovery. Reform economists, however, questioned theories about a worker's value-added contribution to production. They argued that efficiencies in production justified higher wages and saw no threat to the economy in minimum-wage regulation covering only the poorest workers. They accepted the claim that enhancing the income of millions of the lowest paid would stimulate consumption and production and thus reduce unemployment and promote recovery. But the effect of wage and hour regulation on the economy was uncertain, since any disruption would depend on the scope of coverage and the wage and hour standards approved by Congress.

Most businessmen opposed the regulation of labor standards as an unwarranted and dangerous experiment. They were well represented by powerful trade associations and the National Association of Manufacturers (NAM). But a small minority was willing to accept regulation in order to eliminate sweatshop standards and encourage fair competition in the labor market. They were willing to accept higher standards if all employers were required to do so. Some realized that technological improvements in production had increased unemployment and were therefore willing to accept a shorter workweek, minimum wages for the poorest workers, and a ban on child labor. The alternative seemed to be a standing army of unemployed and an unbalanced budget to meet the cost of keeping them on the dole.

Organized labor was also divided on the question of regulation. Although the American Federation of Labor demanded a 30-hour week and a ban on child labor in order to expand employment, it adamantly opposed minimum-wage regulation for men. Regulation threatened collective bargaining, and conservative AFL leaders were afraid Congress would fix the maximum as well as the minimum wage. However, union leaders in mass-production industries supported wage and hour regulation as the best way to eliminate sweatshop working conditions. The split between the AFL and the Congress of Industrial Organizations (CIO) undermined support for regulation and made it impossible for administration attorneys to draft a bill satisfactory to both organizations. The administration's failure to obtain unified labor support was almost fatal to wage and hour regulation in Congress.

The proposal for national regulation also produced a party and sectional split. Sympathetic northern Democrats supported it because uniform rates would elimate the South's cheap-labor advantage and curtail the flight of "carpet-bag" industries to the southern states. But southern Democrats insisted on flexible rates and differentials in order to retain their advantage. Moreover, the powerful southern and western farm bloc opposed coverage of farm workers, both on the farm and in commodity-processing occupations near the farm. Any effort to include farm workers would have been fatal to labor-standards regulation, even though they were among the poorest paid in the nation. Such an attempt would have been constitutionaly dubious, since the Supreme Court considered farming to be a local activity subject to state regulation and beyond the reach of the commerce power.

Another problem involved the coverage of women. Although Roosevelt had promised to help forgotten men, both he and Secretary of Labor Frances Perkins supported the coverage of women and equal pay for equal work as well. State regulation of labor standards for women and children was based on its power to protect their health, safety, and welfare. Congress, however, would base its regulation on its commerce power. Since most women worked in low paid service occupations in localities, they were not engaged in activities in interstate commerce and would not be covered. Hence, initially national regulation would not help millions of poorly paid female workers. Moreover, Congress refused to accept provisions for equal pay for equal work for those women who were covered.

Because national regulation would be a novel peacetime experiment, administration attorneys disagreed over the legislative justification for a law, the agency to administer wage and hour standards, the scope of coverage, and wage and hour rates. Commerce Department officials wanted to incorporate labor-standard provisions in fair-competition agreements to be administered by the Federal Trade Commission (FTC). Justice Department attorneys thought regulation should be limited to only those industries requesting coverage in order to avoid a constitutional challenge. Labor Department officials preferred to have labor standards determined democratically by industry labor-management committees supervised by an administrator in the department. These disagreements undermined support for regulation and aided conservative opponents who claimed that some officials did not enthusiastically support regulation.

All of these problems led to a prolonged and heated fight over the FLSA when it was introduced as the Black-Connery Bill in 1937. In the view of veteran congressmen, never had Democratic party leaders defied their president as they did in the 75th Congress. Many doubted that Roosevelt would be able to rally New Deal supporters and overcome opposition to the Black-Connery Bill. But he made the necessary compromises and finally induced Congress to accept it. The FLSA was, however, far different than the purchasing-power measure the president introduced.

I would like to acknowledge the assistance provided by the staffs of the National Archives (Washington, D.C.), the Justice Department Archives, the Manuscript Division of the Library of Congress, the Franklin D. Roosevelt Library, Butler Library at Columbia University, Alexander Library at Rutgers University, Lilly Library at the University of Indiana, Dinand Library at Holy Cross College, Schlesinger Library at Radcliffe College, the State Historical Society of Colorado, and the State Historical Society of Wisconsin.

Portions of this study have appeared in different form and are reprinted with the permission of the University of Texas Press:

"Ghost of the NRA: Drafting National Wage and Hour Legislation in 1937," *Social Science Quarterly*, 67:2 (August 1986), 241–54.

"The Federal Trade Commission Versus the National Recovery Administration: Fair Trade Practices and Voluntary Codes, 1935," *Social Science Quarterly*, 70:1 (March 1989), 149–63.

This study traces the struggle for national regulation of labor standards, living wages, and purchasing-power recovery from 1933 to 1941. It makes no attempt to cover the postwar amendment of the FLSA or the continuing controversies over wage and hour regulation. These subsequent developments have been examined in other studies.

A Living Wage
for the Forgotten Man

1

By the Sweat of Thy Brow

Masters, give unto your servants that which is just and equal;
knowing that ye also have a Master in heaven.

—Colossians 4:1

FOR centuries Christian fathers in western Europe recognized the right of a working man to a "just wage" and to an income sufficient to maintain himself and his family. Inherent in the just-wage concept was the moral condemnation of unmerited and unnecessary poverty and recognition of the right of workers to their share of nature's bounty. Church fathers accepted a just wage as a natural right superior to man-made laws. Justice, St. Thomas Aquinas taught, required both a fair price for commodities and a just wage for labor.[1]

Although Church fathers advocated a just wage, during the Middle Ages wages were controlled by local custom until the disintegration of the feudal order induced western European governments to regulate them. In Elizabethan England Parliament authorized justices of the peace to set minimum wages locally for poorly paid workers to assure them an adequate income for their labor. But as a result of rapid industrialization, by the early nineteenth century unskilled workers were reduced to almost unbearable poverty. Parliament again responded with factory legislation regulating child labor, sanitary conditions, and working hours for women and for the very young. Nevertheless, continued industrialization produced a surplus of unskilled workers who could not easily be organized by labor unions. They were exploited by unscrupulous employers who required excessive hours, paid wages insufficient to meet the needs of the worker and his family, and maintained working conditions that endangered public health. By the end of the century the evils of this "sweating" system induced humanitarian reformers to organize a campaign for government regulation of wages and hours so that the most oppressed workers could earn a "living wage" at a minimum-subsistence level.[2]

Concerned about industrial evils, injustice, and the spread of socialism, Church fathers transformed the medieval just wage into the living-wage concept. In his encyclical *Rerum Novarum* (1891), Pope Leo XIII recognized the right of everyone to procure what was necessary to live. The dictates of nature, he insisted, were more imperious and ancient than any bargain between master and servant, and required an income sufficient to support the worker and his family in reasonable, if frugal, comfort. If an employer forced his workers to accept harsh conditions, the Church would consider them to be the victims of fraud and injustice. Archbishop Henry Edward Manning of Westminster considered the worker's right to subsistence superior to the right of property.[3]

Concern about obtaining living wages for sweated workers in Great Britain was also stimulated by labor protests, reports on factory conditions, and the activities of women's organizations. Beginning in 1889 local school boards responded to protests over low salaries for teachers by adopting "fair-wage" resolutions. The House of Commons initially approved resolutions favoring living wages for government employees, and after the turn of the century Parliament made the government the "model employer" by adopting the living-wage principle. It also passed the Trade Boards Act (1909), which authorized labor-management boards to set wages in sweated industries. And under the Fair Wage Clause (1909) it required government contractors to accept local prevailing wages. After years of labor trouble in the mines, it also approved the Coal Mines Minimum Wage Act (1912). Although none of the rates set by the boards came close to union "standard wages" and barely met a "human-needs" level, they improved the income of workers in some poorly paid trades. But despite limited progress in the prewar period, several million families lived at or below the "poverty standard."[4]

In America rapid industrialization created social problems and labor disorders very similar to those in Britain, Australia, New Zealand, and western Europe. American reformers were aware of the trade-board laws adopted by these countries but were unable to secure uniform national legislation because regulation of labor activities was primarily the responsibility of the states under their "police powers." Prior to the Civil War a few states began to regulate child labor and the workday in industrial occupations, but with limited success because the laws were inadequately enforced. After the war organized labor and humanitarian reformers were more successful in inducing the states to restrict child labor and the workweek for women in industrial occupations. A number of states also accepted effective legislation limiting hours for men in dangerous occupations in the transportation, mining, smelting, and refining industries.[5]

The Populist movement and the Depression of 1893 intensified the public's concern about unemployment, labor problems, and social justice. Reports on factory standards exposed the evils of the sweating system and shockingly low incomes, particularly for women and children. These studies also revealed that millions of workers existed close to the poverty line. Most workers averaged about 60 hours a week during the 1890s. Those in organized trades might make as much as $18 weekly, or about $900 annually, but many of the unskilled made less than $12.50, or $625 annually, and the average for all workers in manufacturing was about $490. Urban workers needed an annual income of from $600 to $800 to maintain a "reasonable" or "minimum standard" of living for a family of five. Prices for food and clothing were low, but many families were subsisting near the poverty line.[6]

Although the courts upheld state laws setting the workday for women, children, and workers in dangerous occupations, such legislation did nothing to improve their income. The courts had accepted the regulation of the workday in order to protect the health and safety of employees and the public, but there seemed little hope that they would uphold legislation requiring employers to pay wages that would guarantee workers minimum-subsistence wages. Employers would certainly challenge wage regulation as a violation of "liberty of contract" as implied in the due process clause of the Fourteenth Amendment. However, since the exploitation of women and children had become notorious, some reformers thought the courts might be willing to abandon absolute freedom of contract and to accept state minimum-wage regulation for at least women and children in order to protect their health and morals.[7]

The movement for living wages for women and children got underway after the turn of the century. Studies revealed that more than half of all working women earned less than $6 a week, or $300 annually, and somehow managed to maintain themselves at a pauper standard, which was anything less than $500 for a family. Responding to the need, the National Consumers' League (NCL), the Women's Trade Union League, the American Federation of Labor and the Federal Council of Churches of Christ launched a campaign for state minimum-wage regulation.[8]

As evidence of the evils of the sweating system accumulated, support for living wages became quite respectable, even though there was little agreement on the annual income needed to maintain a reasonable standard of living. The Council of Churches' social creed recommended "living wages at the highest level an employer could afford." AFL President Samuel Gompers thought a wage should maintain a family "in a manner that society recognized as indispensable to physical and mental health or as required by national respect of human beings." Unrestricted competition, he explained, should not reduce workers to conditions of slavery or starvation abhorrent to all those moved by a sense of social justice.[9]

Other reformers offered more specific standards for defining a living wage. Professor Simon Patten suggested a standard beyond a subsistence minimum. A worker, he argued, had a right to a home, a family, self-development, leisure, recreation, cleanliness, and "the development of the beautiful." President John Mitchell of the United Mine Workers (UMW) recommended an "American standard," which also went beyond a mere-subsistence minimum. A worker and his family, Mitchell believed, should have a six-room house, including a bathroom, kitchen, dining room, parlor, and bedroom to provide decency and comfort. They should have enough income for food, clothing, furniture, carpets, pictures, and books. Children should be in school until sixteen years of age. An annual income of at least $600 would maintain this American standard and anything less would not be a living wage. The sociologist Albion W. Small of the University of Chicago suggested a higher minimum as well as a maximum-annual income. No worker, he argued, could take care of his family on an annual income of less than $1,000, nor should anyone earn more than $50,000, the president's salary. These idealistic, if not romantic, conceptions of the American standard of living undoubtedly appealed to exploited workers and reformers interested in social justice, but they were visionary, given the entrenched power of employers and the constitutional limitations on state police power.[10]

In the Theodore Roosevelt administration, however, reformers were encouraged when the Supreme Court revealed a willingness to uphold state regulation of hours for women and children. Although it voided a New York 10-hour-day law for bakers in *Lochner* v. *New York* (1905) as a violation of freedom of contract, in *Muller* v. *Oregon* (1908) the "Brandeis Brief" induced it to accept the Oregon hours law for women as a valid exercise of the state's power to protect their health and well-being. Encouraged by the Court's acceptance of the brief, the Consumers' League and other reform organizations intensified their campaign for state regulation of wages for women and children on the same ground. If statistics could convince the Court that state regulation of hours was valid, they might convince it that regulation of wages was equally valid.[11]

As the Progressive reform campaign reached flood tide in 1912, the movement for wage regulation gained increasing public support. Former President Roosevelt accepted living wages, and as the candidate for the Progressive party he endorsed minimum-wage laws. President Woodrow Wilson told the nation that the state was responsible for applying strict principles of equity and justice. The employer who objected to paying a living wage, he intoned, denied the bread of life to the needy and was a man of blood. After years of agitation, the National Consumers' League and other reformers finally induced the legislature of Massachusetts to accept the nation's first minimum-wage law for women and children in 1912. The law not only set a precedent, but was equally important as a model for other states and later for the national government as well.[12]

The weak nonmandatory Massachusetts law established an industrial commission to supervise industry boards composed of employer, employee, and public representatives. Upon complaint, the boards investigated labor standards, held hearings on living costs and industry conditions, and recommended wage rates to maintain a minimum-subsistence standard. When approved by the commission, the nonmandatory rates became the industry minimum, to be "enforced" by public opinion. Nonmandatory enforcement reflected the uncertainty about the constitutionality of this innovative legislation. Despite the uncertainty, ten additional states passed wage laws before the Supreme Court considered their constitutionality. In *Stettler* v. *O'Hara*(1917) the Court, split 4-to-4, upheld the Oregon law and recognized the right of the state to protect the health and morals of women. Thereafter six additional states passed similar laws before the movement was checked in the 1920s.[13]

Reformers won another victory when the Court upheld Oregon's law regulating hours for men and women in industrial occupations. In *Bunting* v. *Oregon* (1917) it sustained the pay-and-one-half requirement for overtime beyond ten hours. Despite the overtime-pay provision, the Court upheld the law as a measure regulating hours, ignored the *Lochner* precedent, and accepted the state's claim that the statute was a health measure. Although it approved the wage provision, there was no guarantee that it would uphold wage regulation for men and women in the future if the challenge to liberty of contract was more direct and if the health and safety justification was less so.[14]

In the period prior to World War I prospects for minimum-wage regulation for men seemed dim. In addition to the constitutional roadblock, reformers would have to overcome both public indifference and labor hostility. If the public accepted wage regulation for women and children in order to protect their health and morals, there seemed little chance that it would accept regulation for men on the same basis. More serious was the outright hostility of the AFL. President Gompers and other union leaders supported laws for women and children to protect the family and to keep them out of the labor market, but they were adamantly opposed to the regulation of men's wages. A minimum wage, they argued, would become the maximum when employers compensated for raising the minimum by lowering higher rates. Despite the AFL's opposition to government wage-fixing, the national railroad brotherhoods won an emergency wage increase under the Adamson Act (1916). Congress forestalled a strike by establishing an 8-hour day for carriers in interstate commerce and by forbidding them from reducing wages below those in effect for the longer day. In *Wilson* v. *New* (1917) the Court accepted the wage-fixing provision as temporary and necessary, because the unions and carriers had failed to exercise their bargaining rights. But once again, although the Court had accepted an emergency increase, there was no indication that it would abandon liberty of contract in the future.[15]

America's entry in World War I soon required government regulation of industrial and labor relations on an unprecedented scale. Exercising its war powers, Congress authorized President Wilson to reorganize government agencies and to regulate agriculture and industry during the war emergency. Inflation led to a substantial rise in living costs and a corresponding decline in real wages. High labor turnover, wage discrepancies in various industries, and labor disputes induced Wilson to set up the National War Labor Board (NWLB) in order to maintain production for the war effort. Formulating an emergency labor policy, the board adopted guidelines on labor standards and working conditions for all government agencies. In order to maintain prewar real wages, NWLB mediation committees approved an 8-hour day and living wages that would maintain their families in health and comfort.[16]

During the war and after the armistice, street-railway arbitration boards applied labor standards adopted by the NWLB. They refused to consider workers as a commodity whose wages should be based on supply and demand. A Connecticut board defined a living wage as an income that would provide a family with good food, warm clothing, decent homes, and medical care and recreation. A Massachusetts board said that under the law of supply and demand strikes over inadequate wages led to interruption of transportation and possible disorder, which was not in the public interest. These decisions sustained minimum-wage regulation as a practical way to settle disputes over the adequacy of worker's incomes.[17]

Since budget studies were necessary for fixing living wages, Columbia University economist William F. Ogburn determined the cost of living in 1918–19 for a family of four at a subsistence and a comfort level. The subsistence standard required an annual income of $1,386 for bare "necessities," below which a family would live in poverty. An income of $1,760.50 would maintain it at a comfort level, providing for necessities, recreation, and education. A more recent study of those budgets devised a "poverty band" consisting of minimum subsistence, minimum adequacy, and minimum comfort standards based on differences between the income of unskilled and skilled workers. The minimum comfort income was also called the "American Health and Decency" standard. A postwar study revealed that 75 percent of the workers surveyed had annual incomes of less than $1,575, which was below the minimum adequacy level. Royal Meeker, chief of the Bureau of Labor Statistics, doubted whether many workers were enjoying a health and comfort standard and said the postwar goal should be an effort to raise them to that level. But the National Industrial Conference Board called the standard a visionary ideal that did not reflect prevailing conditions.[18]

In the immediate postwar period the country went through a difficult economic adjustment brought on by demobilization and by the conversion of industry to peacetime production. Organized labor came out of the war determined not only to preserve the gains it had won, but prepared to fight for additional concessions. After the demise of the NWLB and a year of strikes and disorder, in October 1919 President Wilson convened a National Industrial Conference composed of labor, employer, and public representatives to consult on a program of labor-management cooperation to meet the industrial emergency. Organized labor called for labor-management boards in each industry to make recommendations for labor standards. Employers emphasized individual liberty, freedom of contract, the "open shop," and a limitation on strikes. Both, however, accepted a living wage, equal pay for women, a 6-day workweek, and discouragement of overtime. The conference failed when the employers rejected collective bargaining, but the chaotic situation induced Wilson to call a second session in December.[19]

The December conference recommended a plan for the settlement of disputes with a minimum of government regulation. Congress would create a national industrial board and regional boards of inquiry for the settlement of disputes, but the proposal did not suggest mandatory guidelines. It suggested adjudication of disputes, employee representation, collective bargaining, a 6-day-48-hour workweek, equal pay for women, prohibition of child labor, and wages to maintain the worker's family at the reasonable-comfort standard. Since reliable information about the cost of living was necessary for the determination of wages, it urged the government to extend its reporting on the cost of living and family budgets. If wages fell below the reasonable comfort level for any length of time, labor strife threatened the well-being of the state. If wages fell to the subsistence level, the public was exposed to dangerous discontent.[20]

President Wilson supported labor's demand for minimum-comfort standard wages. Workers, he told Congress in January, needed wages sufficient to live in comfort, unhampered by fear of poverty and want in old age. They deserved sanitary conditions in the home and the workplace, and an income sufficient for their children's health and education. AFL President Gompers objected to basing wages on cost-of-living budgets. Basing wages on the cost of living alone, he said, was pernicious and intolerable because living standards would remain fixed, and workers would no longer accept wages based on family budgets and bread bills. Workers, he argued, were entitled to more than a bare living and should obtain a fairer reward for their contribution to society.[21]

While the conference was considering its recommendations, the Senate Committee on Education and Labor investigated the 1919 steel strike and suggested creating a board similar to the War Labor Board to settle management-labor disputes. The industrial board would supervise compulsory investigations, but there would be no compulsory arbitration. It would accept collective bargaining and an 8-hour day in making recommendations, which would be endorsed by public opinion. The majority of people, the committee believed, accepted living wages that would permit families to enjoy the American standard of life.[22] Committee Chairman William S. Kenyon of Iowa urged Congress to accept a national industrial code. He wanted a national industrial congress to draft a code of standards to govern industrial relations and working standards.[23] His proposal was dropped because of the press of other legislation. Although Congress declined to create a national labor board for all industry, in February 1920 it passed the Esch-Cummins Transportation Act, which returned railroads to private control and established a Railroad Labor Board for the adjustment of wage standards. Congress stipulated that wages would be "just and reasonable" and authorized sectional boards to consider wages for similar work in other industries and the relation of wages to the cost of living. In August the Railroad Labor Board approved a 22-percent increase in wages, which the employees accepted even though they deemed it inadequate. After the 1921-22 recession, it approved wage reductions, the unions went on strike, and President Warren G. Harding arranged mediation. Thereafter, both labor and the carriers became dissatisfied with the board's adjudication, and

Congress passed the Railway Labor Act of 1926, which abolished the board and provided for mediation and conciliation.[24] Repudiated by both labor and management, the first peacetime experiment in the adjustment of wage standards in a declining industry floundered ignominiously.

Despite the failure of the Railroad Labor Board experiment, unemployment and violence in the coal fields in 1922 led to a constitutionally significant bill to regulate the industry. Senator Kenyon sponsored a bill which recognized that the production and distribution of coal was a public necessity and that Congress could exercise its commerce power to eliminate local disputes that interfered with the production and distribution of coal. Consequently, Congress would create a coal-mining board that would resolve them on the basis of a code of standards outlined in his bill.

When a labor dispute threatened to disrupt commerce, it would hold hearings and set "just and reasonable" wages. It would guarantee capital a fair return, recognize the right of miners to organize and bargain, and accept the right of workers to a living wage sufficient to maintain a family in health and reasonable comfort. A 6-day week and an 8-hour day would be the standard.[25] Kenyon's bill was attacked as inadequate because the board lacked the power to enforce its rulings. Although it was shelved, it suggested a code of rights as a solution for labor-management problems and offered a constitutional justification for national regulation of local working conditions.

Before there could be any agreement on a code of labor standards, there would have to be agreement on production efficiency, cost-of-living factors, maintenance budgets, and living wages. During the depression of 1921 there was considerable disagreement among labor leaders, engineers, and economists over these questions. Labor's campaign for an 8-hour day was criticized on the ground that shorter hours were not necessary for human welfare, since a shorter workday might not sustain living wages. What was needed was employment at "going wages" regularly paid. Moreover, some engineers challenged labor's claim that greater efficiency and the elimination of waste justified an 8-hour workday.[26] And many distinguished economists were critical of the production-efficiency theory of wage determination.

John R. Commons of the University of Wisconsin said the productive-efficiency argument for higher wages was meaningless because "value productivity" ignored cycles of overproduction and could be increased by cutting production. Herbert Feis of the University of Kansas thought the relation of wages to production was indirect because it was impossible to determine the contribution of any group of workers to total production. George Soule of the *The New*

Republic noted that real wages had not increased despite greater productivity, because the connection between productivity and wages was not close enough to act as a stimulus. Whether higher productivity resulted in higher wages, he said, depended on both economic factors and social control.[27]

Economists were also critical of the cost-of-living factor as the basis for determining living wages. Commons found it obnoxious because it gave workers no share of increasing wealth. Feis said it was mathematically impossible to determine a standardized cost of living. Minimum wages, he said, were based on compromise and were influenced by public opinion. The living-wage concept was ethical rather than economic, since the public was not concerned about the value of services rendered but instead wanted a wage that would maintain a worker at a socially acceptable standard of living. William F. Ogburn, a budget expert, noted considerable confusion in the relation of wages to the cost of living. There was disagreement over living wages because of confusion over subsistence and comfort standards of living. It was necessary to differentiate between actual and standard budgets and to recognize the difference in costs in many communities. The idea of a just wage is family maintenance, and he found many workers trying to live on less than living wages. Abraham Epstein, the champion of social security, agreed that only organized workers had incomes that met increased living costs as opposed to the mass of workers. Although Paul H. Douglas accepted the living-wage principal, he doubted the practicality of setting uniform-minimum wages. Such a standard, he believed, would be too great a drain on the national income.[28]

Samuel A. Lewisohn, a New York industrialist, found the living-wage concept something of a "rhetorical half-truth," since it was based on the comfort-income factor but ignored national income. There was too much emphasis on family budgets and too little on national productivity. The living-wage movement, he warned, was endangered because the national income was being ignored. The failure to include it in the determination of wages would raise false hopes about the policy in the public mind.[29] These economists accepted the need to improve the worker's standard of living, but were concerned about the effect of living wages on production efficiency and the national income. All of these problems raised serious doubts living wages as a remedy for poverty, but they were soon made irrelevant by the Supreme Court, which dealt the movement a stunning blow.

In *Adkins* v. *Childrens' Hospital* (1923) the Supreme Court once again sanctified freedom of contract and voided the District of Columbia's women's wage law. Justice George Sutherland said the law was class legislation, distinguished laws setting hours from those fixing wages, and suggested that the Nineteenth Amendment had eliminated the differences between men and women. He found no basis for the claim that minimum-wage laws safeguarded the morals of women. Moreover, while regulation protected employees, it ignored the principle that the worker should receive a just equivalent for the services rendered. And if Congress could fix minimum wages, it could fix maximum wages as well. The minority opinion condemned the majority for voiding the law on the basis that it was unwise or unsound. Long hours and low wages were equally harmful to the health and well-being of female workers. And there were many economic theories for determining the value of the labor performed.[30] Since the *Adkins* decision was the law of the land, the implication was that all state minimum-wage laws were also unconstitutional.

Amid a chorus of criticism of the *Adkins* decision led by the National Consumers' League, the courts voided six state laws and only the Massachusetts nonmandatory law was upheld. A few states tried to secure compliance without prosecuting employers for violations, while some employers voluntarily paid the minimum wage because regulation had helped eliminate sweatshop competition. In 1925 Wisconsin passed a new law that sought to comply with the Court's holding that employees receive just compensation for services rendered. Instead of requiring employers to pay a living wage based on the cost of living, the law prohibited them from paying a woman an "oppressive wage," an amount less than reasonable and adequate for services rendered.[31]

The oppressive-wage concept was an important contribution in the campaign for minimum-wage regulation. It suggested that state legislatures might use their police powers in the interest of the community by authorizing labor commissions to determine "fair" and "unfair" wages for services rendered. Given the controversy over the theories for determining the value of labor performed, however, they would have as much of a problem fixing minimum wages on that factor as they did to meet the cost of living. Initially, the Wisconsin commission was able to secure substantial compliance without risking a test case, which it was reluctant to do because of the Supreme Court's hostility to wage regulation. The Court demonstrated it once again when it voided a New Jersey law regulating employment agency fees in *Ribnik* v. *McBride* (1928). It not only denied the state the right to eliminate abuses in employment agency operations, but also insisted that, in the absence of any grave emergency, fixing prices, rents, or wages was beyond legislative power.[32]

Although the Supreme Court limited effective regulation of

women's wages to the brief period from 1912 and 1923, the experiment was of some value. Experience with state regulation helped convince more ethical employers that sweatshop competition could be eliminated. Such laws also induced the public to accept the regulation of private enterprise when it understood the need to help exploited women and children obtain at least a subsistence income. State commissions also gained experience in formulating family budgets and in fixing wages to provide subsistence-living standards. And experience indicated that sweatshop wages could be raised without causing serious problems for the industries regulated.[33]

The brief experiment also revealed that state commissions worked under serious handicaps. Statistics were inadequate for formulating budgets and for setting standard wages, and the commissions could not work rapidly enough to keep minimum wages in line with increases in the cost of living. If regulation improved wages somewhat in sweatshop occupations, the effect of such increases on the income of all workers was impossible to determine. Moreover, it was impossible to determine whether fixing wages for certain classes of women improved the income of many other disadvantaged workers. Studies in the 1920s revealed that millions of women received less than subsistence wages, and of these, black women suffered the most, receiving half the amount of poorly paid white women. Since the laws had done little to raise living standards, mass production and improved purchasing power were more likely to raise living standards than wage regulation. But there was no guarantee that mass production would improve the purchasing power of workers without collective bargaining and agreement on income distribution.[34]

In 1923 the economy improved and the nation soon entered the era of "Coolidge prosperity," which was based on both business expansion and considerable reckless speculation. To a large degree, the prosperity was corporate, and while real wages of many employees improved, some industries declined, and millions of workers were unable to improve their standard of living. Despite an overall rise in standards, large numbers of workers continued to live in precarious economic circumstances. Approximately 76 percent of them were unable to save anything from their wages and had no property of any kind. In the era of Coolidge prosperity all farm workers; half of those in mining, industrial, and clerical employment; and one-third of those in transportation, trade, and public service had incomes that barely met the cost of living. Only 25 percent of those employed were able to purchase the goods produced through greater industrial efficiency, while about 65 percent of the population had not benefited from prosperity or had incomes inadequate to maintain a health-and-comfort standard of living.[35]

Because of the inability of millions of workers to improve their standard of living, the AFL emphasized the need to have wage increases based on improvements in production. AFL President William Green, who succeeded Gompers in 1924, insisted that the living wage, the savings wage, and the cost of living concepts were too intangible and indefinite to be used as a basis for determining an adequate income. Labor's reward, Green said, should reflect labor's contribution to increased production. AFL Vice President John P. Frey agreed on the obsolescence of rhetoric. "A fair day's pay for a fair day's work" and the "value of labor," he argued, were slogans too uncertain for determining wages. Workers were less able to buy what they produced then they had been twenty-five years earlier. Increases in production, he warned, must be accompanied by increases in purchasing power, and industry would have to recognize that its welfare depended upon increasing wages.[36]

In the euphoria of prosperity even many businessmen realized that expanding industry depended on improving worker's incomes. President Samuel M. Vauclain of the Baldwin Locomotive Company believed that the country's economy depended upon the worker's ability to purchase products of all kinds and not merely the basic necessities of life. Owen D. Young, chairman of the board of General Motors, thought higher wage levels were entirely consistent with declining prices. Accepting a "cultural wage," he said employees should be able to take advantage of cultural opportunities to enrich their lives. Needless-to-say, President Coolidge also endorsed high-wage prosperity. The American people, he said, should be so well paid that "they could afford to meet the price of prosperity." Recognizing the need to maintain purchasing power, many prominent businessmen accepted what was known as "the economy of high wages." They were quite happy to have other employers increase wages in order to keep the economy prosperous.[37]

While much lip service was paid to the high-wage theory during the era of Coolidge prosperity, income studies revealed that many workers were not only unable to purchase many of the goods produced, but were actually living in precarious economic conditions. Increased productivity had benefited employers rather than labor by a ratio of 5 to 1. About 3 million were out of work, and of those employed, perhaps one-third received less than a living wage. According to one study, of approximately 30 million workers, about 8 million men in nonagricultural work received an average annual income of less than $1,250 and 2 million women earned less than $700 annually. A Brookings Institution study revealed that of 27.4 million families, 6 million, or 21 percent, had annual incomes of less than $1,000, 12 million, or 42 percent, had less than $1,500, and 20 million, or 71 percent, had less than $2,500. Despite the overall prosperity, the real wages of a majority of families had fallen below the comfort standard, which in 1927 was about $2,050. Since millions had incomes as much as $600 below the cost of living, poverty had become a plague in the richest nation on earth, as was revealed by a substantial increase in relief expenditures.[38]

Economic conditions and wage and hour standards were particularly appalling in the textile and bituminous coal industries. In southern mills the workweek ranged from 60 to 72 hours, women and children over fourteen worked at night, and state protective regulation was ignored. By 1928 there was a wage differential of about 44 percent favoring the southern mills, whose employees earned an average income of $671 per year as compared with $1,012 nationally. Southern employers defended the low incomes, suggesting that cheap company housing and lower costs of living justified the differential, an argument that was disputed by other southern critics of the industry. Excessively long hours, the "stretch out," and other sweating practices led to violent strikes, which were brutally suppressed by local police officers and state troops. Those employees who were not blacklisted were thereafter happy to accept whatever the mill owners were willing to pay.[39]

Conditions in the bituminous coal industry were equally bad, if not worse. Because of increases in output and overcapacity after 1920, the price of coal dropped drastically during the decade. Fiercely competing operators cut labor costs and earnings fell 23 percent by 1929. The 8-hour day moved up to 10 hours and safety standards deteriorated. When the United Mine Workers refused to accept wage cuts, the operators launched a campaign to destroy the union. The result was a labor war in Pennsylvania that became a national scandal and the subject of a Senate investigation. On the initiative of the UMW, Senator James E. Watson of Indiana sponsored a bill in 1928 to stabilize the industry. It was based on the premise that coal mining was an indispensable service maintaining public health and safety. Congress would therefore exercise its commerce power to create a bituminous coal commission, legalize marketing pools, license coal companies to operate in interstate commerce, and require them to accept labor's right to organize and bargain. Mine operators objected to the proposal on constitutional grounds and Congress took no action on it. But the proposal to regulate the industry remained popular with the UMW and the legislation was revived later in the Hoover administration.[40]

Maldistribution of income and rapidly rising charity expenditures by the end of the Coolidge administration should have alerted businessmen to a change in the business cycle. But in the euphoria of prosperity many of them thought the economy would continue to expand and ignored Cassandras crying in the wilderness. President Coolidge assured the public that the blessings of prosperity stemmed from the integrity and character of the American people, rather than from credit and speculation. America's "greatest secretary of commerce," Herbert Hoover, fully shared the president's confidence in the economy and in its ability to eliminate poverty throughout the land. Hoover had great faith in "American individualism" and in the ability of business and labor leaders to cooperate in overcoming their problems. Convinced of the virtues of decentralized authority, he opposed the extension of federal power and was committed to the policy of cooperation, guided by the government. Since he opposed government regulation, he supported trade-association efforts to eliminate business abuses that might otherwise warrant regulation. In nominating Hoover for the presidency, the Republican party offered a leader whose philosophy, experience, and accomplishments seemed ideal for the nation's quest to eliminate poverty. But unfortunately for those who had faith in rugged individualism, the invisible hand had some wrenching adjustments in store for the American people.[41]

Historians agree that President Hoover was not responsible for the excessive credit expansion and reckless speculation that undermined investor confidence in the economy and that led to the stock market crash in 1929. Initially, Hoover looked upon the following economic slump as a natural correction in the business cycle that would eventually restore a proper equilibrium. He opposed direct government intervention in the economy and sought to maintain confidence in its fundamental soundness. Through a series of well-publicized conferences in the winter of 1929, he secured pledges from business and labor leaders to stimulate business, stabilize employment, increase construction activities, and hold the line on wages. During the first year of the recession, his program of voluntary cooperation was well received by the public.[42]

Despite his efforts, Hoover's program failed to deter the business liquidation that he sought to arrest. Although many large employers maintained wages in 1930, almost from the beginning many small companies began cutting pay and laying off employees. The economy turned sharply downward, business failures set new records, manufacturing declined, and factory payrolls, commodity prices, and retail trade went down. By 1931 bankers faced serious liquidation problems, became critical of efforts to maintain price levels and wage rates, and demanded a reduction of pay scales. Hoover organized the President's Emergency Committee for Employment and supported an expanded public-works program[43]

Because of Hoover's reluctance to consider reform legislation, Sen. Robert F. Wagner of New York, who was committed to welfare-state principles, introduced legislation to stimulate employment, which he believed was essential for the country's stability. In 1930 he sponsored a public-works bill for employment stabilization, another for statistical surveys of unemployment, and a third for an expansion of the nation's employment exchanges. Hoover accepted the public works and unemployment-survey measures, but vetoed the employment-exchanges bill on the grounds that it would disrupt the existing system. After Republican losses in the 1930 election, he responded to mounting criticism of his Emergency Committee for Employment's failure to cope with the unemployment problem by reorganizing it as the President's Organization on Unemployment Relief. But by 1931 many business leaders were convinced that voluntary cooperation had failed to relieve the economic emergency and that direct-government action was necessary.[44]

There were a flood of suggestions for restoring economic stability and for coping with the economic crisis. Gerard Swope, president of the General Electric Company, recommended a national council to coordinate the self-governing trade-association organization of industries in interstate commerce. Both the financier Bernard Baruch and Henry I. Harriman, president of the U.S. Chamber of Commerce, endorsed trade-association industrial self-government. Stuart Chase, a liberal economist, also favored industrial cooperation for planned production and regulation of minimum wages and maximum hours. In 1931 a "Progressive Conference" of businessmen, labor leaders, economists, and social workers considered proposals for industrial stabilization, unemployment relief, tariff revision, public power, and agriculture. AFL President Green recommended a 5-day week to provide jobs for the unemployed. No program was adopted, but committees were established to formulate recommendations.[45]

During the 1920s the AFL had demanded a 5-day-40-hour workweek through collective bargaining but only a few trade unions had been able to achieve it. Because of mounting unemployment, the train-service brotherhoods launched a campaign for a 6-hour day and a 30-hour workweek. After watching its membership drop to a low of 2.9 million by 1932, even conservative AFL leaders were ready to abandon the union's traditional policy of self-reliance and to seek government support for labor's objectives. Since collective bargaining was crippled and strikes were hopeless, in 1932 the AFL asked Congress to establish a 30-hour workweek. Its campaign was supported by Secretary of Labor William M. Doak, and Senator Hugo L. Black of Alabama and Rep. Charles A. Karch of Illinois initially sponsored the AFL 30-hour bill. Although the federation accepted government regulation of the workweek as a panacea for unemployment, it remained utterly opposed to wage-fixing.[46]

During the election campaign in the fall of 1932, the American people were offered the choice of continuing Hoover's policy of voluntary cooperation, or abandoning rugged individualism and accepting government intervention and regulation. Democratic candidate Franklin D. Roosevelt condemned Hoover's policy of cooperation for aiding those who controlled the economy and ignoring the "forgotten men" at the bottom of the economic pyramid. He offered the people a rather vague "new deal" and promised government action to help those forgotten men and women whose lives had been blighted by the depression. Although he endorsed a shorter workweek, just what specific policies his administration might adopt were not clear. But the majority of voters were not concerned about specifics. Given the choice of continuing voluntary cooperation or accepting the vague promise of a New Deal, they voted against Hoover and American individualism. By doing so, they repudiated a president who had done more that any previous executive to reverse a depression. But unfortunately for Hoover, his policy had failed to overcome the worst economic collapse the American people had ever experienced. And in the dreadful winter of 1932–33 the economy hit rock bottom as a result of a banking crisis that put people in the wealthiest country on Earth on the bartering system. It also put fear in their hearts and induced a substantial number to abandon their faith in laissez faire.[47]

Nothing was accomplished by Congress in the "lame-duck" session after the election, but Senator Black and William P. Connery of Massachusetts, chairman of the House Labor Committee, cosponsored bills to establish a uniform national 30-hour workweek. Almost identical in two short sections, the Black-Connery bills prohibited the interstate shipment of the product of any mine or manufacturing establishment in which any person worked more than 30 hours a week. Connery's bill extended the prohibition to imported products. There were no provisions for wages, child labor, administrative machinery, flexibility, or discretion. Startling in their simplicity and economic implications, the bills were patterned on the First Child Labor Act of 1916, were based upon a broad interpretation of the commerce power, and were a direct challenge to the Supreme Court's more narrow holding in *Hammer* v. *Dagenhart* (1918), which voided the law. Before Hoover left office, the Senate Judiciary Committee held hearings on Black's bill under the sympathetic chairmanship of Senator George Norris, the Nebraska progressive Republican.[48]

The Judiciary Committee heard fifty-four labor leaders, businessmen, economists, engineers, and attorneys on the 30-hour workweek proposal. Almost all agreed that industrial technology had created grave economic and employment problems, but a considerable number of them did not accept a reduction of the workweek as some kind of miraculous panacea. Most union leaders supported the bill, but were divided on the issue of wage guarantees. President Green thought the 30-hour week would put at least 6.5 million back to work and suggested that the Court might be willing to reconsider its adverse holding in the *Dagenhart* case. The AFL lobbyist William C. Hushing said the federation would not support a minimum wage because employers would make it the maximum, but UMW Vice President Phil Murray and Emil Rieve of the Hosiery Workers endorsed it.[49]

Businessmen also gave conflicting advice to the committee. The National Association of Manufacturers general counsel James A. Emery condemned the bill as a violation of state jurisdiction, citing the *Employers' Liability Cases* (1908), which denied the national government any right to regulate business within the state. He also insisted that any attempt to add a wage clause to the bill would defy the Court's holding in the *Adkins* case, and Black agreed that the only way to overcome that prohibition was through a constitutional amendment. Clarence A. Miller, counsel for the American Short Line Railroad Association, argued that the Court would not abandon the *Dagenhart* holding because of depressed economic conditions. Other attorneys, however, disagreed. The UMW counsel Henry Warrum cited *Gibbons* v. *Ogden* (1824) to affirm the right of Congress to regulate activities related to interstate commerce within the state. Benjamin Marsh, representing the Joint Committee on Unemployment, said there were justices on the Court who could follow the breadlines as well as the election returns. And not all businessmen opposed the bill. A number of representatives from the hard-pressed textile and hosiery industries endorsed it, with or without wage guarantees.[50]

Conservative and reform economists disagreed on the probable effects of a reduced workweek. Professor Wilford I. King of New York University was afraid that a shorter workweek would delay recovery, but Brown University's George E. Bigge said that economic conditions had changed and that some plan would have to take up the slack in employment. The UMW economist W. Jett Lauck also supported the bill. Clearly, the committee received conflicting advice about the effect of a reduced workweek upon the economy.[51]

Despite the doubts as to the bill's constitutionality and its effect on the economy and wages, the committee recommended it to the Senate. Representative Connery's Labor Committee heard many of the same witnesses, received much the same information, and also approved it. The 30-hour week, his committee claimed, would help millions of the unemployed, improve purchasing power, and eliminate the dole. It was quite willing to leave the question of constitutionality to the Supreme Court. Since there was no time to consider the Black-Connery bills so late in the lame-duck season, they had to be carried over to the new Congress. The hearings, nevertheless, publicized the shorter workweek as a remedy for the unemployment problem.[52]

Although the Black-Connery bills raised serious economic and constitutional questions, by the winter of 1932–33 the employment problem seemed to warrant some kind of government intervention in the labor-market place. Not only had unemployment risen to approximately 14.4 million, but widespread wage cuts, work-sharing, part-time work, and the dole had greatly reduced purchasing power and living standards. Extensive unemployment and severe wage-cutting made it possible for sweatshop employers to exploit workers at long hours for low pay. All workers suffered, but none more than women and children, particularly those in sweated industries. Despite some improvement in child-labor regulation, in 1930 the Children's Bureau found over 431,000 fourteen- or fifteen-year-old children, as well as over 235,000 under the age of fourteen, employed. Over 1.25 million children between seven and fifteen years of age were not attending school. Revelations of the deplorable conditions in sweatshop industries intensified support for child-labor and minimum-wage legislation throughout the country.[53]

In his encyclical *Quadragesimo* (1931) Pope Pius XI urged all governments to provide full employment with wages that would enable workers to maintain a decent standard of living. President-elect Roosevelt, defining American individualism differently than Hoover, said it meant equality of opportunity for all and the right of exploitation for none. Professor Edward S. Corwin of Princeton supported reform and assured the people that they were "no longer headed for heaven in a perambulator labeled evolution, laissez faire, or any other uncomprehensible force." John B. Andrews, secretary of the American Association for Labor Legislation, had not seen such widespread interest in social-justice legislation since the zealous days of 1912. Originally, living wages meant an income to maintain a family at a subsistence level, but during the 1920 the public learned that greater production might raise bare survival incomes to the health and comfort level. During the depression, reformers tied living wages to purchasing-power recovery, an expanding economy, and a higher standard of living.[54]

If the time for national regulation of labor standards seemed opportune, there were, nevertheless, substantial obstacles. The Supreme Court majority opposed living wages that simply met the worker's needs and insisted on compensation for services rendered. Moreover, economists deemed studies of industrial wages and living costs inadequate and questioned whether wage and hour regulation would promote recovery and raise the standard of living. And AFL opposition to government wage-fixing seemed to be an insuperable problem. But Roosevelt had promised action on behalf of the forgotten men and women, and millions of voters at the bottom of the economic pyramid anticipated a program to improve their wages and living standards.

2

Wage and Hour Regulation on Trial

The forming of wage boards is a purely practical device to take
the arbitrary exercise of power away from any government official
and to put the finding of proper minimum wage levels in the hands
of a group which would reasonably represent the industry itself
and therefore be productive of a practical working basis of wages.
—Secretary Frances Perkins

THERE is some truth in the aphorism that much of the New Deal
was in the oven when the chef arrived in Washington. In the Hoover
administration, Congress had considered proposals for agricultural
adjustment, public works, relief, public power, banking and a 30-
hour workweek. Although Roosevelt was not committed to any of
them, he had nevertheless promised to act on behalf of those forgotten
men at the bottom of the economic pyramid. But if he and other New
Deal reformers promised to help millions of the poorest of the poor,
they had not accepted the Black-Connery bill's rigid 30-hour workweek as a panacea for recovery or for raising the living standards of
disadvantaged workers. Finding a solution for the recovery problem
and for a way to raise the wage and hour standards of millions of
poorly paid workers proved to be a complicated problem.

Roosevelt brought to Washington something of Jefferson's humani-
tarianism, Teddy Roosevelt's New Nationalism, and Wilson's prog-
ressivism. Although he had received some training in economics at
Harvard, he did not have a systematic economic philosophy. Nevertheless, he accepted the need to improve the nation's economic system, which he believed had been wrecked by business leaders. He
favored controlling the economy in order to achieve a better balance
of the national income, and he thought a better distribution of income
would improve living standards for the underprivileged. As Senator
Huey Long of Louisiana said: Roosevelt was for feeding the hungry
in a land of plenty, clothing the naked in a country with overproduction of clothes, and housing those without shelter.[1]

35

Out of his deep desire to improve people's lives, Roosevelt made minimum security an important part of his New Deal program. Every worker, he believed, had a right to secure his needs and to make a comfortable living through his own labor. The government therefore had an obligation to develop an economic order in which every man had an opportunity to find work. If government regulation of the economy limited free enterprise, it should be accepted to protect the public interest. In his endeavor to improve the lives of the disadvantaged, he had the constant support of Eleanor Roosevelt, who had even stronger convictions on social welfare and progress. Her sympathy for the unemployed and disadvantaged won much support for the New Deal, particularly from millions of women who struggled to make a living.[2]

Because of the depression emergency, Roosevelt and his "Brain Trust" gave particular attention to proposals for regulating the economy. Although his advisors had different approaches to the problem, like the president, they believed in a "balanced society" in which no element would hold preponderant power. They accepted the need to control industry, improve purchasing power and redistribute income. New Freedom and trust-busting were rejected, and business-government cooperation was accepted as necessary. There were differences of opinion, however, as to how such cooperation was to be achieved. Raymond Moley and Adolph Berle wanted to rely mainly on the cooperation of businessmen, but Rexford G. Tugwell distrusted them and preferred to put his faith in government regulation. Since many critics believed the depression had been caused by overproduction and underconsumption, Roosevelt was intrigued with the proposal for improving the economy by adjusting production to demand.[3]

Roosevelt and his advisers looked upon labor as a key element in any recovery program. For both economic and humanitarian reasons, they accepted the need to improve the purchasing power and living standards of poorly paid workers. As a result of his previous experience as assistant secretary of the navy in the Wilson administration and as governor of New York, Roosevelt was inclined to pay more attention to the problems of the poor, unemployed, or aged worker than to unions or collective bargaining. But since he wanted labor support, his relations with union leaders were friendly, even though he had little faith in their abilities. Except for Tugwell, other members of the Brain Trust had little interest in unions. Nevertheless, organized labor had many friends in the administration, including Mrs. Roosevelt, the railroad attorney Donald Richberg, the relief administrator Harry Hopkins, Senator Wagner, and Roosevelt's former New York industrial commissioner, Secretary of Labor Frances Perkins.[4]

Roosevelt's attitude toward labor problems and organized labor was revealed by his selection of Frances Perkins to head the Labor Department. Labor had always considered the department its preserve, and union men had always held the office. The AFL wanted Roosevelt to appoint either Daniel J. Tobin of the Teamsters or Edward McGrady, an AFL legislative representative. Roosevelt, however, did not want his secretary to be the creature of the unions. He believed the department should represent all workers, be neutral among competing factions, and concentrate on national labor policy. Hence, he passed over Tobin and McGrady and chose Perkins instead. Before accepting the office, she reminded him that union men had always held it and committed him to back both an extensive social insurance program and national wage and hour regulation. Close relations with the AFL were maintained with the appointment of McGrady as assistant secretary. He turned out to be one of the best troubleshooters in the department until he got tired of "second fiddling" for Perkins and resigned.[5]

Under Secretary Perkins, the first female cabinet officer, the Labor Department ran smoothly. She took over an organization that had been dominated by the Immigration and Naturalization Service and converted it into an agency which exercised real influence in promoting labor legislation. One of her most important innovations was the creation of the Division of Labor Standards, which assisted the states in improving their labor laws. Among the many able people she appointed was Isador Lubin, commissioner of labor statistics, who was not only an excellent statistician, but also an expert on technological unemployment and the wage system. Congressmen admired her abilities, but some resented her self-righteousness, and some southerners were upset because of her indifference to their partisan demands.[6]

Perkins was an acknowledged expert on labor legislation and social reform. A student of Professor Simon Patten, she accepted capitalism and did not advocate a planned society. She supported industrial democracy and wanted the government to help employers and unions solve their labor problems. She thought workers had an equity in their jobs, a right to be involved in basic decisions in their industry, and a right to a fair wage as well. Collective bargaining should be encouraged, labor's purchasing power should be improved, and the worker's living standard should be raised. She thought minimum-wage and maximum-hour laws would establish a basic economic floor for workers and provide at least subsistence wages. In developing labor legislation, she preferred to rely on advisory boards composed of labor, management, and public representatives.[7]

Initially, some labor leaders were dismayed by the Perkins appointment. Instead of working with a union man in the Labor Department, they would have to contend with a female social reformer. Labor, said President Green in a moment of exasperation, would never be reconciled to her selection. John L. Lewis referred to her as a "mere social worker," and there was a reference to her as the "Secretary Against Labor." Some conservative AFL leaders thought she was too theoretical and were concerned about her support for government regulation of labor-management relations. On the other hand, Perkins thought some conservative labor leaders were narrowly concerned with union problems and incapable of thinking in terms of broad public policy. Despite such early criticism, she was supported by many union leaders and was responsible for making Sidney Hillman of the Amalgamated Clothing Workers (ACWU) an important administration adviser on labor problems.[8]

Early in the hectic "One Hundred Days," while Congress was concentrating on banking, relief, and agricultural problems, the Labor Department worked on improving state labor legislation and supported the campaign for ratification of the Child Labor Amendment. Although child-labor laws had been improved in a number of states in the period from 1923 to 1932, the Children's Bureau held an emergency conference of national organizations, state agencies, and federal bureaus, which recommended improvements in state legislation and set up a steering committee to back proposals. Among the objectives was a campaign for the acceptance of state minimum-wage legislation for working children.[9]

There were those, however, who believed that the time had come for national regulation, and a number of bills were introduced in Congress to ban the products of child labor from entering interstate commerce. In relying on the interstate commerce power, these measures resembled the First Child Labor Act, which had been voided by the Supreme Court. After it had struck down a subsequent attempt by Congress to use its taxing power to eliminate the products of child labor in commerce, reformers were successful in inducing Congress to pass the Child Labor Amendment (1924), which would give it power to regulate the labor of workers under eighteen years of age. Despite an intensive campaign by the National Child Labor Committee (NCLC), the Consumers' League, and numerous other reformers, the amendment faced stiff opposition from those who opposed a national law and was rejected by a number of states. Because of the failure of the amendment, the NCLC again decided to concentrate on improving state legislation.[10]

Deplorable economic conditions during the depression also stimulated interest in minimum-wage legislation. The wage-cutting practiced by the most unscrupulous employers dragged down wage and hour standards in many industries and created an economic morass. Declines of income in major cities between 1929 and 1933 ranged from 24 to 51 percent, and such figures may actually have underestimated the reduction for families. While there were variations in declines among income groups, the poorest paid suffered the most. The great majority of unskilled workers received wages far below the level of decent self-support. Among the poorest paid, untold thousands of women received from $5 to $10 a week in numerous industries both North and South. Unemployment, destitution, and hunger reduced millions of workers to desperation, and to a willingness to work for any wage.[11]

The Consumers' League once again focused public attention on the sweatshop problem and revived interest in state minimum-wage legislation for at least women and children. Since successful state legislation involved drafting a model bill similar to the Wisconsin law that would overcome the limitations of the *Adkins* decision, in late 1932 the league organized a committee of experts, guided by Harvard Law School Professor Felix Frankfurter, and including Mary Dewson, a minimum-wage expert, Josephine Goldmark, an authority on women's hours legislation, and the attorneys Benjamin V. Cohen and Thomas G. Corcoran, both Frankfurter protégés.[12]

Frankfurter's committee distinguished its new model bill from previous state minimum-wage laws for women and children. In the *Adkins* decision, Justice Sutherland offered an opening for reformers by suggesting that a wage law requiring an employer to pay for the "value of services rendered" would be understandable. Hence, there was the possibility that state intervention to require employers to pay women and children "fair wages," rather than living wages, might be upheld. The committee was also encouraged by the Supreme Court's holding in *Highland* v. *Russell Car Co.* (1929), which denied that the liberty of contract protected by the due process clauses of the Fifth and Fourteenth amendments was absolute. Thus, if the state could show a relationship between oppressive wages and the need to protect working women and children, there might be no violation of liberty of contract and state regulation might be upheld.[13]

The committee recognized that freedom of contract had become obsolete, since the realities of the labor market forced women and children to accept wages that had no relation to services rendered.

The evils of oppressive, unreasonable, and overreaching employers who paid "unfair wages" justified state intervention to protect workers who were unable to obtain fair wages. The constant lowering of wages and the widespread sweatshop working conditions reduced the purchasing power of employees, threatened their health and well-being, and contributed to the deterioration of society. Although the measure would require employers to pay "fair wages," rather than living wages, the relationship between low wages and living standards remained the same. State intervention would be required when the employee's income fell below subsistence levels. When substantial numbers of women and children in any occupation received "oppressive and unreasonable wages," a state labor commissioner might investigate to determine if employers were paying wages commensurate with the value of services rendered.[14]

The model bill provided for a democratic determination of fair-wage standards by industrial-wage boards. In his investigation, the commissioner would be guided by the same rules that a court of law would follow in determining reasonable value for services rendered. If the investigation revealed that wages were oppressive and insufficient to maintain workers at a healthful-living standard, he would appoint an industry-wage board of employee, employer, and public representatives to determine a fair wage. After public hearings and consideration of job classifications, services rendered, and local differentials, the board would submit its fair-wage recommendations to the commissioner. He would then establish the recommended fair rates by directory order, and compliance would depend on publicity and public pressure. After nine months, if noncompliance continued, subsequent to another hearing, the commissioner could make the fair rates mandatory, and violations would be subject to penal law. These procedures sought to assure a standard of reasonableness and were based on the experience of state wage boards.[15]

Backed by the labor departments of nine eastern states, early in 1933 the Consumers' League organized an intensive campaign for its model bill. Both Roosevelt and Perkins supported this drive, which was eventually successful in inducing seven states to adopt new wage laws. Neither anticipated congressional action on national wage and hour standards while Roosevelt's advisers were formulating a recovery program. Nevertheless, since administration leaders did not sponsor a measure to reduce the workweek, Senator Black reintroduced his 30-hour bill, which was backed by the AFL and ACWU, early in March. The reintroduction of his new bill complicated consideration of a recovery bill.[16]

Although Roosevelt favored reducing working hours, he opposed

the inflexible 30-hour standard. Neither he nor his advisers anticipated action on Black's bill or were impressed with it as a panacea
for unemployment. Perkins thought Black had erred in accepting the
technocratic argument that America had achieved a static economy.
Senator Wagner thought the 30-hour bill inadequate for recovery, and
Moley regarded it as completely impractical. Attorney General Homer
Cummings doubted that it would survive a Supreme Court test.
Roosevelt thought it ignored the requirements of particular occupations, such as dairymen and the "rhythm of the cow." He was warned
that it would lead to "labor bootlegging": workers holding two jobs
to avoid the limitation, particularly in southern textile mills.[17]

Although she favored reducing hours, Secretary Perkins looked
upon the 30-hour workweek as a "share the work by compulsion"
scheme that would not be taken seriously. A 30-hour week would
mean a reduction of wages and purchasing power that would impede
recovery. Professor Harry A. Millis, a University of Chicago economist, warned her that it would raise production costs and create business uncertainty. She therefore favored Hillman's suggestion to
amend the bill and create industrial boards to set wage and hour
standards. The establishment of industrial boards, she understood,
would not be a unique experiment, since there had been considerable
experience with them.[18]

Roosevelt asked Perkins to induce Black to withdraw his 30-hour
bill, but she was unable to do so. Without resorting to new hearings,
the Senate Judiciary Committee approved a two-year limit, with the
object of making the bill an emergency measure and thus hopefully
strengthening its constitutionality. The committee also considered and
rejected a Perkins amendment to allow the president to set a flexible
workweek of between 30 and 40 hours as conditions might require.
It also asserted the right of Congress to use its commerce power to
regulate hours in an emergency when business conditions produced
widespread misery, destitution, and want throughout the country. It
hoped the Supreme Court would reverse its *Dagenhart* decision.[19]

When the Black bill was taken up by the Senate early in April,
debate centered more on its constitutionality than on its economic
implications. Many senators were committed to doing something
about unemployment but seemed reluctant to accept the bill without
amendment. Senator Arthur Robinson of Indiana referred to the Supreme Court's recent decision in the *New State Ice Co.* v. *Liebman*
(1932) as indicating that it might take social and economic conditions
into consideration, but Senator William Borah of Idaho doubted that
the emergency could be used to justify the measure. Other proponents
of regulation were willing to support the bill and let the Court settle

the constitutional issue.[20] Opposition centered among conservative northern Republicans and those southern Democrats who saw national regulation as a threat to the South's cheap-labor advantage. Conservative Republicans branded the bill economically unsound and a violation of individual freedom. David A. Reed of Pennsylvania said it was "sentimentalism run riot." Senator Josiah W. Bailey of North Carolina defended liberty of contract, states rights, the republic, and the Constitution. The measure, he warned, would lead to socialism and ultimately to communism.[21]

Several amendments were offered to provide for a flexible workweek, to cover imported goods, and to exempt certain industries from coverage. Although the Senate knew a mandatory 30-hour workweek would undoubtedly cause severe industrial dislocation, it rejected Majority Leader Joseph T. Robinson's amendment for a flexible 36-hour week. Sen. Henry Hatfield's amendment to apply the 30-hour standard to imports was also rejected on the ground that it would interfere with the administration's efforts to improve trade relations. No effort was made to include minimum-wage provisions because wage-setting was understood to be unconstitutional. After accepting amendments exempting industries processing perishable goods and authorizing the secretary of labor to issue overtime work permits, the bill was passed by a comfortable margin of 53 to 30 and sent to the House. Forty-one Democrats, nine Republicans, and three independents supported it. Ten Democrats, eight from the South, joined the remaining Republicans in opposition. The amendments made the 30-hour week only slightly more flexible, but despite the economic and constitutional implications, a reduction of the workweek as a panacea for unemployment seemed too appealing politically to resist.[22]

Since the unexpected passage of Black's bill early in April complicated the administration's plans for recovery legislation, Roosevelt immediately asked Perkins to draft a more flexible measure. But Professor Frankfurter told her that Congress could regulate neither wages nor hours within the states. He urged her to seek the legal aid of Robert Szold, formerly assistant to Solicitor General John W. Davis in the Wilson administration. Szold submitted drafts of two flexible 30-hour bills, one based on the commerce power and the other on both the commerce and taxing power. Both would authorize industry boards to regulate wages and hours and contained features similar to those of the Consumer's League's model bill for state regulation.[23]

Szold's first bill would have Congress declare it to be against public policy to allow industries affecting interstate commerce to employ workers for unreasonably long hours or at wages less than fair or reasonable for the value of services rendered, and less than sufficient to meet the minimum cost of living necessary for health. During the emergency, a reasonable standard would be a 30-hour workweek and industry boards would recommend fair wages. Any manufacturing enterprise shipping goods in commerce was covered, with exemptions for agriculture, fishing, canning, and other seasonal industries. The secretary of labor would designate the industries that would have labor boards, appoint their members, accept or reject their findings, investigate wage and hour standards, and issue an order establishing the standard. Szold's second bill was similarly based on the commerce power and utilized industry-board procedures, but in addition would raise revenue by levying a tax penalty on those employers who paid less than the industry wage standard approved by the secretary.[24] The tax penalty levied on employers who failed to pay fair wages was of dubious constitutionality.

Perkins also received several fair-trade proposals for wage and hour regulation. Gerard Swope offered a trade-association plan for industrial self-government which suggested a 48-hour week and Labor Department authority for approving minimum wages. Henry I. Harriman, president of the U.S. Chamber of Commerce, submitted its proposal for transferring the Federal Trade Commission's powers to the secretary of commerce in order to promote fair methods of competition, including agreements on the workweek and minimum wages. Assistant Secretary of Commerce John Dickinson urged Perkins to consider his plan for a national industrial board and for the organization of enterprise under codes of labor standards approved by the secretary of labor. Labor Department Solicitor Charles Wyzanski preferred the Chamber of Commerce's fair-trade approach because regulation would not be based on a ban on goods in commerce and because the administrative burden would be on private parties.[25]

After consulting Black and Secretary of Commerce Daniel Roper, Perkins advised Connery's labor committee that the Black bill's provisions authorizing the Labor Department to grant exemptions from the 30-hour week would be burdensome and impossible to administer. She also warned it about the adverse effect the reduction of hours, income, and purchasing power would have on recovery. When she recommended flexible standards set by industry boards, the committee urged her to draft a bill covering production and competition as well as wages and hours. Richberg, Hillman, and Frankfurter helped her draft what Wyzanski called the "Richberg redraft" of the Black bill. Her Control of Hours, Wages and Production Bill reflected the fair-trade approach and would prohibit commerce in goods produced by unfair competition. All goods made in establishments by employees working more than 30 hours a week would be banned, with exemptions up to 40 hours. If the secretary of labor found that unfair competition was based on unreasonably long hours, he could limit them to adjust production. If a substantial number of workers did not receive fair wages for the value of services rendered or sufficient for a reasonable standard of living, he could establish wage boards to set fair wages. As Perkins explained, procedures for establishing fair wages were based on state experience and represented a democratic method for securing an equitable adjustment of wages.[26]

Although the Perkins production-control bill's flexible wage and hour provisions overcame the rigid workweek problem, there were serious objections to it. Frankfurter was critical of the fair-competition approach and doubted that the Supreme Court would uphold any measure banning goods in commerce because of unreasonable restraint of commerce based on unfair conditions of work. A better approach, he advised, would be to base a bill on the need to relieve commerce from unreasonable impediments. It would then be necessary to show the relationship of business, purchasing power, and the volume of commerce, as well as the relationship between purchasing power and a reduction of the workweek and minimum wages. Wyzanski also found the Perkins bill's provisions for balancing industrial production highly objectionable because of the lack of specific guidelines, and he thought the minimum-wage provisions were unconstitutional as an invasion of state power and violation of due process. The recovery emergency, he warned, did not give Congress additional power. In his view, the minimum-wage provisions rested on nothing more than hope and prejudiced the bill's chances. Moreover, given the lack of statistical data, he doubted that national regulation of minimum wages would be possible.[27]

Much to the dismay of Perkins and other supporters of wage and hour regulation, her bill generated intense opposition from labor and business during the House hearings in April. President Green objected strongly to "pegging wages" in any bill. Matthew Woll said the Perkins bill would make workers serfs. According to Moley, it was more of a shock to employers than the original Black bill. Both Roosevelt and Perkins, he said, were aghast at the commotion it raised, much of which was promoted by the Chamber of Commerce and by the National Association of Manufacturers. He was afraid he might not be able to move fast enough on the recovery measure to head off the "menace of the Black or Perkins bills." Because of the opposition, early in May Roosevelt abandoned both of them before the conclusion of the hearings. The Chamber of Commerce and the NAM took advantage of the controversy over the bills and induced Roosevelt to accept their plan for code regulation. Despite the defeat of her bill, Perkins gave Black and David J. Lewis credit for promoting the shorter workweek as a recovery panacea.[28]

After Roosevelt's decision to abandon the Black bill, Perkins urged Dickinson to include in his national recovery measure provisions for a maximum 40-hour workweek and wage-fixing. Mary Dewson also pressed Dickinson, Senator Wagner, and General Hugh Johnson to consider them. Dickinson assured her that all proposals for industrial regulation included these provisions. Although Roosevelt accepted the trade-association plan, Connery's committee reported out a thoroughly revised version of Black's bill, which provided for a "Federal Trade Regulation Board" and for the licensing of business engaged in interstate commerce. It contained strong labor-standard guarantees. All licensees would have to agree to a 30-hour workweek and maintain wages at the decency and comfort standard.[29]

Perkins opposed both the Labor Committee's licensing bill and the trade-association approach to wage and hour regulation. Licensing, she told Connery, would be experimental, cumbersome, and slow, and if it were necessary, it should be incorporated in other legislation. Minimum-wage regulation should follow the experience of state legislation and should not be combined with licensing or the suspension of the antitrust laws. It would be a serious mistake, she believed, to combine wage and hour provisions in a broader scheme of regulation.[30] But unfortunately for Perkins and for those who favored a wage and hour law based on twenty years of state experience, Roosevelt's advisers decided to incorporate labor standards in the recovery measure.

By early May Dickinson, Hugh Johnson, and Senator Wagner were well along in perfecting their industrial-recovery bill. Although the AFL preferred the Black bill, after Roosevelt abandoned it the federation accepted the inevitable, but insisted on the inclusion of labor-standard provisions in the recovery measure. In return for accepting trade-association codification of industry, organized labor obtained the labor guarantees in Section 7(a), which included the right to organize and bargain, freedom from "yellow dog" contracts, and wage and hour standards approved by the president. But the fixing of maximum-wage rates was banned. John L. Lewis claimed that the United Mine Workers was responsible for the labor guarantees, which were taken from the Davis-Kelly coal bill of the Hoover administration. The Chamber of Commerce and the NAM accepted them because they did not want a divisive issue that would threaten the legislation. This understanding between the AFL and the trade associations expedited approval of the bill when it was introduced in May.[31]

Wyzanski, however, questioned the constitutionality of the recovery bill. He thought the fair competition code-making provisions of Section 3(b) were much too vague and doubted that the commerce power could be extended to all the transactions covered. The recovery measure, he told Wagner, should have emphasized the elimination of unfair practices and the maintenance of fair-labor standards. The attitude of Labor Department officials was revealed when Johnson asked the Bureau of Labor Statistics to recommend a minimum wage. Sidney W. Wilcox, the chief statistician, declined to recommend a figure. One fixed minimum, Wilcox explained, ignored local variations in the cost of living as well as experience in administering wage laws. If a figure were set too low, labor would be alienated, whereas were it too high, it would be visionary. Moreover, a fixed minimum would reduce labor representatives on the code authorities to "rubber stamping" administrative decisions. Labor-management representatives, he insisted, should agree on wage and hour standards for the codes.[32]

Strongly supporting the president, the House passed the recovery bill overwhelmingly. But it faced stiff opposition in the Senate because some conservatives objected to the labor guarantees of Section 7(a) and to the vast authority granted to the recovery agency. Others opposed the suspension of the antitrust laws and warned that the dominant corporations in any industry would write the codes. Senator Wagner defended the bill, explaining that there was no other way of outlawing sweatshops and protecting labor. Supporters carried the day, and the bill was narrowly approved by a margin of seven votes. In signing the National Industrial Recovery Act (NIRA), Roosevelt emphasized the cooperation of industry, labor, and government during World War I and the law's potential for putting millions back to work by reducing the workweek. He also questioned the legality of any business that existed by paying less than living wages.[33] Clearly, the recovery act was an unprecedented peacetime cooperative effort to regulate the nation's market place. But surely Senator Wagner exaggerated when he claimed that there was no other way to outlaw sweatshops and to protect labor.

Before trade-association codes were approved by the National Recovery Administration, employers were asked to accept the president's Reemployment Agreement, which prohibited child labor, set a flexible 35-hour week, and provided for a minimum weekly wage of between $12 and $15. The NRA Administrator Hugh Johnson asked the trade associations to accept a 32-hour week and a 45-cent minimum, which would provide $14.40 a week. But because of weak labor representation on the industry code committees, approximately

85 percent of the codes provided for a 40-hour week and wage rates based on differentials. The average 30-cent rate would provide an annual income of only $600, about half of the amount needed to maintain a subsistence living standard. Since most of the codes prohibited child labor, Roosevelt claimed that it was being abolished. His claim was an exaggeration, since the codes did not cover intrastate activities in which most working children were employed. Grace Abbott of the Children's Bureau thought his claim would set back the child-labor movement in the states.[34]

The major effect of the recovery program came over the summer of 1933 with the reemployment of an estimated 2.5 million workers. The average workweek declined from 43.3 to 37.8 hours, while average hourly earnings rose from 43.8 to 53.6 cents. But minimum rates were so low in some industries that average weekly earnings actually declined, as some employers reduced rates for the skilled to compensate for the increase for the unskilled. Purchasing power did increase by 7 percent, but was offset by a commensurate increase in the cost of living. Recognizing the weakness of the labor provisions of the codes, the National Consumers' League recommended that they be improved, particularly in industries in which labor was unorganized. By the end of the year, it was suggesting a 35-to-40-hour week and a 35-cent minimum with no differentials based on sex, race, or age. Disillusioned by the manner in which trade associations had drafted codes without labor participation, in October the AFL demanded that they be revised to provide for a 30-hour week.[35]

Responding to AFL demands, in March of 1934 Connery's House Labor Committee produced a new 30-hour bill. Recognizing that trade associations would not accept a 30-hour week unless Congress made it the law of the land, the bill required that it be written into the codes. Like the committee's licensing proposal of May 1933, the new bill would establish a board to grant exemptions from the 30-hour limitation. It also required employers to pay the same wages for the 30-hour week that they were paying for a longer workweek. The measure, the committee explained, was designed to carry out the president's appeal to industry to provide employment for millions of idle workers. Since the standards accepted by many of the code authorities had failed to relieve the unemployment problem, Congress was asked to accept the 30-hour week in the interest of putting six or seven million back to work.[36]

Despite AFL support for the new 30-hour proposal, House leaders bottled it up in the Rules Committee, and Connery could not get it to the floor by petition. Nevertheless, Senator Black told Perkins the fight for the 30-hour week would be continued. The blanket 30-hour measure was again rejected by the administration because there were doubts about its constitutionality and because NRA leaders planned to have the code authorities reduce hours and increase wages. Both the extensive delegation of authority contemplated by Connery's proposal and the blanket amending of code agreements by an act of Congress were of dubious constitutionality. Moreover, after a meeting in March, NRA authorities recommended a 10-percent reduction in hours and a 10-percent increase in wages. Despite the president's appeal for shorter hours and "purchasing-power wages," most of the code authorities did not accept the NRA's "10 and 10" proposal. By the fall of 1934 their retention of the 40-hour week seemed to make little difference. Actual hours worked in all industries were only 37.5 and only 34 in manufacturing. By late 1934 it was clear that even though the NRA had been able to improve wage and hour standards for the lowest paid workers, the code program had failed to stimulate a substantial recovery.[37]

However viewed, the first year and a half of the code program had failed to remedy the unemployment problem or to greatly improve purchasing-power wages. Surveys in the fall of 1934 showed the average industrial worker's purchasing power virtually unchanged. In October real weekly earnings were still 16.2 percent below those of 1929. Employment reached only 75 percent of the 1929 level, and at least 11 million remained jobless. The Federal Emergency Relief Administration reported 19 million on relief, more than 15 percent of the population. Dissatisfied with the existing NRA program, the AFL demanded the 30-hour week with no reduction in pay. John L. Lewis suggested a 50-cent minimum, employment insurance, old-age pensions, and equal pay for women. President Green said the AFL wanted government administration of the codes, labor representation on code authorities, and the retention of Section 7(a). Since employers refused to shorten hours, the AFL wanted the 30-hour week written into law.[38]

Responding once again to AFL demands, in January of 1935 both Senator Black and Representative Connery produced 30-hour workweek bills. Since the Rules Committee had bottled up Connery's 30-hour measure the previous session, action on the new bills shifted to the Senate. Black's bill would amend the codes to establish a 30-hour week and to prohibit employers from reducing wages without agreement with employee representatives. The secretary of labor might issue exemptions to meet special requirements in any industry. During Senate Judiciary Committee hearings on his bill, Black emphasized the need to do something about technological unemployment, while President Green warned the country about the social menace of a "standing army" of discontented jobless workers. John L. Lewis read NRA labor Administrator Richberg out of the labor movement for approving a 48-hour week for the auto industry, while the NAM counsel James A. Emery condemned any attempt by Congress to fix a workweek as unconstitutional. Distinguished economists warned the committee about the adverse effects a reduction of the workweek would have on the nation's economy. Harold G. Moulton of the Brookings Institution and O. G. Saxon of Yale University and Willford I. King of New York University thought labor costs, prices, and productive capacity would increase whether or not the 30-hour week was adopted.[39]

By March of 1935 the debate over incorporating the 30-hour workweek in industry codes seemed somewhat academic. Even if the administration could get Congress to extend the life of the NRA, which seemed highly uncertain at the time, there was a good possibility that code regulation of industry would be found unconstitutional by the Supreme Court. Earlier the Court had voided Section 9(c) of Title I of the NIRA in *Panama Refining Co.* v. *Ryan* (1935), denying the president the authority to interdict the transportation of oil in interstate commerce on the ground that Congress had delegated quasi-legislative authority to the executive. Although the opinion did not cover other provisions of the NIRA, it seemed unlikely that the Court would accept the more extensive delegation of congressional authority to the code authorities. Significantly, in voiding the delegation of quasi-legislative authority to the executive, the Court erected a new barrier, not only to code regulation of industry, but also to national regulation of wages and hours through industry boards composed of employer and employee representatives.[40]

Despite the adverse holding in *Panama Refining Co.*, Roosevelt decided to reorganize the recovery agency and asked Congress for a two-year extension of the NIRA. After General Johnson had been eased out and replaced by the National Industrial Recovery Board, the NRA began contracting its activities with the intention of concentrating on labor standards. To prevent code enforcement from breaking down completely, Attorney General Cummings decided to hazard a Court test of the live-poultry code. The *Schechter Company* case had a number of advantages from the government's viewpoint, since the respected New York Circuit Court had already approved the delegation of legislative authority, the process of code-making, and the fair-trade provisions of the code. It had, however, voided the wage and hour provisions on the ground that the slaughterhouse employees of the Schechter Company were not directly engaged in interstate commerce.[41]

Much to the joy of NRA opponents, on "Black Monday," May 27, in *A.L.A. Schechter Poultry Co.* v. *United States* (1935), the Court unanimously voided the code-making authority delegated by Section 3 of the NIRA. Congress, it said, could not transfer legislative functions to others and must itself prescribe policies and standards for enforcement agencies. Moreover, it refused to apply the "stream-of-commerce" doctrine to slaughterhouse operations. These activities, it declared, had only an indirect effect on interstate commerce and were not subject to federal regulation. The national government could not therefore regulate the wages and hours of persons employed in the internal commerce of a state. Although the *Schechter* decision was hailed by those opposed to government regulation, the Court was criticized by legal scholars for its "direct-indirect effect" interpretation of the commerce power. The Court, said Frankfurter and Henry M. Hart of Harvard, should not have considered the scope of the commerce power at all. A weak and ambiguous decision, declared Edward S. Corwin, which left a muddlement worse confounded. Government by "NRA hullabaloo," chided Harvard's Thomas Reed Powell, had been succeeded by government by "abracadabra."[42]

Nevertheless, existing codes were unenforceable and the first experiment in cooperative regulation of industry came to an end at a time when millions of workers could not earn enough to maintain a subsistence standard of living. Estimates of the cost of living in 1935 varied considerably according to geographic location, ranging from $1,080 to $1,544 annually for a worker with a family. A study in fifty-nine cities indicated that a family of four needed $900 annually for an emergency standard of living and $1,260 for a subsistence budget. The unskilled working a 40-hour week for 30 to 40 cents an hour were making from $600 to $800 annually, which did not come close to the subsistence standard. Clearly, millions lacked adequate purchasing power and could hardly contribute anything to economic recovery.[43]

The *Schechter* decision not only voided the New Deal's first experiment in labor-management cooperation, but wage and hour regulation had failed to stimulate recovery. Although the income of the poorest paid had been improved in code industries, employers cut high wages and the overall results were disappointing, particularly to organized labor. After their NRA experience, AFL leaders were determined to avoid regulation by powerful agencies at all costs. Perkins, however, thought the NRA experience had convinced the public that living wages should be maintained by national regulation. The collapse of the code program left Roosevelt in something of a quandry. With reemployment stagnant, purchasing power unrestored, millions on the dole, and recovery incomplete, he sought some way to prevent the return of sweatshop competition and protect employers who tried to maintain fair standards. He had planned to limit the NRA to the regulation of wage and hour standards, but how he might accomplish this objective after the *Schechter* decision and in the face of AFL opposition to wage regulation remained to be seen.

3

Horse and Buggy Days

Necessitous men are not free men. Liberty requires an opportunity to make a living—a living according to the standard of the time, a living which gives man not only enough to live by, but something to live for.
—Franklin D. Roosevelt

ALTHOUGH President Roosevelt had intended to extend a revised National Recovery Administration (NRA) code program for two years early in 1935, the *Schechter* decision upset his plans. Because of the collapse of the enforceable program, the resumption of sweatshop competition, and the threat to the nation's economy, he was induced to accept a hastily conceived plan to maintain the codes on a voluntary basis while Congress considered new recovery legislation. Although the voluntary program floundered in confusion, he authorized a labor-management council to seek agreement on recovery legislation that might be submitted to Congress. The council made its recommendations in 1936, but Roosevelt refused to consider a new measure because he was concerned about charges that his New Deal advisers had no respect for the Constitution. Despite strong support for action on labor standards, those who favored national wage and hour legislation had to wait until after the 1936 election. During the interim, however, some progress was made in the improvement of labor standards.

Early in 1935 Roosevelt asked Congress to extend a revised version of the NRA program, despite criticism from all sides about its inadequacies. Many congressmen were unhappy with price-fixing, organized labor resented trade-association control of industry committees, small businessmen condemned corporate control of code authorities, and farm organizations and consumer groups were upset over rising prices. Despite such criticism, S. Clay Williams, chairman of the National Industrial Recovery Board (NIRB) after General Johnson's departure, favored extending the existing law to preserve the gains already accomplished through Section 7(a) and the fair-trade provisions. But he had doubts about the best way to preserve them.[1]

Unable to reach agreement on a plan, in January the NIRB suggested three options for Roosevelt's consideration. He could ask Congress to extend the NIRA for a limited period without change. Or he could ask it to make the NRA permanent, but to ban price-fixing, make trade-practice agreements voluntary, and require codes on minimum wages, maximum hours, and child labor. A third option was to incorporate these changes in a measure extending the NRA for two years. Donald Richberg, executive director of the National Emergency Council, drafted an NRA amendment to authorize the president to prescribe codes of fair competition limited to minimum wages, maximum hours, child labor, and Section 7(a) guarantees.[2]

In February Roosevelt sent Congress his message recommending amendment of the NIRA, rather than a finished draft of a bill for labor standards. He suggested permanent legislation to authorize Congress and the president to take action to prevent future depressions. He asked Congress for the power to amend the codes of fair competition. If an industry refused to formulate a code, he wanted to prescribe a limited code banning child labor, setting a 30-to-40-hour workweek, and fixing minimum wages. He thought flexible wages should be adjusted within and between industries in order to promote fair competition among them. Wage differentials would be based upon geographic considerations and skilled classifications, but the president could not set maximum rates. Since the NIRB was unable to provide a finished draft, Roosevelt left the decision on NIRA amendment to Congress.[3]

The House was willing to extend the NRA for two years, to limit regulation to industries in interstate commerce, and to ban price-fixing. In addition, it would require that codes contain the guarantees of Section 7(a) and a ban on unfair methods of competition. Nothing would impair the power of the Federal Trade Commission (FTC) to hear complaints and issue cease and desist orders. Existing codes would be continued after the president reviewed them within six months of the extension of the law. If the House was ready to give Roosevelt most of what he wanted, the provisions for FTC enforcement of the ban on unfair-trade practices nevertheless upset NRA officials concerned about conflicts between the commission and the recovery agency over administration of the program. Some critics believed the FTC provision would end self-government under the codes.[4]

Despite strong backing from the Industry and Business Committee for National Recovery Extension, organized labor, and NRA officials, the extension proposal generated stiff opposition in the Senate. Opponents condemned the code program for curtailing competition, oppressing small business, fixing prices, ignoring the rights of workers, and centralizing industry. Senator Borah, who took the lead in opposing price-fixing, favored letting the NIRA expire and incorporating the labor guarantees of Section 7(a) in separate legislation. Senator Pat Harrison's Finance Committee was willing to extend the law to April 1936, which would give Congress time to consider a better law. In order to overcome the opposition, Roosevelt tried to tie NIRA extension to the Wagner labor-relations bill, which the Senate passed, but his strategy was wrecked by the *Schechter* decision. Instead of a two-year extension, the Senate approved Bennett C. Clark's resolution extending the NIRA for ten months. The president would be required to review and approve all codes in a thirty-day period after the extension became law. In the opinion of those who supported the NRA, the ten-month extension and thirty-day review requirement indicated the Senate's desire to kill the code program.[5]

Because of doubts about the constitutionality of the NIRA and the Senate's opposition, Congress delayed action a bill until the Supreme Court handed down its decision in the *Schechter* case. After it voided the code, NRA officials announced that codes were no longer the law of the land, and Justice Department attorneys warned the trade associations that the antitrust laws were once again in full effect. Within a few weeks there were indications that cutthroat competition would revive sweatshop standards and undermine the efforts of employers to maintain fair wages. Roosevelt was soon swamped with proposals for revising and extending the NRA in some new form. Moley and Tugwell recommended a constitutional amendment broadening the commerce power, but Roosevelt had little interest in it. The Chamber of Commerce was willing to accept an extension of the NRA if its role were reduced to approving or rejecting trade agreements. The chamber wanted the "open shop," but would accept provisions for fair competition, including minimum wages, maximum hours, and a ban on child labor. Organized labor was very anxious to preserve the labor guarantees of Section 7(a). President Green predicted an economic and social disaster if the law were allowed to expire.[6]

Anticipating that Congress might not extend the National Industrial Recovery Act, Secretary Perkins thought the Supreme Court might be willing to uphold a more carefully drafted wage and hour measure and had the Labor Department attorney Charles O. Gregory prepare one similar to her 1933 proposal. Her bill would authorize the secretary of labor to appoint wage and hour boards in any industry when wages fell below the subsistence level. After hearings, the boards would recommend minimum wages and maximum hours to the secretary for approval, but no workweek could be more than 48 hours. Although she thought the bill feasible, the constitutional obstacles seemed insuperable, and she received no encouragement from Roosevelt or from Attorney General Cummings. She consulted legal experts and found them unsure of the proper constitutional justification. Cummings discouraged her, saying that the Court had blocked any further action on wage and hour legislation. Roosevelt was reluctant to try a new measure because he was sensitive to the charge that he had no respect for the Constitution. Perkins accepted his decision, and as she noted, put her unconstitutional bill in her desk drawer for consideration at some more opportune time.[7]

Still dreaming of cooperative self-regulation, Alexander Sachs, chief NRA economist, and Simon Rifkind, Senator Wagner's secretary, thought trade associations might be willing to accept voluntary labor-standard agreements. They suggested revising the NIRA to provide for voluntary codes on labor standards that would be exempt from the antitrust laws when approved by the FTC. Just what role the NRA might have in this program is not clear, but presumably it would help labor and industry agree on the labor standards. Another plan was to offer government contracts to those industries willing to accept voluntary labor-standard codes approved by the NRA. If they were exempt from the antitrust laws, the FTC would not be involved. Since the NRA would have no enforcement authority, the contracts would have to be enforced by some other party, possibly organized labor.[8]

Neither Roosevelt nor Richberg had any faith in voluntary agreements and insisted that they would have to comply with the antitrust laws. The president thought legal action would be necessary to make industry members conform to such agreements. Since the antitrust laws were once again in full effect, if businessmen operated under their existing codes on a voluntary basis, they might be open to a suit for triple damages by disgruntled buyers or competitors. All codes contained provisions on machine hours, discounts, and selling that had never been approved by the FTC or by the courts. Hence, trade-association attorneys warned the administration that they would be willing to accept voluntary codes only if illegal practices were clearly defined.[9]

Congress had no time to define illegal practices in the brief period before the NIRA would expire, even if it had wanted to. Since the Senate opposed a two-year extension, the House yielded, and Congress accepted a resolution extending it to April 1936. The president's power to make NRA codes the law of the land was repealed. The exemption from the antitrust laws was restricted to only those agreements incorporating the labor guarantees of Section 7(a). Practices that violated the antitrust laws or constituted unfair competition were prohibited. The resolution said nothing about supervision or administration and was an obvious attempt to induce industry to incorporate Section 7(a) in their agreements on the assumption that they wanted to eliminate sweatshop competition. Not only did Roosevelt fail to get a two-year extension of the NIRA, but Congress left him with a new administrative muddle.[10]

Roosevelt thereafter appointed the NRA official James L. O'Neill, a vice president of the Guarantee Trust Company of New York City, acting administrator of the recovery agency. George L. Berry, AFL vice president and president of the Pressmens Union, was named O'Neill's assistant for labor relations. A division of business cooperation was to help industry prepare voluntary agreements, and a division of review was to study NRA experience and produce reports that would be helpful when Congress considered new recovery legislation. In June, O'Neill began a drastic reduction of personnel and explored the enforcement problems with the FTC. The two agencies were expected to end their two-year feud over the enforcement of the codes and concentrate on approving voluntary agreements. Secretary Roper's Business Advisory Council suggested putting the NRA under the FTC in order to help the commission formulate the agreements. FTC Chairman Ewin Davis thought his agency should be enlarged to as many as nine members to handle the work and that the NRA's role should be confined to simply approving the labor provisions.[11]

Until the FTC and NRA could agree on their responsibilities, the business community was informed that neither was anxious to receive agreements for review. O'Neill admitted that the NRA had not worked out a procedure for considering them. His advisory council, he explained, would proceed slowly in order to avoid having to abrogate decisions at a later time. According to AFL President Green, a council member, the NRA was also considering what concessions would be made to industry for accepting the labor guarantees.[12]

In early July Attorney General Cummings complicated the problem by ruling that NRA-approved wage and hour provisions in the voluntary agreements might violate the antitrust laws. Clearly, Cummings wanted the antitrust laws enforced and did not want the NRA bargaining with the trade associations on labor standards. Equally clearly, Cummings's ruling eliminated any effective NRA participation in the voluntary-code program. Thereafter the FTC went ahead with its own fair-trade conferences on some of the 170 codes already submitted for review. As far as O'Neill was concerned, the Blue Eagle was in cold storage, and he did not know what Roosevelt was going to do about it. Having no enthusiasm for protecting labor's interests in any case, he resigned late in July. Since the NRA would expire in ten months, all Roosevelt needed was someone who could handle the paperwork. He made the NRA official Lawrence J. Martin acting administrator and let him "sign papers."[13]

With the FTC reviewing agreements and the NRA in limbo, Labor Department officials feared that labor's interests would be ignored. Reacting to the confusion, Wyzanski admitted that he did not know what provisions might be in the agreements, what agency was responsible for the labor guarantees, or what industries would be covered. The problem surfaced immediately, when the FTC took up the wholesale-tobacco agreement and the NRA declined to offer any advice, apparently with the intent to force the FTC to accept NRA standards. According to Clara M. Beyer, chief of the Industrial Division of the Children's Bureau, NRA officials refused to cooperate because they believed the extended NIRA was inadequate to protect labor's interests. But if labor standards were left to the FTC, she warned, workers would not be protected, since Administrator Berry believed that he had a mandate to submit agreements with labor provisions to the president for approval. NRA experience proved that industry committees were primarily interested in enforcing trade-practice provisions and discriminated against labor by ignoring the Section 7(a) guarantees. Before the *Schechter* case, she explained, the NRA had some control over the committees through its enforcement division, but such control was no longer possible with the voluntary agreements. The voluntary program, she predicted, would end in failure unless the committees could be made responsible to some government agency.[14]

Early in August Attorney General Cummings ended the administrative confusion by placing responsibility for approving the voluntary agreements with the FTC. All agreements were to have a section on trade practices and a separate title for labor standards. While the FTC reviewed the former, the labor provisions would be sent to the NRA for review and returned to the FTC. If both agencies accepted the agreement, it would be sent to the president for approval. If the president rejected the labor provisions, the associations could ask the FTC to approve the trade practices. They could also submit agreements without the labor provisions, but such agreements would not be exempt from the antitrust laws. Cummings's plan confirmed his intent to have the antitrust laws enforced; left the NRA independent of the FTC; allowed the NRA to review the labor standards; and made it impossible for the associations to bargain with the NRA for exemptions from the antitrust laws. At the same time, Roosevelt asked Congress to begin hearings on a new measure to replace the NIRA. Pending congressional action, he hoped the trade associations would accept the voluntary agreements and maintain NRA labor standards.[15]

Because of interagency jealousy, there was some delay in implementing Cummings's plan. The FTC had no objection to it, but NRA Administrator Martin felt the delay would hurt the plan. Predicting conflicts with the FTC, he wanted the right to send NRA recommendations on labor standards to the president independently of the FTC. Unhappy at being left out of the procedure, Assistant Secretary of Labor A. H. Altmeyer thought the FTC should not take part in the process for approving labor standards. He wanted the agreements submitted to his department for clearance on labor standards and to the Justice Department for legal clearance. Cummings, however, thought that labor's interests would be adequately protected by the NRA Labor Advisory Board and that requiring approval by both departments would be cumbersome. Early in September agreement on procedure was finally worked out and Cummings's plan went into effect.[16]

Later in September, Roosevelt made Berry his Coordinator for Industrial Cooperation. Under this grand title, Berry would remain an NRA administrator, transmit agreements approved by the FTC and NRA to the president, and organize labor-management conferences for recovery. Just how he might promote industrial self-government with the FTC enforcing the antitrust acts was not clear. As Berry noted, he was in a rather difficult position, something like "the innocent bystander who attempts to compromise differences between families and is usually the first person to be shot." He knew that salvaging anything from the NRA would be difficult and that he could not compel anyone to cooperate in carrying out industrial self-government. But he believed that organized labor and businessmen might be willing to cooperate in the elimination of sweatshop-labor standards. Even the AFL's conservative John P. Frey considered the NRA experiment constructive and thought a new NRA program with adequate labor representation would be worthwhile. Some industry leaders knew that even substantial recovery would not solve the unemployment problem, which prevented the administration from balancing the budget. Rather than increase the debt and resort to paper-money inflation, and understanding that a shorter week was inevitable, they agreed that a 36-to-30-hour week might ease the unemployment problem. Berry assured them that they would be consulted before any new legislation was proposed.[17]

Because FTC and NRA procedures for approving voluntary agreements were so complicated, trade-association leaders predicted the immediate collapse of the program unless the rules were simplified. But simplification of the rules was not going to save it. Since the FTC enforced the antitrust laws, the associations could not bargain with the NRA for exemptions. Hence, there was no way for the NRA to induce them to accept the Section 7(a) guarantees. Organized labor had supported the extension of the NIRA on the assumption that they would be incorporated in the agreements. It demanded representation on the industry committees to strengthen collective bargaining and to share responsibility for supervision of the guarantees. But labor leaders soon learned that the associations were sending agreements to the FTC without labor participation on the committees and without adequate Section 7(a) guarantees. In October the AFL convention denounced the program as a mere sham without any social significance whatever. Having lost faith in the program, the federation asked Congress to approve legislation to preserve the gains labor had won through Section 7(a).[18]

Under strong AFL pressure, Congress passed the Wagner National Labor Relations and Guffey-Snyder Bituminous Coal Conservation acts. The Wagner Act, considered by labor as one of the most important New Deal reforms, made permanent the Section 7(a) guarantee of labor's right to organize and bargain. The bituminous coal act, backed by the United Mine Workers (UMW), created a "little NRA for coal" in order to prevent a return to pre-NRA chaos in the industry. A coal commission was to enforce a statutory industry code that covered control of production, collective bargaining, and wage and hour regulation. Roosevelt and Justice Department attorneys doubted the constitutionality of the law's 15-percent tax on producers who refused to accept the code, but the UMW's strike threat induced the president to accept it. Congress also passed legislation creating the Works Progress Administration (WPA), and after some delay, the Walsh-Healey Public Contracts Act. Although the latter would affect only employers receiving government contracts, it kept alive government regulation of labor standards after the *Schechter* decision. Because Congress required that workers be paid local prevailing wages, Labor Department officials would have to determine wage rates in localities throughout the nation.[19]

Assistant Secretary Altmeyer squarely faced the problem of determining prevailing wages that would be fair and that would maintain an American standard of living for employees working on government contracts in any locality in the country. The difficulty, he noted, was that the concept of prevailing wages was illusory. There were many local rates, and even union rates would be difficult to determine where there was little or no unionization. The only way to determine fair wages locally, he suggested, was to gather data on rates for the use of labor-management industry committees and to let them make recommendations. This system would provide for differentials between communities and occupations. The resulting wage, he believed, would be somewhere above the lowest prevailing wage and below the highest, and would maintain a standard satisfactory to labor. The WPA met this problem by paying "security wages" based on local prevailing rates that ranged from $19 to $94 monthly for a 32-to-40-hour week. Although the agency and its wage policy came under considerable criticism, supporters defended it for paying living wages and for pumping money into the economy. For public contracts, Secretary Perkins set a 40-hour week and a median $15 weekly minimum.[20]

Since the administration did not sponsor a new recovery bill, Connery's Labor Committee once again reported out its 30-hour work week licensing bill. It was similar to the committee's May 1933 bill, with almost identical provisions for collective bargaining, child labor, and just and reasonable wages. Since it accepted the labor guarantees, the AFL was willing to support it as a substitute for the NIRA. But despite labor's backing, Connery could not get the House to consider it because Congress preferred a limited extension of the NRA and Roosevelt wanted to delay action on any proposal for business regulation until he obtained information on industry conditions after the invalidation of the codes.[21]

Within a few months of the *Schechter* decision, Roosevelt learned that NRA code labor standards were collapsing and that sweatshop conditions were spreading. In the well-unionized construction, basic materials, and graphic arts industries, code standards were being maintained. But in retail trades and the textile, paper-box, and apparel industries, they were abandoned or widely disregarded. Hours in the apparel industry mounted rapidly from a 36- to a 48- or 54-hour workweek. In the South, not only were blacks being "put back in their place," but there were reports of a ten-cent hourly wage in a New Orleans warehouse and a 78-hour week in a North Carolina bagging mill as extreme examples. The tide of northern "carpetbag employers" fleeing from unions to the South swelled, since poverty-stricken southern towns offered cheap labor, free buildings, power and water, and tax exemptions. Roosevelt passed this information to Senator Pat Harrison and his Finance Committee for consideration when it prepared new recovery legislation. He also set up a cabinet committee to survey the severely depressed textile industry. It found that code standards had reduced unemployment and raised wages significantly. Since some industry leaders were making an effort to maintain standards, the study recommended that Congress support these efforts through whatever legislation might be possible. Although the study did not recommend labor standards, the report indicated that Congress might deal with the stabilization problem industry-by-industry if there were strong objections to more comprehensive recovery legislation.[22]

Amid gloomy predictions about the collapse of the voluntary-code program, Berry went ahead with his plans for a conference on recovery legislation. Early in November 1935 he invited over 6,000 business, investment, labor, and consumer representatives to Washington. Although he received strong support from labor, the response from businessmen was decidedly mixed. Many industrialists condemned the conference as another attempt to regiment business and to create a new legislative mess. Berry's conference got underway in December and was attended by 3,000 delegates. Smaller employers were well represented, but some major industries sent observers with orders not to participate. Berry's proposal for a national labor-management council set off a heated debate that induced hundreds to leave. Only 300 attended the round-table meetings, with labor and management groups meeting separately. There was strong opposition to proposals for reenacting anything resembling the NRA, but eighteen management groups were induced to join labor on a Council for Industrial Progress. Berry assured Roosevelt that the great majority on the council would be sympathetic to legislation for the rehabilitation of industry. Eighteen management groups may have been willing to cooperate, but a *Trade-Ways* survey nevertheless revealed that 78 percent of all trade and industry groups opposed a revival of the NRA, and a NAM survey found 82 percent of 10,000 industrialists opposed to any new recovery legislation.[23]

While Berry was promoting his conference, the FTC became intensely active in reviewing trade-practice agreements. One observer thought that its harassment of businessmen might induce them to support Berry's council and even welcome a new NRA. The FTC approved a few agreements and rejected provisions that violated the antitrust laws. Since the trade associations were unable to bargain with it for including Section 7(a) guarantees, they lost all interest in the voluntary program. By December it was floundering and there seemed no way to save it. Labor Department officials warned Secretary Perkins about the consequences of the floundering program. Under the control of the FTC, Wyzanski explained, the program was certain to bog down, and if it lapsed, the department should not be involved with it. Beyer told Perkins that the program could not be successful because industry committees could not be made competent and responsible. There was danger, she believed, because the floundering program would be used by administration opponents when Congress considered more adequate legislation in the future. Roosevelt accepted the inevitable and terminated the NRA in December, thus ending a second experiment in the cooperative stabilization of industry.[24]

Although Roosevelt shelved the NRA, Berry's Council for Industrial Progress met early in January 1936, with ninety business and thirty labor representatives attending. Berry assured them that the president did not intend to revive the NRA and wanted recommendations on the problems of recovery, economic stabilization, fair-trade practices, and unemployment. The council established seven committees, of which the Committee on Industrial Policy and a Committee on a Maximum Workweek, General-Wages, and Child Labor were the most concerned with labor standards. The Committee on Industrial Policy accepted the need for government regulation of free enterprise and for the improvement of purchasing power by maintaining adequate wages and income. The committee on labor standards defined child labor, excessive hours, and low wages as a form of "unfair competition in the flow of commerce" that was detrimental to the national welfare. It therefore recommended that Congress create independent commissions to limit the workweek, fix minimum wages, and regulate child labor. Despite the fact that some critics of government-sponsored industrial cooperation could not take the council's March reports seriously, Roosevelt extended Berry's job as coordinator and asked the council how the government could promote reemployment and improve wage and hour standards. He also asked it to survey the accomplishments of the NRA, particularly its efforts to improve labor standards.[25]

Although Roosevelt planned to have Congress consider a new recovery measure in 1936, he delayed action for both political and constitutional reasons. After Congress adjourned in 1935, he believed that the country needed a respite from further legislative experiments. Moreover, he wanted to unite his party for the forthcoming election campaign and wished to avoid conflicts with Congress over "radical legislation." Congress seemed equally reluctant to consider legislation on industrial regulation until the Supreme Court reviewed the Wagner and Guffey acts, both of which had set off a flood of litigation. Stalled legislation included Representative Henry Ellenbogen's textile-industry licensing bill; Senator O'Mahoney's FTC-licensing measure;

Representative James A. Shanley's excise-tax licensing plan; another Ellenbogen bill for FTC supervision of fair competition; and Representative Ernest Lundeen's social-insurance bill.[26]

The Labor Department attorney Gerard Reilly questioned the constitutionality or feasibility of all of these bills. He thought Ellenbogen's textile-industry bill better than the Guffey coal act because it did not resort to the taxing power to compel employers to accept a code of fair competition. Instead, it proposed a commission to issue licenses to manufacturers who accepted codes that included labor standards, including a ban on child labor, a 35-hour workweek, and a $15-minimum weekly wage. But banning unlicensed firms from shipping goods in interstate commerce was a direct challenge to the *Dagenhart* decision. The other licensing measures faced the same constitutional roadblock. Reilly also deemed Lundeen's social-insurance bill impractical. It contemplated a guarantee of a minimum standard of living to those receiving less than $20 a week. He estimated that between fifteen and twenty million might be eligible and that the cost would run to $20 billion with a minimum weekly benefit of $10. Lundeen's bill not only failed to provide the tax revenue for the expenditure, but it was also completely out of harmony with Roosevelt's financial program.[27]

All doubts about the Supreme Court's attitude toward regulating production were eliminated in May 1936, when it voided the Guffey coal act in *Carter* v. *Carter Coal Co.* Not only did it find the excise tax a penalty rather than a revenue levy, but it also denied the government the power to regulate production on the ground that the effect of coal production and labor standards on commerce was indirect. Moreover, management-labor agreements fixing wages were a delegation of congressional authority clearly in violation of the Fifth Amendment. By adopting the direct-indirect distinction, the Court once again denied Congress power to regulate activities within the states. Having done so, the Court then denied the states the right to regulate the wages of women. In June 1936 it voided the carefully drawn New York law in *Morehead* v. *Tipaldo* on the ground that such regulation was a violation of freedom of contract protected by the due process clause of the Fourteenth Amendment. Relying on the *Adkins* decision, the Court said the state could not prohibit, change, or nullify contracts between employers and women. The *Tipaldo* decision was a severe blow to the state minimum-wage movement.[28]

Not only did the *Carter* and *Tipaldo* decisions block efforts to regulate labor standards, but they stimulated a campaign to either curb the Supreme Court or amend the Constitution to give the states or the national government the power to regulate wages and hours. Congressmen opposed to increasing national authority supported amendments to expand state powers. Representative Hamilton Fish offered two such resolutions, one to give the states the right to regulate minimum wages for women and children, and another granting the same power to cover men as well. Among other proposals were amendments to submit the Court's decisions to Congress or the people for approval, to increase the number of judicial votes necessary to void an act of Congress, or to simply prohibit the Court from reviewing acts of Congress. Roosevelt knew there was little agreement on any proposal, and even if Congress could muster the two-thirds vote in a year or two, he thought the ratification problem would be overwhelming. He followed Frankfurter's advice to postpone a Court challenge until the issue could be taken to the country during the election campaign. If the Court voided additional legislation, agitation against it would increase, and Roosevelt could ask Congress for an amendment to cope with economic problems after the election.[29]

As Frankfurter predicted, the Supreme Court became a major issue during the campaign. The Democratic platform accepted the need for a clarifying amendment if national economic problems could not otherwise be met through constitutional legislation. Despite the *Tipaldo* decision, the Republican platform declared that the states could regulate conditions of life and labor without altering the Constitution. Roosevelt said almost nothing about the Court during the campaign. Instead, he castigated the economic royalists and told the country that liberty required an opportunity to make a living according to the standards of the time. He also reminded workers that the New Deal had tried to improve labor standards, reduce the workweek, and raise wages. He had tried to help those at the bottom of the economic pyramid by eliminating sweatshops and by improving purchasing power.[30]

Because workers were well-aware of Roosevelt's efforts to aid those at the bottom of the pyramid, organized labor supported him wholeheartedly. Labor, said John L. Lewis, had gained more during the Roosevelt administration than any other and had a duty to support it. Under the leadership of Lewis, Hillman, and David Dubinsky of the International Ladies Garment Workers Union, the newly formed Congress of Industrial Organizations (CIO) gave the president its unqualified support during the campaign. Lewis, Hillman, and George Berry organized Labor's Non-Partisan League (LNPL) for participation in the campaign on a grand scale. Roosevelt acknowledged its support and promised Berry that his administration would promote justice for the nation's wage earners. Consequently, Lewis, Hillman, Berry, and other labor leaders anticipated that labor would have a prominent voice in formulating the administration's forthcoming legislative program.[31]

Given his overwhelming victory, Roosevelt could rightly claim that the majority of voters had endorsed his New Deal policies. Public opinion polls revealed that substantial majorities favored national regulation of labor standards, with 68 percent favoring an 8-hour day, 63 percent supporting minimum wages, and 82 percent favoring a child-labor amendment. Although it opposed national regulation, even the National Association of Manufacturers (NAM) accepted the need for basic standards. It endorsed a ban on child labor, a workweek consistent with the health and welfare of employees, and a general wage level for similar work in localities. Robert W. Johnson of the Johnson and Johnson Company, which operated textile mills in a number of states, urged Roosevelt to move ahead with some plan to control hours and expressed the hope that the best of the old NRA could be revived. And the AFL counsel Charlton Ogburn assured the president that the federation was anxious to cooperate on his legislative program. Secretary Perkins sent her "unconstitutional" wage and hour bill to the White House for consideration by the new Congress.[32]

Early in November Charles O. Gregory, soon to replace Wyzanski as solicitor, studied the constitutionality of labor standards legislation. Given the Supreme Court's decisions, he had little new to suggest for overcoming the constitutional roadblock. Any resort to a coercive excise tax seemed blocked by the *Carter* decision. Federal licensing to require labor standards also seemed doubtful. Legislation promoting state-mandated labor standards would depend on state cooperation and would challenge the *Tipaldo* decision. Expanding the coverage of the Walsh-Healey Public Contracts Act would be constitutional, but would be restricted to government projects. Perhaps, he concluded, the best approach would be to incorporate labor standards in legislation for particular industries that would accept regulation, such as textiles and coal.[33]

Coordinator Berry asked his council's Maximum Workweek, General Wage, and Child Labor Committee to review its position on the Supreme Court's decisions and called a council meeting in December. It was the occasion for much speechmaking, which seemed intended primarily for publicity. President Green took an exceptionally aggressive tone in demanding legislation for a 30-hour week and for strengthening collective bargaining. Edward Filene, a Boston businessman, convincingly argued that cutthroat wages would have to be raised in order to create greater purchasing power and to overcome the depression. More important, however, were the committee reports.[34]

The Industrial Policy Committee paid lip service to the high-wage purchasing-power theory of recovery, but its report was not persuasive. The Maximum Workweek, General Wage, and Child Labor Committee's report sketched the function of national commissions for the regulation of hours, wages, and child labor. Its recommendations set off an argument over the constitutionality of labor standards legislation. Those accepting the need for a constitutional amendment urged delay, while those desiring action agreed that any labor legislation would have to be narrow in scope. The Fair Trade Practice Committee suggested either FTC-supervised labor-standards agreements or state fair-competition legislation, if national regulation were deemed unconstitutional. Overall, the council recognized the national character of the recovery problem and the need to end sweatshop competition, stabilize business, and enhance purchasing power.[35]

Berry did not keep Roosevelt informed about the council's work, and the press soon noted contradictions in its recommendations for FTC participation and for the creation of a "new NRA." Roosevelt confirmed the serious breakdown of wage and hour standards and emphasized the need to restore minimum wages and maximum hours, but he asked the press not to say he was trying to restore the NRA. He did not know when legislation would be ready, but he said the states could not handle the problem without federal help. Attorney General Cummings also ruled out state action. Sweatshop and child labor, he told the Washington Bar Association, must not be allowed to deprive workers of an opportunity to maintain American standards of living. Moreover, it was futile to argue that unemployment and recovery were merely state problems. Prophetic language from the attorney general, but he did not reveal how the administration intended to overcome the constitutional roadblock.[36]

Despite the roadblock, prospects were not completely hopeless. Justice Department attorney Robert L. Stern recognized that the Supreme Court had established precedents that could be used to justify regulation. Although it had denied that mining and production were directly related to interstate commerce, it had also recognized that strikes interfering with production would be subject to national commerce power if the effect of a local dispute restrained the supply of goods or altered the price of products entering commerce. And the Court had upheld the regulation of stockyards, packers, and grain-futures trading on the ground that whatever obstructed or unduly burdened trade practices came within the commerce power. Congress had the right to consider the danger, and the Court would not substitute its own judgment unless the relation of the subject to commerce and its effect were clearly nonexistent. If the Court were willing to accept these precedents, Congress might regulate all interrelated elements in interstate industries. The *Schechter* case, Stern believed, had one saving grace. In considering the local poultry market, the Court did not pass on the power of Congress to control trade practices or labor relations in major industries in interstate commerce. Hence, the *Schechter* case could be distinguished when and if regulatory legislation were attempted.[37]

Because new recovery legislation was postponed, in 1936 the nation experienced a further deterioration in wage and hour standards. Employers reduced labor costs by hiring children, paying as little as $3 to $9 a week in some sections of the country. Such exploitation was a threat to the living standards, security, and well-being of workers everywhere. In 1935 there was a 55-percent increase over the previous year in the employment of 14- and-15-year-olds. In 1936 two and one-half times as many left school as in the previous year and took unskilled work in low-paid occupations. President Green was appalled by the exploitation of 13- and 14-year-olds in New Jersey silk mills and said that ratification of the pending Child Labor Amendment was the only solution.[38]

Although economists insisted that shortening the workweek was not a panacea for the unemployment problem, the AFL clung to the 30-hour week. Industrial production in 1936 was still 12 percent below that of 1929 and payrolls were 14 percent below those of that year. Production had increased by 43 percent between 1932 and 1935 while man-hours in manufacturing rose only 26 percent. Hence, the federation said the 6-hour day was justified. Not only was reemployment lagging because of increases in productivity, but average weekly earnings remained 18 percent below those of 1929 and much of the improvement in earnings had been offset by the increase in the cost of living. Because an estimated twelve million remained jobless, the AFL insisted that there would be no industrial recovery without a shorter workweek with no reduction in pay.[39]

As his first administration drew to a close in the winter of 1936, the public knew that Roosevelt understood the plight of the nation's exploited workers and that he remained firmly committed to the improvement of labor standards. Press reports revealed that work on new recovery legislation was already under way, despite the constitutional obstacle. How it could be overcome remained unclear. But quite in keeping with his penchant for experimentation, Roosevelt was anxious to try a new approach. The activities of Berry's council indicated that he was keeping his options open. Very little was known about his plans, and all the public could do was speculate about them until his inauguration in January.

4

Ghost of the NRA

The employment of men or women or children at wages or under
work conditions which imperils the health or morals of such men,
women, or children constitutes economic slavery.
          —Representative William P. Connery

AFTER Roosevelt's resounding victory in 1936, prospects for national
wage and hour regulation seemed bright. The president was committed to a new labor-standards proposal; Congress was solidly Democratic; and a majority of the public supported regulation of wages,
hours, and child labor. There remained the constitutional roadblock,
but a well-drafted law might induce the Supreme Court to follow the
election returns, if not the breadlines. Since there was little agreement
among administration attorneys on labor-standards legislation, Roosevelt asked that all proposals be sent to the Justice Department for
consideration. Justice Department attorneys were reluctant to draft
a wage and hour bill until the Supreme Court handed down a decision
on the Wagner Labor Relations Act. Berry's attorneys contemplated
incorporating labor standards in fair-trade legislation, while Labor
Department officials preferred the determination of standards
through industry committees. Because there was little agreement
among them, Roosevelt faced a problem similar to that in 1933 over
the drafting of the NIRA. But there was no comparable emergency
in 1937 that might frighten Congress into accepting new experimental
labor legislation. Hence, Roosevelt would first have to overcome the
constitutional obstacle.

In January Roosevelt reminded the public that despite all the New
Deal's efforts, one-third of the nation remained ill-housed, ill-clad,
and ill-nourished. He confirmed his commitment to a shorter workweek and decent labor standards but ruled out state action or a constitutional amendment. The government, he explained, should assist
people in their efforts to improve their lives, enjoy personal liberty,

and pursue the happiness that comes with security and opportunities for recreation and culture. The most serious problem was unemployment and the lack of balance it created in the economy. What the country needed was a modern interpretation of the Constitution by a Supreme Court that respected the will of the people. How the "Four Horsemen" on the horse-and-buggy Court could be induced to accept the will of the people, he did not explain. Nor did he suggest specific wage and hour legislation.[1]

Since Roosevelt failed to submit a labor-standards proposal to Congress in January, a number of congressmen offered their own bills for consideration. Senator Black and Representative Connery once again submitted their 30-hour bills. Senator Francis T. Maloney proposed a national unemployment commission to set a 30-to-40-hour workweek, and Senator O'Mahoney again suggested regulation of labor standards through Federal Trade Commission (FTC)-licensing. Representative Harry B. Hawes thought Congress should help the states enforce their labor laws. Other bills would regulate individual industries, such as coal and textiles. All of these measures revealed considerable disagreement on the constitutional basis for regulating wages and hours.[2]

Berry's council also had considerable difficulty agreeing on a proposal. In January its Legal Committee approved two fair-competition bills, which were drafted by David Drechsler and Siegfried Hartman and sent to Solicitor Stanley Reed. Drechsler's bill proposed direct FTC regulation of fair wage and hour standards. Oppressive labor standards were defined as a form of unfair competition that caused labor disorders and obstructed commerce. The FTC would investigate substandard conditions and issue cease and desist orders to those employers failing to maintain fair standards. Hartman's bill also defined substandard labor conditions to be an unfair-trade practice that burdened commerce. In an approach similar to the voluntary agreement plan, his proposal would authorize industrial associations to submit fair-trade agreements with labor guarantees to the president for approval. The FTC, attorney general, and courts would be responsible for compliance and enforcement. Since the president asked that all wages and hour proposals were to be submitted to the Justice Department, Cummings created a special team in Reed's office to review them. He preferred to have experienced attorneys who had participated in the *Schechter* and *Carter* cases responsible for drafting the wage and hour bill.[3]

Since the AFL opposed FTC regulation of wages and hours, it abandoned Berry's council and offered its own bill. The federation counsel Charlton Ogburn's proposal contemplated a national commission authorized to promote labor-management conferences on labor standards. Agreements on wages and hours would be considered part of fair competition, and Congress would not arbitrarily fix standards. While supporting Ogburn's bill, President Green made it clear that the AFL would press its demand for a basic 30-hour week, with flexibility for different occupations and industries. He backed Senator Black, who said the fight for the 30-hour week would go on and that he favored a constitutional amendment, if one were necessary. The CIO's John L. Lewis explained that its legislative program had not crystallized because it did not know what the administration would do about an amendment. In February Labor Department officials urged Black to redraft his bill and criticized proposals offered by Senators Maloney and O'Mahoney.[4]

Since there were doubts in the Labor Department regarding standards and coverage, Solicitor Gregory asked 30 leading academic economists for advice. Only 16 responded and their replies may not have been helpful. Six favored basing minimum rates on the cost of living alone, 3 preferred fair value for services rendered, and 3 would utilize the cost of living and other factors. Eleven favored covering men as well as women and children, while 3 would cover only women and children. Thirteen favored covering all occupations, and only 2 would limit coverage to sweated industries. Eleven preferred individual rates for each industry while 4 favored the same minimum for all. Nine favored geographic differentials while 5 opposed them. Seven opposed variations according to the size of the community, while 5 approved them. Six favored regulation by a national board, 4 preferred regional boards, and only 1 recommended regulation by state boards.[5] Admittedly, the sample was small, but the majority favored covering men and all occupations and basing wages on the cost of living factor.

By mid-February Gregory completed his redraft of the "National Labor Standards Act," which resembled the Consumers' League's model bill. When the secretary found that substandard-labor conditions in any industry obstructed the flow of commerce, he would authorize an investigation by a labor-management council. After hearings, the council would formulate articles of labor standards for the industry, which would be administered by the secretary. A national advisory board of representatives from the industrial councils would be responsible for recommending uniform practices. The secretary would also appoint officials to enforce the articles in each industry. The federal courts could enjoin and punish violations of the articles. Those receiving public contracts had to accept the standards set forth in the articles for their industry.[6]

Gregory's bill simply assumed that Congress could eliminate from commerce obstacles created by local labor-management disputes over wages and hours. He sought to overcome the Supreme Court's prohibition against delegation of congressional authority to management-labor boards by having the secretary appoint their members. The Court might then accept them as officials and approve their right to make wage and hour recommendations. Recommendations approved by the secretary might then be part of the process of administrative discretion under basic standards set by Congress. The ban on child labor simply assumed that the Court was ready to abandon the *Dagenhart* decision. Clearly, the constitutionality of the National Labor Standards Act depended on the willingness of the Court to uphold the National Labor Relations Act.

Attorney General Cummings and Representative Connery were equally concerned about the constitutionality of the wage and hour measure. Connery suggested having Thomas G. Corcoran cooperate on the drafting project. Corcoran was a protégé of Frankfurter and a member of the legal staff of the Reconstruction Finance Corporation. He worked closely with Benjamin V. Cohen, another Frankfurter student, who was on the legal staff of the Public Works Administration. Both had worked with Frankfurter on the Consumers' League's model minimum-wage bill and were asked to cooperate with Reed's staff on the labor-standards measure. They relied on Associate Justice Louis D. Brandeis for advice on constitutional issues. Brandeis promoted his proposals through Frankfurter, who passed supporting material to Roosevelt. The president relied on Corcoran, who enlisted the aid of the best administration "Harvard Brains," and then delivered the finished bill. Roosevelt delegated overall responsibility for coordinating the labor-standards project to his son, James, who was not much of an asset on Capitol Hill, where some congressmen resented dealing with "an emissary from father."[7]

Very few details about the wage and hour proposal were revealed, because Roosevelt did not have a bill. Early in February he did say that the law would be broad and that it might be ready for Congress "pretty soon." He flatly denied that it depended on the Supreme Court's decision in the pending NLRB cases. When he conferred with Richberg, who submitted a Business Advisory Council draft of a fair-competition wage and hour measure, the press reported that the administration was considering an omnibus measure whereby Congress would reenact the old National Recovery Administration (NRA) codes, including a blanket code, with flexible standards. In response, Roosevelt said his mind was open to all suggestions for dealing with unemployment. His primary concern was wages and hours, and trade practices were of secondary importance. Congress, he suggested, could decide whether trade practices and labor standards would be combined in the same measure. Actually, he had already ruled out trade practices early in the month. All he wanted was a bill regulating wages and hours.[8]

In February Roosevelt gave the nation a shock instead of a wage and hour bill. Since the Supreme Court remained the roadblock, he decided to challenge it. He sent Congress Attorney General Cummings's Judicial Reorganization Bill, which sought to pack the Court in order to obtain a majority favorable to New Deal legislation. It stunned the country and Congress and turned out to be a serious political error. In a spurious approach to the issues between the New Deal and the Court, his "Court-packing" plan proposed adding forty-five judges to the lower courts and up to six to the bench. Not only did he fail to focus attention on its tortured interpretation of the Constitution, but he misjudged his proposal's impact on the public, his party, and pending reform legislation. The Court bill set off a congressional donnybrook that tied up all legislation from February to June, dismayed his congressional leaders, and pleased his Republican opponents. Some loyal party leaders reluctantly supported it, but many southern conservative Democrats joined the Republicans in condemning it and any further New Deal experimental "radical" legislation.[9]

Although the Court-packing bill split the Democrats and alienated some party leaders, loyal Democrats, social reformers, and organized labor supported it. Understanding that labor's program was threatened by the Court, John L. Lewis assured Roosevelt of the CIO's backing. The AFL also endorsed the bill, believing that economic progress would be made more rapidly by its acceptance. Roosevelt was supremely confident that the opposition would collapse and held up other legislation in order to induce reluctant congressmen to cooperate. Despite such pressure, New Deal opponents launched a crusade to "save constitutional government," and Congress was swamped with protests. Encouraged by the uproar, hostile senators threatened to filibuster against the bill, and dissension among Democrats lasted long after it was defeated. Justice Brandeis undermined Roosevelt's assault on the Court by having Senator Burton K. Wheeler publicize Chief Justice Hughes's letter defending it. Corcoran thereafter refused to see Brandeis, whose influence on the administration virtually ended.[10]

During the fight over the Court bill, Reed's attorneys made little progress on the labor-standards measure. They reviewed wage and hour proposals and waited for the Supreme Court's decision on the NLRB cases. They rejected Berry's fair-trade bills because they were naively drafted and were based upon congressional control of industrial-trade practices that had been rejected by the Court. Walter L. Pope, who headed Reed's drafting team, also found Senator O'Mahoney's FTC-licensing bill both impractical and unconstitutional. Licensing was inexpedient because it would not cover individuals or partnerships engaged in interstate commerce without a corporate franchise. And since the Court had limited the conditions that could be imposed on corporations engaged in interstate commerce, any licensing plan for regulating labor standards would be found unconstitutional. Because of the delay on the wage and hour bill, when Assistant Attorney General Robert Jackson asked Pope about progress on it, Pope advised him to wait for the Court's decision on the NLRB cases.[11]

Pope opposed proposals for omnibus coverage and favored regulating individual industries. He wanted to start with those in which there was the greatest need before undertaking the more difficult task of regulating all industry. He thought there would be considerable support for a law in the coal and textile industries, whereas an omnibus bill would be strongly opposed. Since each industry had its own problems, the factual basis for regulation could be more easily determined than it could for all industries. Even though regulation of specific industries might put them at a competitive disadvantage with others, he believed the most expedient step would be to proceed with the Ellenbogen textile-industry bill and to redraft the invalidated Guffey coal act.[12]

In drafting a new coal-industry bill, Pope utilized the Ashurst-Sumners Act's conditional-state ban of prison-made goods, which the Supreme Court upheld in the *Kentucky Whip & Collar Co.* v. *Illinois Central Railroad Co.* (1937). The Court upheld the right of Congress to exclude from commerce prison-made goods destined to states that banned their receipt. Pope's bill would make unlawful the transportation of coal mined under labor standards inferior to those of the state of destination. In addition, producers operating under substandard labor conditions could not ship coal to any interstate market also supplied by competitors maintaining fair standards. Pope's draft specified an 8-hour day, fair wages commensurate with the value of services rendered, and a ban on child labor. Although the United Mine Workers (UMW), Richberg, and Berry's attorneys reviewed it favorably, its dependence on state cooperation was a serious weakness in obtaining effective national regulation of wage and hour standards.[13]

In March, Roosevelt recognized the growing opposition to his Court bill and took the issue to the country. Before the end of the month, however, the Supreme Court undermined his attack by upholding the Washington state minimum-wage law for women in *West Coast Hotel* v. *Parrish*. Speaking for the majority of five, Chief Justice Hughes set aside the *Tipaldo* decision on a technicality and overruled the *Adkins* decision. The Constitution, he explained, does not speak of liberty of contract; rather, it prohibits the denial of liberty without due process of law. But regulation that is reasonably related to its subject and is adopted in the interest of protecting the health, safety, morals, and welfare of the community is due process. Considering the exploitation of female employees, he said the community did not have to subsidize unconscionable employers. Reformers were pleased with the *Parrish* decision because the Court abandoned absolute freedom of contract, a major obstacle to action on minimum-wage laws. As Attorney General Cummings noted, the legislative rights of forty-eight states were reinstated. Although the decision stimulated state action on minimum-wage laws, Roosevelt continued to believe that state regulation was inadequate to meet the national problem.[14]

Early in April the Supreme Court dealt another blow to Roosevelt's Court plan by upholding the Wagner Labor Relations Act. In *N. L. R. B.* v. *Jones & Laughlin Steel Corp.* it agreed that acts that directly burdened or obstructed the free flow of commerce, including those growing out of labor disputes, were within the reach of congressional power. Congress could therefore regulate intrastate activities that had a close and substantial relationship to commerce. Such activities might be subject to regulation even though the industry might be considered local. Although the Court's extension of congressional authority to control activities related to production that obstructed commerce pleased administration attorneys, there was no guarantee that it would uphold wage and hour legislation. In order to justify national regulation, it would have to be convinced that disputes over hours, wages, and child labor caused labor strife that burdened or obstructed commerce. Both supporters and opponents of the Court bill agreed that the Court might not approve national regulation on the basis of the *Jones & Laughlin* decision. Moreover, the constitutional "no man's land" had become "Owen J. Robert's Land," and Roosevelt was unwilling to trust future New Deal reform legislation to a Court whose favorable decisions depended on the swing vote of Justice Roberts. He therefore pressed Congress for action on the Court bill.[15]

After the Supreme Court handed down its *Jones & Laughlin* decision, Reed asked Pope to drop his work on the coal and textile industry bills and to prepare an omnibus wage and hour measure. Pope rejected a flat ban on goods made under substandard-labor conditions because it would be a direct challenge to the *Dagenhart* decision. As to the right of Congress to eliminate obstacles in commerce, he thought the *Jones & Laughlin* decision was grounded on a very narrow basis, a specific finding that an unfair-labor practice led to a dispute resulting in an obstruction of commerce. And he doubted whether the Court would consider long hours, low wages, and child labor as causes of labor strife. Pope also dismissed the conditional-state ban because it would be impossible to administer. He therefore prepared a bill that would make sales of goods produced under substandard-labor conditions an unfair method of competition. The unfair-competition approach, he explained, had been recommended by Harvard Professor Thomas Reed Powell and would probably be easiest to defend in the courts. His bill's provisions for investigation and enforcement were similar to those utilized by the FTC and would require complaints about substandard labor practices. If Pope thought his bill would meet the Court test, Labor Department Solicitor Gerard Reilly, who replaced Gregory in February, thought it completely impractical. The administrative machinery, Reilly believed, would never carry out the bill's objectives, and it would be impossible to investigate the vast number of complaints that would arise.[16]

After the *Jones & Laughlin* decision, Corcoran and Cohen drafted a fair-standards bill with the aid of Frankfurter and Reilly. Since their bill differed from that proposed by Reed's attorneys, they met with them to resolve differences. Since their bill contemplated omnibus coverage, fair-wage standards, and a child-labor ban, Roosevelt accepted it. Cohen thereafter got a reluctant agreement from the Children's Bureau, the Consumer's League, and the National Child Labor Committee (NCLC) to include the ban and by April 30 completed a new draft providing for regulation by a national wage and hour board. Corcoran then prepared a résumé of the bill's provisions and the president's wage and hour message.[17]

The Cohen-Corcoran bill was based on the right of Congress to eliminate evils caused by substandard labor conditions. The employment of workers under such conditions "caused the channels of commerce to spread conditions detrimental to their health, efficiency, and well being"; burdened "commerce and the free flow of goods"; was an "unfair method of competition"; led to labor disputes that "burdened and obstructed commerce and the free flow of goods"; caused "undue price fluctuations and impaired the price of goods and services"; and "interfered with the orderly and fair marketing of goods." The correction of these conditions required Congress to prohibit the shipping of goods produced under substandard-labor conditions and to provide for the "elimination of substandard conditions in occupations in and directly affecting commerce."[18]

Wages and hours would be determined by either Congress or a Fair Labor Standards Board. A 40-hour-40-cent standard was contemplated but Congress would set the "nonoppressive" standard. An "oppressive wage" would be a rate lower than that set by Congress or the board, and an "oppressive workweek" would be hours longer than those fixed by Congress or the board. "Oppressive child labor" would be the employment of children under 16 years of age or between 16 and 18 in dangerous occupations. "Oppressive labor practices" included strikebreaking, use of labor spies, or the maintenance of company unions. Fair wages and a reasonable workweek would be commensurate with the value or nature of the services rendered. Fair-labor standards would be achieved where no oppressive conditions existed.[19]

Upon complaint about unfair wages, the Labor Standards Board would investigate low rates and services rendered through advisory wage and hour boards. If low wages threatened to undermine fair wages of other workers, the board would set fair rates, taking into account the cost of living, value of services, collective agreements, and fair wages paid by other employers, but it could not set rates providing an annual income of more than $1,500, or $30 per week. Agreement on this figure was not certain, and an income of $1,200, or $24 per week, was still under consideration. Similarly, the board would examine the hours suitable to services rendered, and if they undermined fair standards, it would set a reasonable workweek based on considerations of health, efficiency, and reasonableness for the work done, the number of persons available for work, and hours accepted in collective bargaining agreements and in voluntary agreements, but not a workweek of less than 35 hours. Agreement on this limit was also uncertain, and the 30-hour floor remained under consideration. In addition, workers would receive pay-and-a-half for overtime. There were exceptions for apprentices, the disabled, board and lodging, and special cases. Administration, including investigations, advisory boards, hearings, and enforcement, was similar to that developed by Corcoran and Cohen for the Consumers' League's model bill.[20]

The Corcoran-Cohen draft did not please other attorneys working on wage and hour regulation, because regulation by a board was much too cumbersome and complicated. Sullivan Jones, Berry's assistant coordinator, deemed it "foolhardy" and urged Pope to reconsider the council's unfair trade-practice bill. Pope thought the Corcoran-Cohen draft would arouse strong opposition because it was all-inclusive, complicated, and too much like the NRA in fixing labor standards. Solicitor Reilly agreed that it was truly an omnibus, if not a "blunderbuss" bill. Prohibiting the shipment of goods made under substandard labor conditions, he noted, simply assumed that the *Dagenhart* decision was no longer law. It also had the child-labor ban and failed to provide for industry committees to formulate labor standards. Since the wage and hour board might set standards for all industry because of substandard conditions in a few factories, he was sure such extensive regulation would alarm the business community.[21]

After further consultation with his bill's critics, Cohen worked out a new draft that sought to overcome their objections. Since the April 30 draft had omitted specific provisions for the labor board, a new section authorized the president to appoint one of three members. It would be required to make investigations and inspections through the secretary of labor, who was in turn authorized to utilize industry committees and state agencies. And in order to placate organized labor, it would accept collective bargaining agreements providing for higher minimum wages or shorter hours than those fixed by Congress. The board was to make the wage and hour provisions effective as rapidly as possible without curtailing employment opportunities, and it would vary them to maintain minimum standards of health and efficiency. The 35-hour workweek floor and annual $1,500-income ceiling were retained, but a $20-weekly wage and a 30-hour floor were still under consideration.[22]

Cohen's May 12 draft made no significant changes in the scope of the proposed legislation and failed to overcome the objections of Justice and Labor Department attorneys. Pope congratulated Cohen on his splendid draftsmanship, but told him that his bill was too well done, too inclusive, and too complicated to administer. He predicted that it would raise a storm of protest that would injure the movement for wage and hour regulation. He recommended scrapping it and preparing separate measures for banning child labor and for regulating individual industries. The best plan, he suggested, was to put wage and hour standards in the Ellenbogen textile-industry bill, build experience, and then extend regulation to other industries. Cohen objected to the individual-industry-approach because he wanted to avoid entangling labor standards with fair-trade practices. He preferred to deal exclusively with labor standards on a broad front.[23]

Officials in the Labor Department wanted to delete the child-labor ban because they believed a separate child-labor bill had a good chance of passing. Senator Alben Barkley sponsored the Children's Bureau's bill, and Perkins asked Roosevelt to delete the ban in the wage and hour bill. But he refused to do so in order to make the labor-standards measure easier to get through Congress. And by the middle of May, he had good reason to be concerned.[24]

Tangled in a mass of legislation, Congress seemed to be in a coma. In order to force favorable action on the Court bill, Roosevelt delayed action on farm and labor legislation, and congressional leaders struggled to break the logjam. Angered by the Court bill, hostile southern Democrats were "off the reservation," putting on war paint. While Roosevelt enjoyed a two-week fishing cruise in the Gulf of Mexico, Congress marked time, ignorant of his intentions regarding the labor-standards bill or other legislation. After he returned to Washington, he denied that he would insist on any legislation, which conflicted with reports that congressional leaders had received a "must list" that included the wage and hour bill. His problems with the Court bill were further complicated when Justice Willis Van Devanter announced his retirement. While New Dealers were happy to have one of the four horsemen retire, his departure helped to undermine support for the Court bill. For several weeks Roosevelt's congressional leaders urged him to compromise, but he remained adamant. Despite intense pressure, and much to the president's chagrin, Senator William F. Ashurst's Judiciary Committee finally rejected it, and Roosevelt suffered an embarrassing defeat.[25]

Cohen quickly completed his May 20 draft of the "Fair Labor Standards Act" (FLSA), which differed only slightly from that of May 12. On the following day it was handed to Representative Connery and Senator Black and thereafter became known as the Black-Connery Bill. The wage floor and ceiling for hours remained unspecified, and it was assumed that Congress would accept a 40-cent minimum and 40-hour maximum. The limitation on the maximum annual income was reduced from $1,500 to $1,200, and the board could not set a wage rate higher than 80 cents. Oppressive standards were distinguished from rates that might be unreasonable in certain industries or geographic areas. Where standards were clearly oppressive, regulation would be automatic, but where they depended on particular circumstances, regulation would become effective only after investigation by the board. As rapidly as possible, it would exclude from commerce goods made under oppressive or unfair conditions and establish a floor for wages and a ceiling for hours.[26]

Beyond eliminating oppressive standards, a five-member board would establish fair standards industry-by-industry, with due regard for local diversity. If it found that substandard wages and hours in any industry undermined fair standards maintained by some employers, it would fix fair standards for the entire industry. Once they had been fixed, goods produced under substandard conditions would be banned from commerce. The same ban would apply to goods made by children under conditions found to be detrimental to their health and well-being. In addition to the banning of such goods, the board would also eliminate other conditions that led to labor disputes that burdened or obstructed commerce. Such provisions were supplementary to the ban on goods and provided an alternative legal basis for regulation. Cohen admitted that there was some overlapping of these provisions, but he saw no inconsistencies. Since the board could grant exemptions from the labor standards, he believed the bill was not arbitrary. Moreover, the legislation did not seek to cover purely local activities or intrastate trade.[27]

Without doubt, Corcoran and Cohen were expert legal draftsmen, but Cohen's final draft failed to satisfy those most closely involved with the proposed legislation. Blackwell Smith thought such a powerful board would have trouble resisting pressure groups unless its activities were more rigidly defined. Like Pope, he wanted it to set basic standards in important industries where they could be enforced. Above all, he warned, it must not be diverted from compliance, which had been the NRA problem. Hartman complained to Pope about the Cohen draft's direct government regulation of standards. He thought his own fair-competition bill was better, particularly since it would cover intrastate as well as interstate activities. Ogburn sent the AFL unfair-competition bill to Perkins, explaining that it covered intrastate as well as interstate activities and would decrease geographic differentials. Roosevelt asked him to confer with Black and Perkins and suggested a united front on labor legislation.[28]

Labor Department officials were highly critical of Cohen's bill. Concerned about the constitutionality of wage and hour regulation, they wanted the child-labor ban under a separate title as well as complete authority over child labor. Although Reilly sympathized with the Children's Bureau, he nevertheless thought Roosevelt correct in approving the inclusion of the ban in order to make the bill more acceptable to Congress. He thought it would be embarrassing for Perkins to insist on a separate title. Not only would she upset the president's strategy, but she would be placing the interest of the bureau ahead of the broader objectives of the legislation. Since Cohen anticipated that the first test of the legislation would probably be a child-labor case, it would be unfortunate and undesirable for the bureau to disregard the president's policy and insist upon a change.[29]

Clara Beyer thought Cohen's resort to a standards board to deal with comprehensive wage and hour regulation was ill-advised. If a board were necessary, she believed it should act in a purely judicial capacity. Since it would depend upon the department for investigations and enforcement, she wanted its responsibilities spelled out. She thought the secretary should have the power to investigate labor conditions, enforce wage and hour regulation, and direct state labor officials. State agencies should carry out most of the administration in order to avoid creating a large federal staff in the states. She also supported the Barkley child-labor bill because it provided for very close cooperation between the department and state agencies. Her remedy for all of these problems would be to put the standards board in the department.[30]

Solicitor Reilly, however, questioned the desirability of relying upon state agencies. Not only did state labor departments have little standing with their congressional delegations, he thought the Labor Department's operation would be impaired if it insisted on cooperation. Compliance would be more difficult to obtain if federal inspectors had to consider local political factors in making appointments and thus operate in a "roundabout system." In addition, the former compelling need to build up state labor departments would no longer be essential if Congress provided for a national system. Given all the issues, Reilly recommended a review of the suggestions made by Blackwell Smith, labor organizations, and the department's bureaus. Roosevelt was calling for a united front, and Perkins could not criticize the bill openly without playing into the hands of its opponents and endangering its prospects.[31]

Given the hostility generated by the Court fight among New Deal opponents, the wage and hour bill was in trouble the day Black and Connery received it. When news drifted over to Capitol Hill that Corcoran and Cohen had drafted it, those congressmen who resented the former's close relationship with Roosevelt were provoked. Moreover, the bill was not the product of the labor committees of either house, which had held up other legislation at the request of the president. And most unfortunately, it failed to get the enthusiastic endorsement of the AFL. After a conference with Roosevelt, John L. Lewis and Hillman commented favorably on it, but President Green denounced government wage-fixing and the proposed 40-hour week. Not only was the AFL afraid that mandated standards would lower those already established by collective bargaining, but Green said that employers would cut costs by lowering skilled rates to compensate for increasing minimum wages. The National Association for Manufacturers (NAM) also denounced the bill, denying that the country needed new restrictive and experimental legislation that would increase production costs and create confusion detrimental to economic recovery. In addition, many southerners opposed it because omnibus coverage of all industry by a national board would deny the South its cheap-labor advantage. According to Cummings, the bill stiffened the resistance of many southern senators who "actually froth at the mouth when the subject is mentioned."[32]

Despite the criticism, the administration's Fair Labor Standards Bill was finally in Congress. But it had been drafted in considerable haste by Roosevelt's "assistant attorney generals," who had overcome or brushed aside the objections of those most concerned about regulation of labor standards. By insisting on broad omnibus regulation through a powerful board, Corcoran and Cohen ignored the Justice Department's preference for the gradual industry-by-industry approach, Berry's council's support for fair-competition wage and hour regulation as part of a fair-trade program, AFL opposition to wage-fixing, and the Labor Department's concern about regulation by an independent agency. Moreover, it was new experimental legislation, which was compared to the NRA by opponents who questioned its constitutionality. It was opposed by both the NAM and AFL, two of the most powerful lobbying organizations in Washington. And it was delivered to Congress as "must legislation" when discontent was deep, elections were distant, and congressmen wanted to go home. Some critics doubted that Roosevelt could get Congress moving again before it insisted on adjourning. Under these circumstances, some wondered if "that man" in the White House yet retained his magic. Given these problems, it seemed that only a skilled magician would be able to get the Black-Connery Bill through a rebellious Congress.

5

The Senate Abandons Living Wages

Common sense also tells us that it will help create those jobs and supply necessary purchasing power, if we shorten unreasonably long hours and raise the wages of the whole lower-income third of our industrial population to an American standard of living.
—Senator Hugo L. Black

IN his message to Congress recommending wage and hour regulation, President Roosevelt reminded the country of the need to improve the purchasing power of workers and tied it to stabilizing the market for farm commodities. In a richly endowed self-respecting democracy, he explained, there was no justification for child labor, for stretching workers' hours, or for chiseling their wages. Goods produced under substandard conditions were "contraband" and should not be allowed to "pollute interstate trade." Distinguishing clearly oppressive labor standards from those that were not fair or reasonable, he recognized that fair standards would require wage differentials between industries and localities. By establishing basic standards, he thought it would be possible to build up fair standards industry-by-industry. And he hoped the proposed law would stimulate state action to cover intrastate activities. The objective, he explained, was to establish standards that would enable workers to fulfill the promise of American life.[1]

Initial response to Roosevelt's message and the Black-Connery Bill was mixed and cautious. The *Washington Evening Star* found his objectives admirable but thought that congressional delegation of power might run riot. The *Boston Herald* said his objectives were so sound that they would not provoke much opposition. The *New York Herald Tribune* discovered a new note of reasonableness in his consideration of social problems. The *Philadelphia Inquirer, Cleveland Plain Dealer,* and *Portland Oregonian* said that the elimination of child labor and regulation of wages and hours were worthy objectives. On the other hand, the *Providence Journal* could not imagine northern and southern congressmen agreeing on differentials. The *Baltimore Sun* thought mandatory standards would interfere with reemployment, while the *Hartford Courant* said regulation would fix standards of living at the existing level. The *Los Angeles Times*, expecting the worst, warned its readers that John L. Lewis, Secretary Perkins, "and the rest of that communist crew" were behind the words of the president.[2]

Although early passage of the Black-Connery Bill had been anticipated, Roosevelt faced a tough fight. Senate opponents compared it to the NIRA, because it sought to restore the labor provisions of the old National Recovery Administration (NRA) codes. Senator William H. King of Utah, a staunch foe of the NRA, said it was worse than the NIRA, infringed on states' rights, and would create something like Mussolini's fascism. Senators Arthur H. Vandenberg of Michigan and Pat McCarran of Nevada agreed, suggesting a delay and a study of wage and hour regulation by the labor committees of both houses during the summer recess. Vice President John N. Garner said regulation of labor standards was too complicated for immediate consideration and should be postponed until the next session. Many senators were on the fence, waiting to see what basic standards would be written into the bill before committing themselves. Congressional conservatives quickly organized a bipartisan coalition to limit the board's wage-fixing authority.[3]

Unfortunately for the bill's backers, it failed to get solid support from organized labor. Although John L. Lewis and Hillman said they would back it, the latter favored a 30-hour workweek. President Green's original response was noncommittal, but after a meeting of the AFL Executive Council, the federation agreed to support it if Congress accepted amendments limiting regulation to industries in which collective bargaining was ineffective. The council opposed the board's wage-fixing authority because it was afraid the board would try to fix maximum wages. It also thought the bill's ban on child labor would undermine support for the pending Child Labor Amendment. Because of its opposition to government wage-fixing, it recommended the continuation of the Council for Industrial Progress.[4]

Secretary Roper's Business Advisory Council also opposed the bill. While council members approved its objectives, they suggested that it be made more practical. They preferred a weak board, which would merely administer and enforce the statutory wage and hour standards. They suggested dropping the flexible wage and hour provisions of Section V, the heart of fair-standards regulation. Dropping them, the council believed, would not prejudice later efforts to obtain fair standards as soon as the board successfully established the basic nonoppressive standards. It doubted that enforcement of higher fair standards could be defended, since no court had upheld broad regulation of wages in higher brackets for both male and female workers. It therefore recommended starting slowly with a weak board and making more progress in the long run.[5]

Labor Department officials were concerned about the authority of the Labor Standards Board. Clara Beyer wanted wage and hour regulation in the department and favored utilizing state agencies in order to avoid creating a large federal staff of administrators. Katherine Lenroot did not want the board to be responsible for the enforcement of the child-labor provisions and wanted exclusive bureau enforcement of them. Moreover, she wanted department authority over learners, apprentices, and handicapped workers. Reilly thought Perkins should support the bill and leave desired amendments with the congressional committees or sympathetic congressmen.[6]

Dorothy Sells, an expert on British trade-board regulation, deemed the Labor Standards Board's arbitrary rate-setting authority to be paternalistic. It would hand down wage rates rather than allow industry labor-management representatives to set them. She also objected to following the pattern established by state minimum-wage regulation for women and children, because setting industrial-wage rates nationally was a much more complicated problem. The Black-Connery Bill, she believed, was flawed, because it would not encourage collective bargaining. British trade-board experience had encouraged the shift from compulsory to voluntary bargaining, and there were many advantages in that system. Industry boards had been able to set realistic standards, and the democratic process of negotiating wage agreements helped to promote industrial peace. The system also facilitated administration and compliance. Sells urged Perkins to consider establishing wage boards in as many as nine regions and offered to cooperate in drafting a trade-board measure.[7]

Perkins clearly favored the industry-board approach suggested by Sells. Late in May she asked a House labor subcommittee to place a proposed textile-industry commission in her department. One commission for each industry, she explained, was the proper approach to wage and hour regulation. Since she anticipated the passage of omnibus regulation, if the textile-industry bill passed, she wanted the commission made part of a larger board in order to coordinate administration and to avoid too many investigations. Competition among industries would have to be considered in setting standards, and all related industries should be subject to the same authority in a department reporting directly to the president.[8]

Perkins declined to suggest an appropriate minimum wage for the textile industry and warned the subcommittee about setting one. She preferred to have the commission, rather than Congress, set the minimum. Perkins also believed regional differentials were not a critical issue. Improved machinery, production, and management in all sections of the country, she explained, enabled textile workers with the same training to acquire the same skills in any region. Moreover, she told the subcommittee there was no constitutional authority to set fair wages above the minimum.[9] No action was taken on the textile-industry bill after Congress received the Black-Connery Bill.

Since the wage and hour bill had been introduced late in the session when many congressmen were anxious to go home, Black and Connery arranged a joint hearing and limited witnesses to key industry and labor leaders. Leading off for the administration, Assistant Attorney General Jackson defended the bill's constitutionality and distinguished it from the NIRA. There was no delegation of congressional power to trade associations to draft codes of competition and trade practices were excluded. The due process clause of the Fifth Amendment, he argued, did not prohibit the regulation of labor standards in the interest of the public welfare because its guarantee demanded only that the regulation should not be unreasonable, arbitrary, or capricious. Since the reasonableness of regulation depended on relevant facts, there could be no objection to providing a board to investigate them. Jackson also defended the child-labor provisions by suggesting that a separate ban would be more difficult to sustain in court. The inclusion of the ban, he argued, made it clear that the bill was a genuine attempt to regulate all unfair-labor practices affecting commerce.[10]

Labor Department officials advised Secretary Perkins to make no demands for extensive revision of the Black-Connery Bill. Although they wanted the board in the department, Reilly deemed it wise to let Congress settle the question when it took up the executive-reorganization bill. And although the Children's Bureau favored the Barkley bill, he warned her against challenging Roosevelt's decision to retain the child-labor provisions in the wage and hour bill. Instead, Perkins defended the bill's broad recovery objectives, offered the committee suggestions for the improvement of its provisions for administration and enforcement, and submitted eleven amendments for consideration.[11]

Perkins considered the bill to be more than merely a wage and hour measure. It should be viewed, she argued, as an effort to limit economic fluctuations and to bring security to industry, investors, labor, and consumers. It would stabilize employment, income, marketing, production, and prices. All industrial nations, she reminded the committee, had attempted to assist industry and labor by accepting some system of wage and hour regulation. One of the most successful efforts was the British trade-board system, which had helped Britain weather two severe depressions.[12]

Perkins also emphasized the return of sweatshop conditions after the demise of the NIRA and explained how a few competitors could undermine standards in an entire industry. The only solution was regulating standards nationally to curtail "parasitical practices." By removing labor costs from the basis of competition, she argued, efficient production and high quality would become the standard of competition. Moreover, industry would operate more securely if oppressive standards no longer caused labor disputes. Since industrial security was the objective, she said wage and hour regulation should not be regarded as merely a welfare measure offered for humanitarian purposes.[13]

Rather than have Congress set the basic nonoppressive standards, Perkins preferred to have them fixed by the board. Because conditions in different industries varied so greatly, she argued, the board should set the basic nonoppressive standard industry-by-industry in the same way it set fair standards. She justified this practice by emphasizing the administrative advantages of relying upon advisory boards. Reliance upon them, she emphasized, would not be a return to NRA code authorities because the formulation and enforcement of lawful regulations would be through sworn officials. Echoing Sells, she said it would be desirable to have employer and labor representatives participating in the proceedings before a wage board because their participation would make enforcement easier.[14]

Responding to labor's concern about collective bargaining, Perkins said the Labor Standards Board's authority should be limited to those industries in which bargaining power was insufficient to obtain reasonable standards. It had no authority over job classification, which was left to collective agreement, and no power to fix graduated-wage scales by occupation. Moreover, since it was limited by the annual $1,200-income maximum, high-wage occupations would not be affected. But if employers forced workers to accept collective bargaining agreements providing for oppressive standards, the board could raise them despite the agreement.[15]

On the controversial issue of differentials, Perkins took a flexible position. She wanted to avoid differentials that induced industry to migrate to low-wage areas. And she opposed differentials that gave a competitive advantage to industry in one section of the country that sold in the national market. Since she opposed rigid standards, the board should fix differentials to maintain a balance among all areas.[16]

In regard to the bill's child-labor provisions, Perkins frankly said they would do little to protect children because they were limited to activities in interstate commerce. Hence, she supported the campaign for the Child Labor Amendment. On the question of coverage, she recommended that the board be allowed to exempt employers, rather than have Congress authorize exemptions based on the number of employees. Employers with few workers, she pointed out, were most likely to resort to sweatshop standards. Admitting that the government had no experience regulating minimum wages, fair wages, or differentials, she urged Congress to make the regulation as simple as possible. If it were overly complicated, she anticipated much confusion.[17]

Because Perkins was critical of regulation by the Labor Standards Board, her testimony cannot be considered a strong endorsement of the bill. Although she supported its recovery objectives, she opposed fixed basic standards and preferred to have flexible industry-committee standards approved by the board. Her endorsement of differentials was conditioned on the need to avoid inducing industry to move to low-wage areas. The child-labor provisions, she admitted, would do little to protect children. And she thought the bill too complicated for effective administration. Given Roosevelt's request for unified support for the bill, her criticism was forthright and detrimental to its chances in Congress.

Isador Lubin, commissioner of labor statistics, provided some shocking evidence on living standards but was unable to predict how regulation would affect hours, wages, or purchasing power. Competition, he argued, had failed to work as economists had prophesied. The result was a chaotic market system in which some unscrupulous employers adopted standards that were detrimental to workers, industry, and society. A study of family incomes in 1935–36 revealed that one-third had an income insufficient to meet a subsistence standard of living. They had no gas or electricity for hot water or cooking and lacked food for an adequate diet. He explained that he could not estimate the number of people who would be affected by regulation, since coverage would be determined by the board's definition of activities in interstate commerce. He thought 2 million might be affected by the minimum-wage provision but could not estimate the number affected by the regulation of hours or how much purchasing power might be increased.[18]

If Lubin was reluctant to offer estimates on the bill's coverage, Leon Henderson, former director of research for the NRA and economist for the Works Progress Administration (WPA), was quite willing to do so. As of March 1937, he estimated the total working force to be

52.8 million, with 10.8 million in agriculture. Of 42 million nonfarm workers, only 34.1 million were employed, leaving an estimated 7.9 million jobless. Wage and hour regulation, he suggested, would cover 12 million in manufacturing, mining, transportation, and public utilities. In these industries he found 3 million making less than 40 cents an hour and 6 million working more than 40 hours a week. He estimated that a 40-hour workweek might result in the reemployment of 1.5 million, while a 30-hour week might create jobs for as many as 8 million. Total wages and salaries, he explained, made up about 67 percent of the national income. Since technology had made it possible to increase production with fewer workers, he urged Congress to pass the bill in order to increase the income of the underpaid and avoid another impasse in the form of a deficit in purchasing power.[19]

Powerful business organizations condemned any experiment in wage and hour regulation. James A. Emery of the NAM submitted a list of forty-one manufacturing organizations opposed to the bill and denounced the ocean of authority granted to the board. He predicted rising costs, falling production, and dislocation of the economy if the bill were passed. Noel Sargent, an NAM economist, agreed, claiming that the purchasing-power theory as a remedy for unemployment had been condemned by some of the world's leading economists. He criticized the bill for failing to provide a yardstick for fixing wages and thought regulation would increase costs, reduce exports, raise imports, and worsen the depression. Speaking for the Chamber of Commerce, George H. Davis emphasized the problems involved in regulating wages and hours and condemned the bill for the vagueness of its provisions. Experience under the Public Contracts Act, he claimed, proved that any attempt to use advisory-industry committees would fail because the determination of wages and hours was too difficult. James D. Battle, executive secretary of the National Coal Association, explained that the bituminous industry was operating on a 35-hour week under its own law and should be exempted. Regulation of wages and hours, he warned, would weaken collective bargaining.[20]

A few businessmen, however, supported the bill. John G. Paine, chairman of the management group of the Council for Industrial Progress, endorsed the bill because it carried out the council's legislative proposals. He recommended a flexible 30-to-40-hour workweek and dropping the $1,200 limitation on annual-wage incomes. Robert W. Johnson of the Johnson and Johnson Company believed the partial recovery of the nation's economy had not raised wages or improved purchasing power. Since wages in the textile industry were averaging between $10 and $11 a week, they were well below the $16-weekly wage needed to maintain a worker at a subsistence level. He thought a 6-hour day would promote efficiency, because forcing workers to speed up on an 8-hour shift was too great a drain on their energy. And despite the fact that his company operated mills in the South, he opposed geographic differentials as detrimental to southern workers.[21]

Unfortunately for the bill's proponents, organized labor's support was lukewarm and ambiguous. Since the AFL Executive Council refused to endorse it, President Green offered several amendments to protect collective bargaining. Whatever wages and hour rates were fixed for any industry, unions would have the right to bargain for better standards. The board was to accept rates established through collective bargaining for a substantial part of an industry, unless higher rates were necessary to prevent unfair competition. It was also to consider craft employment as a separate classification. The AFL, warned Green, was opposed to having the board supplant unions in bargaining for wages and hours. Government wage-fixing, he said, was contrary to industrial democracy and self-government. He accepted the 40-hour-40-cent standard as a step in the right direction but condemned the $16-weekly minimum as inadequate. He also said the AFL was strongly opposed to geographic differentials.[22]

The CIO's John L. Lewis joined Green in opposing any authority of the board to override collective bargaining agreements. He thought the bill could be greatly simplified by eliminating the fair-wage-fixing provisions of Section V. A simple 40-cent minimum could be easily enforced, he said, and anything else would be wage-fixing by government fiat. He recommended a 35-hour week, but admitted that it would be a calamity to consider $14 weekly to be a living wage. Hillman flatly disagreed with Lewis on scrapping Section V. If the board could not fix fair standards, he warned, it would not be able to protect ethical employers from cutthroat competition. Moreover, the board would have to adjust wages when it reduced hours in order to maintain annual income. Explaining his disagreement with Lewis on Section V, he said labor-management experience in the garment industry was much different than that of the coal industry.[23]

Merle D. Vincent, legislative counsel for the International Ladies Garment Workers Union (ILGWU), supported the bill's standards, opposed geographic differentials, and argued that improvements in production justified the legislation. Between 1922 and 1929, he explained, labor costs declined by 14 percent, production increased by 37 percent, and industrial profits rose by 85 percent. But industrial wages increased by only 8 percent and were offset by higher living costs. Referring to a study showing that $1,260 was the minimum income a family needed to live at a standard of decency, he defended the $1,200-annual income provision.[24] Although union leaders supported a reduction of the workweek and agreed that regulation must not supplant collective bargaining, their conflicting views on Section V and on the right of the board to fix rates above the nonoppressive standard revealed a lack of unity that would be fatal to higher fair wages and the purchasing-power objective.

Katherine Lenroot joined Secretary Perkins in urging ratification of the Child Labor Amendment. The number of working children, she explained, had risen sharply since the Supreme Court voided the NRA codes and a large number of them were employed in intrastate activities. Since the bill's provisions would cover only 25 percent of those working in industry, passage of the amendment was essential. She also objected to the bill's conditional state ban on child labor because new state laws would be required in all but three states and because administration and enforcement would be difficult. She preferred the simple direct ban on goods made by children and wanted the issue to go to the Court. In order to provide for effective regulation, she recommended that the child-labor provisions be administered by her bureau, which had years of experience in cooperating with state agencies. She was supported by Courtenay Dinwiddie of the National Child Labor Committee (NCLC) on the conditional state ban and by Lucy R. Mason of the National Consumers' League (NCL) on bureau administration. Dissatisfaction with the bill's child-labor provisions encouraged proponents of separate child-labor legislation. A number of child-labor bills were under consideration, and opponents of Black-Connery Bill knew they could weaken it by deleting its ban on child labor.[25]

The hearings not only revealed serious disagreement over the bill's wage and hour and child-labor provisions but also disclosed many other problems. Railway workers, truck drivers, seamen, and oil-field workers sought to have their industries, covered by other legislation, exempted from coverage. Farm organizations, seasonal commodity producers, apple and citrus growers, turpentine producers, sawmill operators, and even jewelers sought exemptions from one or all of the bill's provisions. Another controversy arose over whether to allow the board to restrict imports if wage and hour regulation increased costs and threatened domestic industry. And one of the most troublesome questions was whether to base coverage on the number of workers employed.[26]

Even before the hearings ended, the conservative congressional bloc opposed to the bill was gaining support. In the Senate it centered around Carter Glass of Virginia and Josiah Bailey of North Carolina. Both were Democrats who resented New Deal liberals and Roosevelt's association with CIO leaders. In July a bitter debate broke out when Senate Majority Leader Robinson offered a compromise Court bill which strengthened the anti–New Deal coalition that also opposed the Black-Connery Bill. In the House the wage and hour bill's prospects suffered when Representative Connery died during the hearings. He had toiled loyally on behalf of labor legislation and had literally worked himself to death. In addition, Speaker John Bankhead was in poor health and had difficulty controlling the House, while Sam Rayburn was so anxious to succeed Bankhead that he did not wish to offend anyone. Aware of his strained relations with Congress, Roosevelt joined a party outing on Jefferson Island in Chesapeake Bay in an attempt to restore harmony, but artificial conviviality failed to resolve fundamental policy issues. New Deal opponents advised business organizations that congressional conservatives and Labor Department officials would welcome opposition to the bill.[27]

Responding to business and labor criticism of the board's broad power to fix both nonoppressive and fair wages and hours, early in July the Senate Committee on Education and Labor drastically reduced its authority. In redrafting the bill under Black's guidance, the committee restricted it to setting a workweek no lower then 40 hours or a wage no higher than 40 cents. Hence, the board could set only nonoppressive standards and had no power to fix higher fair wages. The resulting maximum $16-weekly wage would provide an annual income of only $800, which was far below the $1,200 needed to maintain a family at a subsistence level. By adopting the lower standard, the committee simplified the measure and accepted the AFL argument that wages above the oppressive rate should be left to collective bargaining.[28]

According to Senator David Walsh of Massachusetts, who sponsored the lower standard, the committee accepted it to avoid any abrupt change in wages and hours that would wipe out thousands of small business concerns employing from 50-to-80 percent of all workers. Despite the lower standard, he claimed, the board would still be able to reduce hours and raise wages without serious injury to workers and businesses operating under substandard conditions. The policy, he explained, was to maintain working standards at levels of efficiency and to promote the well-being of workers and the profitable operation of business.[29] Walsh's explanation revealed the committee's willingness to protect exploited workers and its rejection of higher fair wages regulation as a panacea for recovery.

As to coverage, the redrafted bill abandoned any attempt to exempt employers on the basis of number of workers employed. Instead, all of those employed in executive, administrative, or professional capacities were exempted. In addition, farm labor, railroad employees, seamen, fishermen, local-retailing employees, apprentices, and the disabled were also exempted. In a bow to the protectionists, the Tariff Commission would be able to investigate the effect of regulation on costs to determine whether an increase in duties was justified. Provisions covering such unfair practices as strikebreaking and corporate labor espionage were dropped because such activities could be better regulated by the National Labor Relations Board (NLRB).[30]

The Labor Department was well satisfied with the redrafted bill. Senator Walsh supported the department's amendments and worked closely with Reilly on them. All but two were accepted: industry labor-management councils would participate in the formulation of wage and hour standards; industrial homework was prohibited; hours schedules would be posted; the Children's Bureau would regulate age limits; working certificates would be issued by the department; the bill's provisions were integrated with those of the Walsh-Healey Act; the ship-building industry was covered; and administratively impractical subsections were eliminated. But the department failed to eliminate the provision for wage differentials based on age or sex. And it also failed to obtain authority to regulate learners, apprentices, and the handicapped because Senator Black balked at having two sets of regulatory agencies. Benjamin Cohen was disturbed by the lower wage and hour standard because he thought the board would set hours higher than 40 and wages lower than 40 cents. Reilly thought the amended bill was in harmony with the one the department originally submitted and believed that Cohen would be satisfied if the House restored a 35-hour floor and 65-cent ceiling as well as the oppressive practices provision.[31]

The amended bill failed to satisfy either the business community or organized labor. The Chamber of Commerce thought it was as bad as the original because there was no specific wage and hour standard, the provisions were obscure, and the rights of the states would be violated. The NAM remained opposed to it, as was the National Committee to Uphold Constitutional Government. Southern businessmen, determined to retain their low-wage advantage, condemned it. The Southern Lumber Industry Committee said farmers would pay more for manufactured goods and urged them to oppose it. The Southern States Industrial Council, claiming to represent 17,000 employers, said regulation would cripple southern industry and denied that there was a demand for it in any section of the country.[32]

Unfortunately for its supporters, the amended bill failed to win unified support from organized labor. Powerful conservative trade union leaders in the AFL, including "Big Bill" Hutchenson of the

Carpenters, John P. Frey, J. W. Williams of the Building Trades Department, and Ira M. Ornburn of the Union Label Trade Department, condemned government wage-fixing and challenged President Green on the issue. Hutchenson, a staunch Republican, denounced both the New Deal and the CIO. Frey and Williams condemned wage-fixing as a threat to the Walsh-Healey Act. But Green endorsed the bill, even though it did not meet labor's expectations. In view of the need for wage and hour regulation, he explained, the AFL wanted the Senate to pass it so it could be amended in the House. He was confident that the House would accept the federation's amendments and that Roosevelt would reject any changes the AFL found unacceptable. When Frey broke openly with Green and asked the Senate to delay the bill, the latter warned him that its enemies would justify their opposition on AFL criticism and shift the blame for its failure to the federation.[33]

Although John L. Lewis and Hillman disagreed on the fair-wage-fixing provisions of the board, the CIO supported the amended bill. Lewis was critical of its provisions but said regulation would be a boon to millions of underprivileged workers. United Mine Workers (UMW) officials found the wage and hour standards inadequate but supported the bill as a foundation on which to build. They organized a petition drive on its behalf and accused businessmen of resorting to layoffs to pressure Congress to reject it. Hillman called for action on it before Congress adjourned, and Eli L. Oliver, vice president of Labor's Non-Partisan League (LNPL), warned Democratic congressmen that failure to support it would be considered a repudiation of their campaign pledges. Workers, he said, had "voted for wage and hour legislation" in 1936, and if Congress refused to pass a law they would remember when they voted again in 1938. The league was dissatisfied with the 40-hour-40-cent limitation and demanded instead a 35-hour-60-cent standard. It thus recognized the reemployment potential of shorter hours and the purchasing-power potential of a higher wage.[34]

Senator Black and Cohen moved quickly to eliminate the tariff issue before the bill was taken up by the Senate. They agreed that the bill's provisions would not compromise Secretary of State Cordell Hull's reciprocal-trade program. Black opposed a clarifying amendment as offering a possible opening to the protectionists. But he promised to substitute one prepared by Hull if he could not stop an effort to amend the tariff provisions from the floor.[35]

In early July there was no opportunity for the Senate to consider the Black-Connery Bill because of the Court-packing fight. The deadlock was finally broken by the untimely death of Majority Leader Joe

Robinson, who suffered a heart attack. His death led to a critical struggle for Robinson's post between the conservative Pat Harrison and the New Deal loyalist Alben Barkley. Although Roosevelt claimed to be neutral, Tom Corcoran lobbied intensively for Barkley, who defeated Harrison by a few votes. After Roosevelt rejected a compromise on the Court bill, the Senate killed it and was ready to adjourn. According to Rep. Fred M. Vinson of Kentucky, the Black-Connery Bill had helped kill the Court bill. There were protests from constituents and lobbyists that linked both proposals. There were also rumors that conservative senators delayed action on the Court bill in order to kill the Black-Connery Bill. Clearly, the issues were linked by those who opposed an expansion of national power and Congress was in no mood for another fight over wage and hour regulation.[36]

Despite the desire of many congressmen to adjourn after an exhausting session, Roosevelt asked them to either pass the pending farm and labor legislation or recess and come back in October. Many of them deplored his demand for action on the Black-Connery Bill, suggesting that such a complicated measure deserved close study before being brought up for a vote. But because of Roosevelt's demand, loyal Senate leaders brought it to a vote after only a few days of debate. Their decision to ram it through the Senate upset many conservative southerners, who for the first time refused to support the president on a major New Deal proposal. Senators Harrison, Glass, Bailey, James Byrnes, "Cotton Ed" Smith of South Carolina, and Walter George of Georgia joined the Republicans in opposition. The fight for it was led by Barkley, Black, Walsh, Claude Pepper of Florida, Lewis Schwellenbach of Washington, and Sherman Minton of Indiana.[37]

Overall, the bill's supporters were able to defeat crippling amendments. Senator Bridges's statutory 40-hour-40-cent standard was rejected, as was Senator Maloney's proposal for an employment board with authority to regulate the workweek. Henry C. Lodge's amendment to restrict the importation of goods made under standards lower than those proposed by the bill was easily defeated. The most important change was Senate acceptance of the Wheeler-Johnson child-labor substitute. It combined the direct ban on goods made by children in interstate commerce with the conditional-state ban. Wheeler explained that the Interstate Commerce Committee preferred the dual approach as a safeguard against judicial invalidation of the direct ban. Although the conditional-state ban was opposed by the Children's Bureau, its acceptance pleased some senators and reportedly won votes for the bill.[38]

One of the most difficult issues was the exemption of seasonal industries. Sens. Charles L. McNary of Oregon and Warren R. Austin of Vermont led the drive to exempt seasonal occupations, and as the debate developed, McNary's list broadened considerably to include numerous occupations in agriculture and food processing. Over Black's objections, McNary's seasonal-occupations amendment was accepted, but Robert McReynolds of North Carolina and John Overton of Louisiana failed to exempt tobacco-warehousing and cotton-ginning. Also exempted were bus, airline, and farm-to-market transportation.[39]

During the debate, Senator Black emphasized the bill's potential for raising the living standards of the lower third of the nation's industrial workers. Specialization and subdivision of labor, he explained, had increased productivity by an estimated 70 percent over a period of twenty-five years. But there had been no comparable increase in the standard of living of workers. Instead, millions had been thrown out of work and the result was a growing sense of insecurity and fear of the future. The existing "economy of scarcity," he believed, was caused by a lack of purchasing power of farmers and workers. The result was great prosperity at the top, millions of unemployed at the bottom, and a tax burden for the support of the unemployed that threatened the budget. Clearly, he argued, the income of farmers and workers must be sufficient to buy the output of the nation's economic system.[40]

Senator Borah went on record in favor of abolishing substandard wages just the way he would abolish slavery. Completely impractical, he recommended scrapping the board and prescribing a uniform 40-hour-30-cent standard without differentials for every industry in the country. Given southern support for differentials, his proposal did not have a chance. Walsh defended the flexible 40-hour-40-cent standard and claimed that the 40-cent rate would improve the wages of 36.7 percent of all employees in seventy-one industries. He also warned his colleagues that if they shelved the bill they were likely to get the House version with a 35-hour-70-cent standard.[41]

Opponents cited studies of NRA experience proporting to prove that board regulation of flexible standards would not work. According to one analysis, the NRA failed because it tried to do the job industry-by-industry. The experience indicated that standards for all competing units must be set at the same time and not individually by a board. Therefore, Congress should set the standards with differentials and allow the board to make exceptions, which would greatly reduce its work. Charles Roos, former NRA research director, produced a highly critical analysis of the effects of the bill. He predicted curtailed employment within the first year of operation; a decrease in production and average living standards; lower consumption of raw materials and lower farm prices; and higher costs for farmers. Under the NRA, he pointed out, the minimum wage of some workers was raised, but the wages of a substantial proportion were lowered to the minimum. He therefore predicted that the bill would level down wage scales.[42]

By the third day of the debate, the bill's backers were fighting off a concerted bipartisan movement to send it back to the committee by amending it to death. To head off this move, Barkley won an agreement to consider amendments without debate in order to reach a decision. After a number of them had been rejected, Senator Tom Connally of Texas made the critical motion to recommit, which was defeated by a vote of 48 to 36. Thereafter the amended bill was passed by a comfortable 56-to-28 margin.[43]

Barkley and Black saved the bill without the help of the southern Democratic hierarchy, but the vote was close. On the Connally motion, only seven more votes would have sent the bill back to committee. This vote revealed the sectional and urban-rural split within the Democratic party. Of the 36 favoring recommittal, 22 were Democrats, half of them from the South. Only 5 of those from the most urban states voted to recommit. On the final vote, 7 Democrats and 1 Republican switched over to support the bill. Two Republicans, James J. Davis of Pennsylvania and Lodge of Massachusetts supported it. Neither were considered progressive and both represented industrial states. Davis, a former steelworker and secretary of labor, responded to labor pressure, and Lodge understood that the bill would reduce the low-wage advantage of the South.[44]

While Barkley and Black may be given credit for marshaling the votes, a number of factors account for their success. The acceptance of the Wheeler-Johnson amendment pleased those who wanted the board's authority reduced. The CIO's endorsement and the AFL's conditional approval satisfied those subject to labor pressure. Some of the Democrats who defied Roosevelt on the Court bill were anxious for a truce, and enough industry and occupational exemptions had been accepted to satisfy several hesitant senators. And those who were not pleased with the amended bill could vote for it with the assurance that if the House changed it, a House-Senate compromise would be necessary.

By eliminating the board's authority to set fair standards above the nonoppressive level, the Senate rejected the original plan to spread work and raise purchasing power. Hence, the amended bill would be clearly a humanitarian measure to eliminate oppressive sweatshop standards imposed upon the most exploited workers. If this change was in line with Roosevelt's concern about the forgotten man at the bottom of the economic pyramid, it nevertheless abandoned the concept that the government could guarantee subsistence incomes to that one-third of the nation living on relief or earning substandard wages. Recovery could best be promoted, the Senate decided, not by disrupting thousands of business concerns, but by setting basic standards that would simultaneously promote the well-being of workers and prosperity of industry.

Because of the Senate's amendment of the Black-Connery Bill, the effect of wage and hour regulation on industry would be greatly reduced. If the board reduced the workweek to the 40-hour floor, probably fewer than 1.5 million workers would be affected. As for wages, not even expert statisticians could predict how many workers might be affected if the board raised wages to the 40-cent ceiling for all industry. Even with a $16-weekly wage, many workers would have an annual income of $800, well below the $1,200 subsistence level. WPA annual security wages ranged from $300 in the deep South to $680 in the Northeast. The Senate standard came close to the WPA emergency level, but it would benefit southern workers.[45] There was little possibility of reaching a national 40-hour-40-cent standard, however, since southerners were determined to preserve their differentials and the South's low-wage advantage.

By August prospects for the bill seemed dim. Its chances in the House were clouded by a split among Democrats, as well as by Connery's death, sectional antagonism, and weak leadership. Roosevelt found Congress in a state of turmoil and thought it might as well adjourn so that congressmen could get back to their constituents. With bumper crops being harvested, those from agricultural states would want crop loans, and he made it clear that there would be no farm bill without a wage and hour bill. But despite his resounding election victory and an overwhelming Democratic majority in the House, a humanitarian proposal for the elimination of sweatshop standards seemed to have little chance of success.

6

No Rule in the House

The American Federation of Labor believes that the fair labor
standards bill should be amended by incorporation of provisions
therein for a shorter workday and a shorter workweek.

—President William Green

By the time the Black-Connery Bill was taken up by the House
Labor Committee, the loss of Connery created a serious leadership
problem. House leaders wanted to pass the chair to Mary Norton of
New Jersey, a seven-term congresswoman who chaired the District
of Columbia Committee. She would have been happy to have it passed
to Robert Ramspeck of Georgia, a relatively liberal member of the
Labor Committee from Atlanta who had attended the hearings and
who was familiar with the bill. But the bill's backers preferred Norton, and Frank Hague, the anti-CIO boss of Jersey City who had
provoked labor by opposing an anti-injunction law, pressured her to
take the post. She yielded, explaining that she represented a labor
district and wished to serve working people. Despite her explanation,
those friendly to labor considered her an amiable but inadequate tool
of Boss Hague.[1]

Early in July Norton's Labor Committee began consideration of
the Black-Connery Bill with the understanding that southern opponents on the Rules Committee would block it unless satisfied with its
provisions in advance. The major issue was the scope of the board's
wage and hour authority. The Labor Committee member Ruben T.
Wood of Missouri, a twenty-four-year president of the Missouri AFL,
backed a 35-hour-70-cent standard. Ramspeck opposed it and instead
supported the flexible 40-hour-40-cent standard. With a number of
members absent, and with Norton casting the deciding vote, the committee adopted Wood's formula. In order to protect collective bargaining, however, the AFL opposed the Wood standard and any
flexible wage over the 40-cent rate.[2] President Green submitted the

98

AFL amendments to the Senate committee, but they were not incorporated in the amended Senate bill. Green won Roosevelt's support to have them accepted by the House committee. Since AFL backing for the bill was vital, Roosevelt agreed that the wage and hour board would not interfere with collective bargaining, fix rates below prevailing wages in any locality, or interfere with the Public Contacts Act. He also assured Green that he would oppose any changes in the bill the AFL deemed unsatisfactory. Perkins told Norton to accept the amendments to avoid AFL opposition on the floor. Hence, after the Senate acted, the House committee repudiated the Wood formula and accepted the AFL amendments. The federation was therefore responsible for the elimination of the higher fair wage provisions in the House.[3]

The AFL amendments would not only eliminate the high fair-standard provision, but would also reduce the board's power by maintaining prevailing wages. Green thought the amendments would convert the bill into an effective collective-bargaining statute and eliminate the fear of "fascist control" of labor and capital. Although geographic differentials would be preserved, he anticipated that prevailing wages and hours in the South would be improved as those in the North were raised by collective bargaining. The conflicting interests of the sections, he believed, would thus be eliminated. The board would have jurisdiction only if collective bargaining in any industry was inadequate, and wages and hours set by agreement would be the standard for any occupation. The board could not lower prevailing standards or establish classifications that adversely affected them in other localities. In addition, prison-made goods would be banned, the union label "nuisance" would be dropped, and standards for government workers would remain under the jurisdiction of the Public Contracts Act. Capital, Green explained, had been unhappy with the original wage and hour standards of the Black-Connery Bill, while labor was unhappy with those of the amended Senate bill. The AFL amendments, he believed, resolved the issue, and the federation would support the bill if they were accepted.[4]

Early in August, Norton's committee included the AFL amendments among fifty-nine revisions of the Black-Connery Bill and recommended it to the House. Among other important revisions, the committee dropped the Wheeler-Johnson child-labor provisions and restored the board's authority over child labor. But it would be required to rely upon the Children's Bureau for all investigations and enforcement. In addition, local retail trade would be covered and competing imported goods would be banned. In order to please southerners, two board members would be chosen from the South. The committee accepted differentials based on local factors affecting production costs. The definition of substandard labor was broadened to ban the employment of women and children on the midnight shift. And the committee tried to please women's organizations by requiring the board to set standards without regard to gender.[5]

Although the committee did its best to satisfy many of the bill's critics, it could do nothing to overcome the opposition of southern conservatives on the Rules Committee. This committee, highly privileged and powerful, controlled all legislation. Once the House adopted a body of rules at the opening of a session, all proposals for amendment of the rules were referred to it. It could present special rules fixing the order of pending measures to be considered, limit debate on a matter, stipulate sections of a bill that might be amended, and decide the nature of possible amendments. It was privileged in obtaining the floor and might interrupt debates or introduce a rule on a different bill regardless of the regular order of procedure. It also might draft a bill and require its consideration and could rely on special rules to control proceedings.

Postmaster General Jim Farley warned Roosevelt that angry southern state chairmen and even national committeemen were supporting the campaign to defeat the bill. Martin Dies of Texas, a leading opponent on the Rules Committee, predicted that it would not get more than four votes from fourteen committee members. Edward Cox of Georgia, another committee opponent, circulated a letter from Charles F. Roos, who condemned wage and hour regulation for delaying recovery. Conservative Democratic Lawrence Lewis of Colorado, another member, compared the board's authority to that of Stalin, Hitler, or Mussolini. John Rankin of Mississippi, a leading opponent, said the bill would destroy collective bargaining, raise the tariff, harass industry, destroy small business, strengthen monopoly, check southern progress, concentrate industry in the East, and penalize it in the North and West. Rankin's litany sounded much like the conservative denunciation of the National Industrial Recovery Act (NIRA), which the administration insisted was not being revived.[6]

Unfortunately for Speaker Bankhead and Majority Leader Rayburn, the ten Rules Committee Democrats were evenly split. In addition to Dies and Cox, southern opponents included Howard W. Smith of Virginia, William J. Driver of Arkansas, and J. Bayard Clark of North Carolina. Smith was from a rural district and had no love for unions. Driver and Clark were convinced that regulation would harm the south. Northern Democrats included Chairman John J. O'Connor of New York, Adolph Sabath of Illinois, Arthur H. Greenwood of Indiana, and Byron B. Harlan of Ohio, all of whom supported the bill. Lawrence Lewis's support was conditioned on the amendment of features he deemed oppressive and unconstitutional. The Democratic split left four Republicans holding the balance and the fate of the bill. J. W. Taylor of Tennessee, Charles E. Mapes of Michigan, and Donald H. McLean of New Jersey opposed it, and Joseph W. Martin of Massachusetts was doubtful. As O'Connor explained, nobody was lending him any votes. But if any three Republicans joined five Democrats, an unlikely event, the bill could be brought out. O'Connor labored in vain.[7]

Despite strong administration pressure, Rayburn was unable to get a rule. Since the farm bloc had helped to tie up the Black-Connery Bill in the Rules Committee, Roosevelt jolted southern and western Democrats by announcing that there would be no more crop loans until the farm bill was passed. But tying the farm bill to the wage and hour bill only deepened the split in Democratic ranks. Since congressmen wanted to go home and a discharge petition was out of the question, Rayburn agreed that the bill would not be brought up under any suspension of the rules. The bill's backers, led by Arthur D. Healey and Maury Maverick of Texas, then made a last-ditch effort to save it. They called a party caucus to commit all Democrats to support it, but southerners hid in the cloakroom and refused to respond to the roll call. Although the bill's backers failed to get a quorum, Bankhead and Rayburn promised to put it on the preferred list for the next session. Roosevelt accepted the inevitable, agreed to allow it to go over to a special session, and even promised 12-cent cotton price support for the farm bill. Congress then adjourned after a long exhausting session.[8]

The Democrats disbanded in an unprecedented state of disharmony. Roosevelt blasted "Tory opposition" for the failure of his program. Senator Guffey, chairman of the Senate Campaign Committee, castigated Wheeler, O'Mahoney, and Burke for opposing the Court bill. The three "ingrates" in turn accused Guffey of fascism and demanded his removal as chairman. Rayburn exonerated O'Connor for his failure to get a rule for the Black-Connery Bill and thought Roosevelt would have to modify his program in order to restore party harmony. The president, Rayburn believed, should sign the sugar bill, abandon any further attempt to pack the Court, consult with congressional leaders before proposing legislation, see more of his friends and fewer of his "yes men," and avoid a special session in the fall.[9]

Disappointed by the administration's failure to get the bill out, organized labor condemned Democratic leaders. President Green castigated the Rules Committee and thought Roosevelt should have kept

Congress in session until the bill passed. John L. Lewis accused the administration of failing to carry out the party's pledges and hinted that the country needed a new party. The CIO blamed the AFL for taking an ambiguous position on the bill and accused federation leaders of not "giving a damn" for those at the bottom of the economic heap. Hillman denounced southern Democrats for defying party leaders. New York socialists ridiculed the Democrats and urged LNPL to support the creation of a farmer-labor party. E. L. Oliver blamed Bankhead for the failure to get a rule and threatened political retaliation. Defending his committee, Cox said that Hillman and Oliver did not speak for the party. Communists, he warned, were invading both parties through the CIO. The Republicans sat back and enjoyed the show.[10]

Upset by defections in Democratic ranks, Roosevelt decided to carry his fight to the people on a speaking tour of the West. Amid rumors that he planned to purge opponents, he condemned the "plutocratic dictatorship" that was opposed to majority rule and economic and social reform. He derided those opponents who paid lip service to improving the life of the worker and then voted against reform. In Minnesota, he emphasized those twin pieces of legislation, the crop-control and wage and hour bills. No section of the country, he said could be prosperous if worker's incomes were below those in other sections; but he indicated that he would accept differentials based on variations in living costs. Back in Washington, he said the people were with him and that three-quarters of the congressmen he had spoken to favored a special session. Representative W. D. McFarlane of Texas, for example, told him that 90 percent of his constituents supported the president's program and a special session. Hence, in the middle of October he asked Congress to convene on November 15 to consider a five-point program, including the wage and hour and crop-control bills.[11]

Public opinion polls confirmed Roosevelt's claim that the public supported wage and hour regulation. According to a series of polls, by July 1937 about 58 percent of those surveyed thought Congress should set a minimum wage; in August 88 percent favored a 40-cent minimum. But there was doubt as to whether hours could be reduced without cutting wages: 37 percent thought wages could be maintained, 39 percent thought they would be cut, while the remainder were uncertain. By December 1937, support for national regulation of the workweek had risen from 55 to 60 percent of those surveyed. These polls revealed that southerners were as interested in higher standards as those in other sections.[12]

Despite the favorable opinion polls, support for wage and hour regulation as a purchasing-power panacea for recovery had been seriously undermined by a number of studies of employment, wages, and purchasing power. A National Industrial Conference Board study of the effect of machinery on production concluded that technology was a minor factor, accounting for less than 4 percent of the jobless in 1930. The answer to the employment problem was an increase in the volume of production, which would raise purchasing power and lead to full employment.[13] This study challenged organized labor's claim that technological unemployment justified a shorter workweek and validated the concern of the bill's opponents that a reduction of hours would curtail production and endanger recovery.

Harold G. Moulton of the Brookings Institution also condemned the shorter workweek panacea. Reducing hours, he argued, would freeze production at the current level and thus lower living standards. Spreading the work and increasing the pay of workers without increasing production would increase unit costs and prices. Under the National Recovery Administration (NRA), an increase in purchasing power had been thwarted because price increases took effect before wage increases raised consumer income. Consumption was governed by the flow of goods and any decrease in production reduced the aggregate income. To pay more than the market rate for wages, he insisted, was needless and unstabilizing. Technological development had not made it possible to simultaneously reduce the workweek and increase production. A 43-hour workweek, he suggested, would be necessary to increase production and improve living standards. A longer workweek, greater production, higher wages, and increased consumption, he predicted, would eventually eliminate unemployment.[14]

Paul Douglas challenged the high-wage purchasing-power theory of regulation. Under the law of marginal productivity, he explained, workers received what they added to the social product. If wage regulation made it impossible for employers to lower rates, workers would be laid off permanently, unless their marginal productivity could be raised to the level of the new minimums. Douglas devised a ratio to determine the effect of wage changes on marginal productivity. A wage increase of 1 percent above labor's marginal productivity would result in a decrease in employment of three or four times as great as the increase in the hourly rate, and total income would be reduced by the same ratio. Conversely, a 1-percent wage reduction would result in a 3- or 4-percent increase in employment and a 2- or 3-percent increase in total income.[15]

Douglas nevertheless understood that wages were not fixed by natural law. There was much evidence that they were held under their true marginal-production value because there was little competition among employers, which justified government regulation of minimum standards in some industries. The danger was government wage-fixing in all industries. Regulation, he suggested, should be confined to those industries in which the basic rate for unskilled labor was below the general wage level for the region as a whole.[16]

Carroll R. Daugherty of the University of Pittsburgh warned that recovery could not be achieved through arbitrarily raising wages, since increased production costs would have a deflationary effect on the economy. Moreover, raising wages and decreasing hours would discourage investment in new plants in competitive industries in which wages were low and labor costs were a large part of production costs. But he agreed that such arguments were not valid in the existing economic system when "modest" wage and hour regulation was necessary to prevent exploitation in sweated industries. Leo Wolman, a former member of the NRA Labor Board, however, attributed the tenacity of the high-wage doctrine to the competition between the AFL and CIO, which were recruiting workers by promising higher wages. The subsequent rise in production costs, he predicted, might be much greater than that contemplated by the Black-Connery Bill's supporters.[17]

Support for the Black-Connery Bill also weakened when the AFL's grudging endorsement turned into open hostility. President Green was unable to smother a rebellion of some of his more conservative Executive Council members, which was revealed at the federation's Denver convention in October. Vice President Frey, backed by Hutchinson and Williams, offered a resolution opposing any measure granting wage-fixing authority to a board. The delegates were told that the AFL had not prepared the Black-Connery Bill, had not introduced it, and had not been consulted about its provisions; nor had it been drafted by the labor committees of either house. Senator George Berry of Tennessee, former chairman of the Council for Industrial Progress, said he would prepare a simple bill fixing the workweek. The AFL Executive Council was therefore directed to consult with union officers before taking any action on wage regulation. Having rejected the bill, the convention once again declared the 30-hour week to be the AFL's primary objective. The council then authorized Green to prepare a substitute bill with statutory standards.[18]

Despite his condemnation of wage-fixing, Berry sent Roosevelt a statutory 40-hour-30-cent standard bill which provided for an emergency workweek up to 48 hours with overtime pay; the board was eliminated and federal district attorneys would be responsible for enforcement. Although the 30-cent minimum was low, Berry argued that it would eliminate the southern demand for differentials. A 40-cent minimum, he cautioned, would increase wages by 100 percent in many southern industries. Since he thought the Black-Connery Bill would fail, he said his proposal would solve the problem. If the South were upset by the elimination of the board, it would be placated by the low 30-cent minimum wage. Solicitor Reilly found serious flaws in Berry's bill. The statutory standard would result in regimentation that would cause serious dislocation in industry. If a 30-cent minimum were accepted, the $600 annual income would be well below that needed to maintain a family at a subsistence standard of living. Coverage of local activities was a mistake and unfortunately, Berry had omitted child-labor provisions. Labor Department officials preferred to rewrite the Black-Connery Bill.[19]

Reilly told Perkins that the best strategy was to get the Black-Connery Bill out of the Rules committee and back to the Labor Committee for amendment. Because geographic and industrial diversity could not be ignored, he wanted standards established industry-by-industry. He found little validity in opposition claims that the bill would lead to sectional discrimination and that it was unconstitutional. Since the board could allow differentials, there would be no sectional discrimination. In the National Labor Relations Board (NLRB) cases the Court had accepted regulation of local activities in production that impeded the free flow of commerce. And there was no improper delegation of legislative authority to the board, since Congress set the basic standards and the board would determine the facts. Clara M. Beyer also recommended redrafting the bill, since some of its provisions were difficult to understand and would lead to controversy and litigation.[20]

Although the International Ladies Garment Workers Union (ILGWU) wanted a 30-hour-60-cent standard, Beyer opposed more flexible rates and thought the basic 40-hour-40-cent standard should be retained. Because of AFL opposition to the board, however, she thought it should be dropped in favor of an administrator in the department. AFL amendments requiring the acceptance of standards determined by collective bargaining would have to be scrapped because they would restrict the work of the industry committees and the administrator. Because of the split in the labor movement, she would omit any reference to workers by class, craft, or industrial units. And because of opposition to a large bureaucracy, she also opposed provisions for deputy administrators in every state. Since state labor departments favored cooperation with the Labor Department in administrating a national law, she had their backing.[21]

Grace Abbott, former head of the Children's Bureau, wanted the

Labor Standard Board's power over child labor completely eliminated. She was afraid it would curtail the authority of the bureau if it remained independent and preferred to have the secretary of labor made responsible for child labor through the bureau. She also wanted the bureau's power to exempt children from the work ban limited to those between 14 and 16 years of age in occupations other than manufacturing and mining. Understanding that amending the child-labor provisions should not complicate the bill's chances, she worked closely with Katherine Lenroot to improve them.[22]

Anticipating the introduction of substitute wage and hour bills by Berry, Ramspeck, and others, Beyer met with Green and Frey to determine whether the AFL would support a simplified bill. Green was sympathetic and thought one might win the approval of his Executive Council if it contained a strong guarantee against any interference with union activities. AFL experience with the NLRB had convinced it that government boards should not be allowed to disrupt collective bargaining. Green feared that the wage and hour board might base its determination of standards on precedents established by the NLRB's interpretation of the National Labor Relations Act. Despite the AFL's reservations, Beyer formed a department committee to write a new bill.[23]

Beyer's committee attempted to simplify the bill and to overcome the concerns of the AFL. Regulation would be confined to unorganized industries in which wages were extremely low and hours unduly long. There would be no arbitrary government action interfering with union activities. The 40-hour-40-cent standard would be retained and provisions for higher fair wages would be dropped. Administration would be in the department, and the administrator would appoint industry committees to recommend wages and hours. Setting flexible standards in unorganized industries would eventually raise them to the level of those that were organized. Procedures would follow those approved by labor and utilized by the states limiting the workweek and establishing minimum wages.[24]

Solicitor Reilly incorporated these recommendations in the department's National Labor Standards Bill, a measure of only twelve sections whose title reflects the abandonment of higher fair wages. The secretary would appoint nine-member labor-management committees in industries in which issues over wages and hours obstructed the flow of commerce. They would submit articles of labor standards, which, when approved by the administrator and the president, would become law, but they would have no administrative or enforcement authority. A national advisory council of representatives of the committees, management, and labor would advise the secretary on policy and administration. Employers would register with the administrator, who would be responsible for enforcement. Violations of the articles would be prosecuted by district attorneys and orders would be enforced by the district courts.[25]

In addition, the government would not purchase goods from any enterprise operating in violation of the articles for its industry. Violation of the National Labor Relations Act would be a violation of the code of labor standards. The workweek was limited to no more than 40 hours, with provisions for seasonal variations. Minimum wages were to be commensurate with the value of services rendered, but industry committees could consider the cost of living and wages paid by employers voluntarily maintaining minimum-wage rates. No person under sixteen years of age could be employed. And collective-bargaining agreements in conformity with the National Labor Relations Act would be part of the articles of agreement.[26]

Clearly, the department's bill sought to overcome the AFL's concern about collective bargaining. Regulation would be limited to only unorganized substandard industries; labor participation on industry councils was guaranteed; collective bargaining agreements in the articles would have the force of law; the more democratic process of fixing minimum wages by industry had been approved by organized labor at the state level; and the controversial board was replaced by an administrator in the department. But the National Labor Standards Act did not induce the AFL Executive Council to abandon its support for a simple statutory-standards bill.

When Congress reconvened on November 15, Roosevelt sent it a conciliatory message, which it received politely but unenthusiastically. He recognized the seriousness of a business recession and promised tax relief and aid to small business. Once again, he reminded Congress that purchasing power had been curtailed by low wage and hour standards. He favored a flexible plan for wage and hour regulation that would enable industry to adopt higher standards but did not insist on uniform rates. Norton's committee faced the problem of reconciling the conflicting provisions of the well-amended Black-Connery Bill, an AFL statutory-standard bill, and the National Labor Standards Act. Its first problem, however, was to get the Black-Connery Bill out of the Rules Committee so that it could be amended.[27]

As soon as Congress convened Norton introduced a discharge petition to extract the bill. She could not bring it out under a suspension of he rules because a two-thirds vote would be required and only forty minutes of debate would be allowed. Congressional leaders assured Roosevelt that the necessary 218 signatures could be quickly obtained.

Seven days thereafter, the bill could be called up for debate on the second or fourth Monday of the month. Norton obtained 158 signatures within a week, but her campaign bogged down amid considerable confusion. Because of conflicting statements about her support for the bill, Perkins assured Norton that she supported it and urged her to get it to the floor so it could be amended. Any delay, she warned, would jeopardize its enactment.[28]

Norton's ability to extract the Black-Connery Bill was already compromised. Green told Norton that it was inadequate, because it would not remedy the unemployment problem. It would have to be amended to provide for a shorter workweek. He therefore refused to support her petition. John L. Lewis also gave it a lukewarm endorsement, saying that it had serious limitations. Because of criticism of the bill from all sides, the Labor Committee voted 19 to 2 to rewrite it.[29]

By the end of November it was clear that House leaders had lost control of their overwhelming Democratic majority and that the Black-Connery Bill was making congressional history. House veterans said it was the first administration bill blocked by the Rules Committee, and the petition was the first ever employed to extract an administration bill from a House committee. Representative Dies defended his committee, arguing that the House should not pass the bill without adequate consideration merely because the president wanted it. Lawrence Lewis thought his committee's refusal to grant a rule would undermine House leadership and fragment the majority. O'Connor, however, could do nothing to overcome the opposition of nine of his committee members.[30]

At the end of the month the petition still lacked twenty-five signatures for the deadline, if the bill were to be brought out on the thirteenth, the second Monday of December. The fourth Monday fell after Christmas, by which time Congress would have adjourned. Just before the deadline, administration pressure and labor lobbying became intense. The ACWU and Labor's Non-Partisan League (LNPL) helped to secure ten signatures. A deal with the farm bloc seemed certain when Marvin Jones of Texas, sponsor of the farm bill, signed the petition. Florida's Lex Green and Joe Hendricks also signed, allegedly to gain support for the Florida ship canal. And the relief administrator Harry Hopkins helped to line up the Louisiana delegation. In a brief moment of drama, Joseph J. Mansfield of Texas rolled down to the clerk's desk in his wheelchair and added the 218th signature amid cheers from the bill's backers and cries of deals and fraud from opponents. Among those signing were 196 Democrats, 8 Progressives, 5 Farmer-Laborites, and only 9 Republicans. Union lobbying and congressional logrolling finally enabled Norton to extract the bill.[31]

The Labor Committee's task was further complicated by the introduction of a number of bills providing for statutory standards or Federal Trade Commission (FTC) regulation. Lawrence J. Connery, who took his brother's seat in the House, offered a statutory 40-hour-40-cent standard bill, declaring that his brother would never have accepted the amended Black-Connery Bill. His bill protected collective bargaining, eliminated differentials, prohibited imports not made under the same standards, and would rely on Justice Department enforcement in the courts. Dewey W. Johnson of Minnesota also offered a bill with the same statutory standard, explaining that it would let unions organize industry, accept the highest wage standards in a locality, and exempt employers who voluntarily maintained decent standards. Alfred N. Phillips of Connecticut, Glen Griswold of Indiana, and Byron B. Harlan of Ohio, a member of the Rules Committee, also introduced similar bills. Representatives Lamneck, Adolph J. Sabath, and James M. Meade of New York introduced bills providing for FTC enforcement of wage and hour standards.[32]

The most serious threat to wage and hour regulation, however, was the AFL demand for a simple statutory 40-hour-40-cent national standard. Rejecting both the wage and hour board and the Labor Department's bill, Green urged the House to accept statutory standards. He condemned the proposal to give an administrator the power previously granted to the board as an effort to create a "labor czar." The AFL statutory-standards bill, he insisted, would promote collective bargaining and eliminate differentials. Its greatest advantage, he argued, was its simplicity. Although it was a short bill of only ten sections, it also had serious disadvantages. A statutory standard for all industry was clearly impractical, and southerners insisted on differentials. Norton tried to head off certain disaster by warning Green that her committee would not substitute the federation's bill for the Black-Connery Bill. But despite Rayburn's warning that a bill with inflexible statutory standards would not be accepted by either house, Green had John F. Dockweiler of California introduce the AFL bill.[33]

Facing a deadline early in December, Norton's committee labored in vain on amendments for the Black-Connery bill. Since it was swamped with proposals for sweeping changes, the bill's backers caucused to decide whether industry-committee administration should be substituted for regulation by the Labor Standards Board. Ramspeck argued that the administrator would be powerless to fix wage and hour standards because he was required to either accept or reject the findings of industry committees. If he rejected a second finding, he would be required to form a new committee. Since differentials were not specifically guaranteed, most southerners remained opposed to an administrator. But a compromise was accepted whereby northerners agreed to vote for differentials in return for southern acceptance of an administrator and industry committee regulation. The caucus also agreed that other objectional features could be eliminated later by a joint-conference committee. Thereafter, the Labor Committee approved the substitution of an administrator by a 9 to 6 vote. Bankhead and Majority Whip Boland then urged all loyal Democrats to support the bill. After the House voted to take it up by a comfortable 285-to-123 margin, Norton opened the debate, admitting that she was the adoptive mother of a baby left on her doorstep.[34]

Norton assured the House that her committee's revised bill, the Norton substitute, did not resemble the NIRA or strike at the South, collective bargaining, or employers. It incorporated sixty changes in a draft of twenty-four sections. The most important was the acceptance of an administrator and industry committee regulation. Aware of southern hostility toward Secretary Perkins, she emphasized that the administrator would be in the Labor Department but not subject to the secretary. The Children's Bureau would administer the child-labor provisions. She also assured the House that there was nothing radical about the administrative provisions for industry-committee formulation of standards, which were modeled on the minimum-wage laws of twenty-two states.[35]

Reaction to the Norton substitute was strongly negative, with some critics condemning it as a collection of last-minute proposals, few of which originated with the committee. The *New York Times* condemned House leaders for bringing out a complicated bill and allowing only four days of debate. Predicting a drastic restructuring of industry if it were passed, the *Times* asserted that no one knew how many workers would be covered, how much unemployment and the relief budget might increase, how geographic differentials would be affected, or whether the reciprocal trade policy would be nullified. During the debate, many supporters and opponents of wage and hour regulation agreed that the Norton substitute lacked adequate study and insisted that it be returned to committee.[36]

House leaders were unable to line up support for the Norton substitute because southerners and supporters of statutory standards united against it. Hope for the bill faded when the anticipated compromise with southerners on differentials failed to materialize. Rebellious northerners, led by Griswold, Dockweiler, Connery, and Lamneck supported statutory standards or the AFL bill. Healey made a strong plea for the Norton substitute, producing a mass of statistics to prove that substandard wages and hours in any part of the country under-mined those in other sections. But when Celler of New York claimed that regulation would promote reemployment, Sam McReynolds of Tennessee and Sam Hobbs of Alabama warned the House that it would destroy unions and collective bargaining. Ramspeck said that both the substitute and the AFL bill were unconstitutional. Dies provoked a chorus of rebel yells when he claimed to have lined up 135 Democrats and 69 Republicans for recommittal.[37]

Great excitement ensued when Norton moved to substitute her amendment for the provisions of the Black-Connery Bill. Several op-ponents said some of its sections were not germane. Jere Cooper of Tennessee objected to the import ban as an alteration of the tariff. The chair overruled most of the objections but threw the House into confusion by upholding Cooper's on a technicality. Rayburn ripped the offending section out of the amendment, and Norton, coached by O'Connor, reintroduced it. Griswold then offered the AFL bill as a substitute for the Norton amendment, and the chair ruled it ger-mane. After a grueling session, supporters of the amendment and southern opponents of wage and hour regulation defeated the AFL bill by a vote of 162 to 131. Their success turned out to be a pyrrhic victory for backers of the Norton substitute. Frustrated by the defeat of the AFL bill, President Green sent telegrams to all members urging them to recommit the substitute for further study.[38]

After disposing of Lamneck's FTC bill, the House began consider-ing amendments to the Norton substitute. Ramspeck's attempt to replace the administrator with the Labor Standards Board was de-feated, as was another effort on behalf of the AFL bill, and one to substitute the Wheeler-Johnson child-labor provisions. Although southern attempts to exempt cotton-ginning, tobacco-warehousing, and fishing were defeated, the House accepted twenty-three amend-ments exempting farm labor, food-processing, and mining occupa-tions. Rayburn and O'Connor then pleaded for support of the thoroughly amended Norton substitute, admitting its defects but re-minding Democrats of their party's pledge. The House accepted it and the bill was brought to a final vote.[39]

The AFL's last-minute pressure against the bill was intense. Green's telegrams were followed by AFL lobbyists, who called House members off the floor just before the final vote. The roll call on Hartley's motion to recommit was taken in breathless silence, with even the packed galleries in strict order. As the ayes alternated with the nays in almost monotonous regularity, it was impossible to predict which way the vote would go. Finally Bankhead announced the result: 216 for recommittal and 198 against. There was an immediate outburst of cheering among the bill's opponents that lasted for several minutes. Norton slumped in her seat as though stunned by the result. She was soon surrounded by the bill's backers, who congratulated her on the effort she made under such difficult circumstances.[40]

With the aid of the AFL, the southern Democratic-Republican coalition dealt the Roosevelt administration the most smashing defeat it had yet received in the House. The vote on the bill clearly revealed both sectional and urban-rural conflicts. Of the 218 who had signed the discharge petition, 85 voted to recommit. Of the 216 voting to recommit, 133 were Democrats and comprised more than one-third of the party in the House. Of 99 southern Democrats, 81 voted to recommit. And 74 percent of those voting to recommit represented primarily rural districts.[41]

The vote also revealed serious dissension in the New Deal farmer-labor coalition. Because of the AFL-CIO split, conservative Republicans and Democrats from urban districts were able to vote against a proposal to eliminate oppressive-labor conditions. As John Martin of Colorado noted, the split furnished an alibi for those who opposed regulation because they had no social conscience. More bluntly, Eli Oliver said labor had been double-crossed by members who had agreed to support the bill. There was a report that Jersey City Boss Hague had ordered his Hudson County delegation to vote to recommit on the assumption that he was striking blow at the CIO. In Louisiana a feud between Mayor Robert S. Maestri of New Orleans and Governor Leche resulted in a sudden switch of seven votes for recommittal.[42]

The defeat of the Black-Connery bill intensified the feud between the AFL and CIO. Since Green's telegram and AFL lobbying gave urban opponents an alibi for voting to recommit, John L. Lewis berated Green for killing the bill and ridiculed him as the toady of his Executive Council. Ramspeck concurred, describing Green as helpless in face of his council's opposition to the bill. Well aware of the CIO's effort to condemn the AFL for the bill's defeat, Green hailed the vote as a victory for workers. He in turn comdemned the CIO and LNPL for the defeat of the AFL bill and for supporting one that would create a "labor czar" and allow differentials. The "dictators" of the CIO, he said, thought more of their prestige than the plight of the workers, while the AFL tried to wipe out sweatshops and differentials.[43]

It would be inaccurate, however, to place the blame for the defeat of the amended Black-Connery bill primarily on the AFL and on the split in organized labor. Opponents were able to form an effective coalition against it because the administration and congressional leaders simply failed to produce an acceptable bill. During the debate, there was much evidence that a majority would support regulation if the Labor Committee could produce an acceptable compromise. But both the committee and the Labor Department faced the insuperable problem of drafting a substitute that could satisfy the AFL and the southerners. Norton was sincere but inexperienced; perhaps William P. Connery could have done better. Yet, given southern demands for differentials and the board, AFL insistence on national uniform statutory standards, and Labor Department preference for industry committee regulation, her efforts were hopeless. Moreover, the bill's backers and House leaders were unable to work out an agreement that could avoid loading down the bill with undesirable amendments. Such agreement depended on bargaining with rural representatives, and unfortunately for the bill's backers, the farm bill had been approved first. Basically, however, the problem originated in Roosevelt's decision to accept the Cohen-Corcoran draft without a thorough review of its provisions by both labor committees before it was introduced. Instead of a careful study of the problem of national regulation by a conference of experts, the labor committees received a bill that went beyond eliminating oppression, which the AFL and Labor Department considered unsatisfactory. In short, the bill was badly handled from the beginning.

The defeat of the Black-Connery Bill was also due to factors over which the bill's backers had no control. Roosevelt's prestige in Congress suffered because of the Supreme Court fight. The nation was also undergoing a recession, which made many congressmen more cautious about a bill that would have a dislocating effect on industry and business. Sit-down strikes and resulting labor disorder upset the public and alarmed those congressmen who were concerned about communist infiltration of the CIO. Moreover, there was a reaction against further reform that became overt when the conservative southern-Democratic and Republican coalition issued a formal anti-New Deal declaration. After four years of reform, a reactionary wave was mounting against any further economic and social experimentation.

Despite this defeat, Roosevelt insisted that the fight for the bill go on. According to Postmaster General Farley, the president was afraid the public would think the Democratic party had repudiated one of its campaign pledges. He resented the betrayal of southern Democrats and planned to retaliate against those who had deserted him. Secretary Ickes believed Roosevelt had failed to assert his leadership, allowing Congress to have its way during the special session on the assumption that it would have to come to him for help. If such is a valid explanation, Roosevelt intended to reassert command of his troops.[44]

Calling congressional leaders to the White House, he chided them on their failure to pass the bill and asked that it be introduced again early in the following session. There seemed to be a lack of enthusiasm. Speaker Bankhead refused to make any predictions about the future of the bill. Senator Ellenbogen thought it would be lost without a national campaign on its behalf.[45] Clearly, New Deal supporters had not effectively utilized their political clout with their congressional delegations. If the bill were to be saved, Roosevelt would have to offer effective support, and the bill's backers would have to organize a vigorous campaign on it behalf.

7

Thou Shalt Eat Bread

> We are interfering with economic law, not however to make the
> rich richer, but to help the poorest of the poor. This law will raise
> the lowest wages. It will reduce the longest hours. The forgotten
> men and women, at least, are being remembered.
> —Representative Herbert S. Bigelow of Ohio

SINCE Roosevelt considered wage and hour regulation to be a party
pledge, the struggle over a bill was resumed when Congress reconvened in January 1938. In a conciliatory message, he once again reminded it and the nation that underpaid workers who had little
purchasing power could contribute little toward recovery. In urging
acceptance of a floor for wages and a ceiling for hours, he did not
insist on uniform standards and sought to assure labor that it would
not lose its bargaining rights by agreeing to the elimination of starvation wages. The press deemed his message the most moderate since
he had taken office and his appeal for regulation quite reasonable. He
avoided blaming any group for the defeat of the Black-Connery Bill
but insisted that the fight would go on. Perkins said supporters would
force the farm bloc to accept it and mobilize public support. In this
quest Roosevelt had the enthusiastic backing of loyal New Deal congressmen. Representative Maverick told him that a bloc of almost
forty New Dealers had agreed to push the bill through.[1]

Early in January Roosevelt met with seven southeastern governors
in an effort to overcome southern resistance to wage and hour regulation. He won their endorsement by agreeing to a reexamination of
southern freight rates and the inclusion of freight-rate differentials as
a factor to be considered by the Labor Standards Board. Critics as-
cribed his success to the victory of Lister Hill over Senator Thomas
Heflin in the Alabama Democratic primary. Hill had endorsed the
full New Deal program, including wage and hour legislation. Roosevelt also induced Josephus Daniels of North Carolina, ambassador to

115

Mexico, to ask southern congressmen to accept wage and hour regulation.[2]

Roosevelt's prodding and Lister Hill's victory produced a change in attitude on regulation among some southerners. Representative Dies announced that a wage and hour bill could be quickly revived with a proper compromise. McReynolds said the southern bloc was already drafting its own bill, which was based on the premise that federal regulation would be needed in only a few industries. It proposed a flexible 40-hour-40-cent standard, with state labor departments authorized to vary national standards. Roosevelt immediately rejected the proposal because state variation of national standards would limit the improvement of purchasing power in those sections needing it most. The plan, he said, was the weakest and most dangerous that he had yet received.[3]

Secretary Perkins organized a national committee of business, industry, labor, and public leaders to back wage and hour regulation. She was assured of strong support from northern garment and textile industry employers. In an effort to overcome southern opposition, Labor Commissioner Arthur L. Fletcher of North Carolina was asked to organize southern state labor department officials behind a bill. Beyer thought there was more support among southern workers than their congressmen admitted and wanted the Labor Department to concentrate on convincing them that their workers favored such a law. If the Black-Connery Bill had been limited to fixing only minimum wages and maximum hours from the start, she believed, there would have been much less opposition. Assistant Secretary Altmeyer favored a limited law covering only those industries in which labor was clearly exploited.[4]

Early in January the administration's plans for reviving the Black-Connery Bill had not crystallized. It considered having the bill reported out with only child-labor provisions and then restoring the wage and hour sections in conference, but this devious strategy was abandoned. Cohen thought the Labor Committee should report out the original Senate bill and endure another fight. He urged Reilly to sound out loyal Democrats on the Rules Committee to see if there were any change in the attitude of the Dies-Cox bloc. Norton said her committee would write a new bill, retain the 40-hour-40-cent standard, and incorporate flexible provisions to satisfy all sections. Her committee, she explained, was in doubt about the constitutionality of flexible standards but was optimistic about the chances of Rules Committee cooperation in getting the bill out.[5]

Because of Norton's illness, her committee made little progress on a bill for over a month. In the interim, the Labor Department prepared two bills, one for flexible standards and the other for statutory differentials. Bill A, apparently the National Labor Standards Act, would create a division of labor standards in the department and authorize an administrator to appoint industry boards to set standards within the 40-hour-40-cent limit. Bill B accepted a 40-hour workweek and a minimum wage of $11 for the South and $13 for the North, with an administrator authorized to grant variations up to 10 percent of the statutory standard. It adopted the NRA standard of 1934, which accepted differentials. Perkins preferred Bill A because Congress would not accept statutory standards and industry-board rates would be more flexible. Bill B's differentials, she pointed out, could hardly be justified on economic grounds. In order to monitor the legislation, she appointed Rufus Poole as an assistant to Solicitor Reilly and charged him with evaluating wage and hour proposals and with following their progress in Congress. Poole canvassed scores of congressmen, learned that a dependable majority favored a bill, and was even able to predict support for amendments.[6]

In order to overcome southern opposition, Roosevelt endorsed Bill B's proposed differentials, and a Gallup poll revealed that the public also accepted them. Nationally, those polled favored a 44-hour-40-cent standard which yielded $17.60. While northerners favored an $18 minimum, southerners accepted a 48-hour-25-cent standard and $12.00 weekly. While the Labor Committee was considering a standard, the District of Columbia wage board approved a $14.50 minimum and 44-hour week for female laundry workers. Hence, in the nation's capital a 44-hour week was "nonoppressive" and a 32-cent minimum was deemed "reasonable" for female employees.[7]

Later in February the administration's strategy was upset when the AFL had Representative Michael J. Stack of Pennsylvania introduce its statutory 40-hour-40-cent standard bill. Like the AFL's previous measure, it did not authorize differentials, had no provisions for administration, relied on Justice Department enforcement in the courts, and imposed $100 fines for each offense. Child and convict labor were prohibited by banning goods made by such labor in interstate commerce. Employers under a union agreement accepting higher standards were exempted. The AFL justified its support for statutory standards by arguing that it was not safe to permit either a government agency or administrator to make the determinations for fair pay. It cited the inability of the Bituminous Coal Board to cope with complicated economic and social factors in setting fair rates.[8]

When Norton's committee finally resumed consideration of wage and hour legislation, it could take up any of at least eighteen bills, many of which had been introduced by its twenty-one members.[9] It was, however, primarily concerned with Bills A and B and the AFL measure. Norton deemed the AFL bills unconstitutional, as did the Rules Committee, which would not allow the House to vote on them. Hartley, a leading opponent on the Labor Committee, condemned Bill B's NRA standards as being below 1937 wage levels. It would, he claimed, depress wages raised above the subsistence level by collective bargaining and conscientious employers. Because of irreconcilable differences, the committee abandoned all the bills, and Norton appointed a seven-member subcommittee chaired by Ramspeck to draft a new bill with standards within 40-to-44-hour and 30-to-40-cent parameters. It included Jennings Randolph of West Virginia, James H. Gildea of Pennsylvania, Albert Thomas of Texas, George J. Schneider of Wisconsin, and Republicans Richard J. Welch of California and Clyde H. Smith of Maine. Norton said it would deliberate without any preconceived ideas, an unlikely prospect, and hoped to have a bill by April.[10]

Prospects for a bill were not particularly bright when Ramspeck's committee began its work. Rayburn said many congressmen were opposed to regulation because Norton's committee could not agree on a bill. Some preferred to have an expert committee study the problem of wage and hour regulation and to delay action for a year. Roosevelt took a conciliatory position, promising to make no attempt to ram a bill through Congress unacceptable to the Rules Committee. Despite its opposition to fixed standards, Ramspeck's subcommittee considered a statutory sliding scale whereby a 44-hour week would be reduced to 40 hours and a 30-cent minimum would be raised to 40 cents over three or four years, with administration in the Labor Department. President Green objected to the sliding scale and the low minimum, but after Roosevelt met with conservative AFL officials, Green said the AFL could be flexible on the 40-cent minimum in order to save the bill. O'Connor thought the initial minimum was not as important as the need for flexibility in order to provide for differentials. He also considered administration of minor importance and was willing to have a subdivision of the Labor Department administer the standards.[11]

After three weeks of deliberation, Ramspeck's subcommittee deadlocked over a 20- or 25-cent minimum and statutory or flexible increases. John L. Lewis considered a 20-cent rate far too low, but Green said the AFL would accept a 30-cent minimum with mandatory increases and would demand a 30-hour week if Congress abandoned minimum-wage regulation. Green and Lewis were not very far apart on standards: both accepted a 40-hour ceiling; Lewis favored a graduated minimum, but not lower than a 35-cent rate. Analyzing the problem, Poole thought labor leaders were more interested in their unions than in aiding the mass of unorganized workers who would benefit from regulation. What was needed, he said, was broad support from sympathetic pressure groups. His criticism of union leaders was not entirely fair. Clearly, they understood the need to protect collective bargaining rights, and CIO leaders backed wage and hour legislation to help unorganized workers in mass-production industries. They understood the humanitarian objective and the need to enhance the purchasing power of workers.[12]

The failure of Ramspeck's subcommittee to agree on a bill upset leaders of the CIO, Labor's Non-Partisan League (LNPL), and the American Labor Party. John L. Lewis condemned the administration for failing to offer a constructive program to cope with the recession. John W. Edelman, CIO regional director for eastern Pennsylvania, pleaded with Roosevelt to fight to get a bill out. Workers, he said, were convinced that the future of the New Deal depended on the Democratic party's ability to respond to the economic needs of the country. There was an uneasy feeling, he claimed, that the administration was wavering on a bill. Eli Oliver told Congress that its failure to pass a wage and hour bill was contributing to a business slump. Workers, he said, had suffered wage cuts and thousands had been added to the relief rolls. Merle Vincent said low wages were cutting the heart out of the nation's markets. A wage and hour law was therefore indispensable for expanded markets and reemployment. O'Connor was condemned for knifing the wage and hour bill and found it necessary to explain that he was not responsible for its defeat.[13]

Unwilling to accept further delay, early in April the five Democratic members of Ramspeck's subcommittee drafted a bill without the cooperation of their Republican colleagues. The Ramspeck bill retained a wage and hour board, accepted a 48-hour-40-cent maximum standard, and provided for annual 5-cent increases above weighted-average wages for any industry. In determining a weighted-average wage, the board would consider many factors: wages paid, the cost of living, the number of employees in an industry, services rendered, local material costs, the value of goods produced, wages fixed by collective bargaining, and standards maintained by fair employers. In setting the workweek, the board would consider the health and well-being of workers, the number of workers available, hours fixed by collective bargaining, and hours maintained by fair employers. Annual increases in wages and reductions in hours, Ramspeck explained, would eventually achieve a 40-hour-40-cent standard and give industry time to adjust. Since the board could classify employers and employees by locality and population, the bill would provide for differentials. But they would be narrowed because the board would base wage rates on weighted-average wages for an entire industry divided by the number of employees. Since the bill accepted a wage and hour board and differentials, it was described as a trial balloon sent up to get a reaction from the unions and from the Rules Committee.[14]

If Ramspeck's bill was indeed a trial balloon, the AFL quickly shot it down. Since it retained a geographically selected board and provided for flexible standards and differentials, the AFL condemned it. Calling its provisions baffling and confusing, Green said it was more objectionable than any of the previous bills. He criticized the board's authority to determine weighted-average wages as subjecting industry to arbitrary-wage decrees. He reiterated the AFL's willingness to accept a 30-cent national minimum. The CIO and LNPL, however, believed the Ramspeck bill wold provide for effective regulation and would meet the broad requirements of the situation. Oliver urged members of Norton's committee to subordinate minor objections and efforts to perfect a bill, which he claimed would only delay or defeat the legislation. John L. Lewis also thought it would be wise to accept imperfections in the bill in order to get Congress to pass the legislation.[15]

Norton's committee remained deadlocked on the question of whether to approve Ramspeck's weighted-average or a statutory escalator-clause substitute. Norton's substitute accepted a 25-cent minimum and a 5-cent annual increase until the 40-cent maximum was reached; a 44-hour week would be reduced by 2 hours annually until the 40-hour floor was reached. The secretary of labor would determine the industries to be covered. Agricultural labor, fishing, retail trade, and transportation workers under the jurisdiction of the ICC were exempted. Administration would be in the Labor Department with Justice Department enforcement. Norton pleaded with her committee to come to a decision. The president insisted on a bill and she wanted to get one out and put pressure on the Rules Committee. She was sick and tired, she complained, of having her committee meet and adjourn without accomplishing anything.[16]

After a caucus of House members indicated that the Ramspeck bill had no chance, Norton's committee finally came to a decision. On a motion by Griswold, by a narrow margin of 10 to 8, it rejected Ramspeck's bill. It then approved the Norton substitute by a 14-to-4 margin. According to Lambertson, the committee's rejection of Ramspeck's bill was highly arbitrary. Before it had even been discussed, he complained, Norton offered her substitute, which came from the Labor Department. Her "half baked" substitute was not considered for more than an hour before the committee voted it out. The House would probably pass it, he predicted, because of the primaries and the political campaign.[17]

Ramspeck refused to support the substitute, calling its escalator provisions arbitrary, discriminatory, and unconstitutional. In the *Parrish* case, however, the Supreme Court had accepted the Washington state legislature's authority to set an inflexible minimum wage to meet living costs. If Congress established a similar fixed minimum, the government would merely have to show that it was not in excess of the amount required to meet living costs in any section of the country. Since the lowest emergency standard was about $800 in Wichita, Kansas, it would be reasonable to assume that the Court would sustain the 40-hour-40-cent standard, which would provide an annual income of only $800 after four years. And because provisions for guiding the secretary of labor had been based on recent Court decisions upholding the jurisdiction of the NLRB, it was reasonable to assume that the administrative provisions of the substitute bill would be upheld. Such delegation of administrative authority had been upheld where specific standards for guidance had been provided and where Congress could not treat all circumstances.[18]

After Norton's committee reported her substitute, she met with the Rules Committee in an effort to overcome its opposition by distinguishing her substitute from the Black-Connery Bill. In her substitute, she explained, the power of the secretary was very limited, and there was virtually no administration. Provisions covering child labor, exemptions, learners, apprentices, and handicapped workers were identical in both bills. And her substitute dropped the special exemptions for processing farm commodities, fruits and vegetables, and seafood. Representative Dies, however, wanted to know how many workers would be affected by the proposed standards.[19]

Secretary Perkins assured Dies that although only a small percent of approximately 13 million workers in the industries covered would benefit directly, the legislation would help all workers in such industries indirectly. She thought the 40-hour week would benefit an estimated 4 million workers in the food-processing, cottonseed-oil, lumber, machine-tool, and railroad-equipment industries; and the 40-cent minimum would affect from 1.25 to 2 million workers. Although the ban on the shipment of goods produced in violation of the minimum standards followed that of the 1916 child-labor law voided by the Supreme Court, she thought it was now ready to uphold the ban, given its holdings in the NLRB cases.[20]

Amid rumors of early adjournment and a resort to Fabian delaying tactics by Rules Committee opponents, Norton's committee met with it to discuss the substitute. There were a few agreements on exemptions and much friction. As tempers rose, O'Connor had trouble keeping order. Welch scolded Rules Committee opponents, Sabath clashed with Cox over his exam of Welch, and Lambertson defended Cox. Roosevelt's support, Norton's pleas, and union lobbying were of no avail. The Rules Committee denied a rule by an 8-to-6-vote. Only one Republican, Joseph W. Martin of Massachusetts, joined the northern Democrats in support of a rule; Taylor, Mapes, and McLean joined the five southern Democrats against it. Once again, the conservative southern-Democratic-Republican coalition succeeded in blocking wage and hour legislation. But on this occasion, they could not justify their opposition on the AFL's refusal to accept such legislation. When opponents said a flat 40-hour-40-cent standard would be substituted when the bill reached the floor, President Green said the AFL would not support such a move, nor would it support the Senate bill in conference. Nevertheless, the bill's backers were again forced to resort to a discharge petition, despite Roosevelt's agreement not to ram anything unacceptable to the Rules Committee through the House.[21]

Since House leaders had suggested adjournment by the first of June, the bill's backers had little time to gather 218 signatures. The petition could not be filed until May 5, and if Congress adjourned as scheduled, the last Monday the bill could be considered was May 23. On this occasion, however, Norton had the vigorous support of northern Democrats, urban Republicans, and organized labor. Healey's steering committee threatened to fight adjournment until the House was allowed to consider the bill. Some state delegations promised unanimous support. A group of ILGWU, ACWU, and American Labor Party delegates met with their New York representatives to remind them that the garment industry was fleeing to low-wage states. Oliver sent groups of southern hosiery workers to see their representatives. John L. Lewis denounced the Rules Committee vote as a travesty on representative government, and the CIO had Hillman lobbying in Washington for a week. President Green sent telegrams to all congressmen asking them to sign the petition the day it was filed. Clearly, this intensive lobbying campaign convinced dubious congressmen that it would be politically wise to sign during the primary campaigns. Before the petition was laid on the table, the steering committee claimed to have two hundred pledges.[22]

Three days before the petition was laid on the table, New Deal Senator Claude Pepper defeated Congressman Mark Wilcox in the Florida primary. In stark contrast to the situation the previous December, there was a veritable stampede to the clerk's table when the petition was offered. Norton led the rush, and such a scramble ensued that a line had to be formed! On this occasion, there was no misunderstanding, and Mayor Maestri delivered the entire Louisiana delegation. In what certainly must have been a record, 218 signatures were obtained in 212 minutes. Among them were 183 Democrats, 22 Republicans, 8 Progressives, and 5 Farmer-Laborites; but only 18 were southern Democrats. President Green, John L. Lewis, and Oliver congratulated House leaders on their success. Some commentators attributed the petition's success to Pepper's victory, since he had supported wage and hour regulation. Obviously, however, his victory failed to put the fear of God in the hearts of those southern Democrats who refused to sign the petition; nor did labor's lobbying campaign impress representatives from rural districts.[23]

Although the Norton substitute would be considered, success was not certain. Ramspeck said it would be amended on the floor, and he had the support of southern senators. Senator Pat Harrison organized a drive among his colleagues for differentials and was supported by Senate Labor Committee Chairman Elbert B. Thomas. Dies said flexible wage provisions would be inserted on the floor. McReynolds favored eliminating them and confining the bill to the regulation of hours. The National Grange and other farm organizations threatened to oppose the bill if hours exemptions for food-processing industries were not restored. Undaunted by these threats, Healey said loyal supporters would block undesirable amendments and any move for adjournment until a vote was taken. A poll indicated that 59 percent of those surveyed favored the passage of the bill before Congress adjourned. In New England an overwhelming 76 percent supported it, and even southerners favored it by a 56-percent margin. Given such support, Norton thought its prospects were much more hopeful then they had been the previous session.[24]

In offering her motion to take up the bill, Norton characterized it as entirely different in form, approach, and administration than the recommitted Black-Connery Bill. A large majority favored taking it up, and it was discharged by an overwhelming 322-to-73-vote. Favoring discharge were 249 Democrats, 62 Republicans, 7 Progressives, and 4 Farmer-Laborites, with only 53 Democrats and 20 Republicans opposed. Debate was limited to five hours and amendments were considered the following day. Leading off, Norton emphasized reassuring improvements in the bill. Differentials and exemptions had been dropped and statutory standards accepted so that employers would know exactly where they stood. The authority of the secretary of labor had been greatly reduced and was considerably less than the rate-setting power of the original board. Norton also asked the House not to emasculate the bill by loading it down with unwelcome amendments. Congress, she said, had an obligation to help those living in misery, and she asked the House to pass the bill in order to give the underprivileged at least the necessities of life.[25]

Representative Healey sought to assure the business community that the statutory standard posed no threat to industry. The maximum-annual income provided by the eventual 40-hour-40-cent rate, a mere $800 for fifty weeks, would not even reach an average $903-emergency budget, much less the $1,261-subsistence budget, neither of which provided a satisfactory "American" standard of living. Several Labor Committee members said the South would not suffer. Randolph did not think the South could prove it was entitled to a differential. Southern textile mills, said Wood, had not closed when the NRA raised worker's wages to $11 weekly. William F. Allen of Delaware thought an industry unable to pay $11 a week had no right to exist. NRA wages and hours, Kent Keller of Illinois claimed, had saved the country. Republican Meade of New York claimed the bill would deter the sweatshop exploitation of workers. And Maverick found it necessary to deny the claim that the bill was the result of a conspiracy hatched by Moscow, the CIO, and John L. Lewis.[26]

Southern opponents emphasized the bill's threat to the South's economy. Cox said the House was creating a Frankenstein which would violate states rights. The bill, he claimed, would keep the South under an economic handicap it had endured for a hundred years. McReynolds said southern workers would suffer if their products could not compete. Ramspeck recommended his bill, saying it was more in line with the president's support for flexible rates. When he cited Assistant Attorney General Jackson's statement that the Supreme Court had not specifically upheld statutory standards, Norton responded that it would not necessarily void them. Dies warned the House about the power bestowed on Secretary Perkins. Mapes claimed the bill would actually increase unemployment and industrial strife. Lambertson labeled the bill a second NRA and a marriage of the administration and the CIO. In his fifteen years in Congress, said O'Connor, outside of Prohibition, he could not remember an issue so hotly debated.[27]

The bill's backers successfully defeated most of the fifty amendments offered. Ramspeck's weighted-average-wage bill lost by a 139-to-70-margin. Lawrence Connery's 40-hour-40-cent standard, Phillips's 30-hour workweek, and Dies's state-administered flexible standard were also rejected. Another attempt to substitute the Wheeler-Johnson child-labor provisions failed, as did amendments to cover federal employees, exempt firms with annual-wage plans, and eliminate the secretary of labor's power to designate the industries to be covered. Most of the farm bloc's amendments were defeated, but an hours exemption for the food-processing and dairy industries was accepted. Also exempted were small county newspapers and child actors. On the whole, the bill's backers successfully prevented opponents from loading it down with unwelcome amendments.[28]

After a tumultuous session lasting far into the night, the bill was finally passed by an overwhelming 314-to-97-vote. Favoring it were 256 Democrats, 46 Republicans, 7 Progressives, and 4 Farmer-Laborites. Of 56 Democrats opposing it, 52 were southerners. Neither Senator Pepper's victory or labor's lobbying broke their resistance. Explaining the overwhelming vote, Norton emphasized the AFL's willingness to abandon its own 40-hour-40-cent standard bill and to accept the escalator clause instead. She also received strong backing from Healey's steering committee, Republican committee member Welch, and many Democrats and Republicans from urban districts.[29]

Editorial comment on the Norton substitute was mixed and revealed much concern about its economic consequences. The *New York Times* thought it had been drafted without proper study and would cause economic dislocation. The *Christian Science Monitor* called the attempt to fix statutory standards preposterous and a face-saving effort by Norton's committee on behalf of the AFL. The bill's real purpose, claimed Walter Lippman, was to deprive the South of its low-wage advantage. The *Washington Daily News* thought the weekly $16-wage merely subsistence income, but the *Washington Post* said Congress could anticipate an expansion of the relief rolls unless flexible rates were accepted. Prosperity, the *West Virginia Charleston Gazette* declared, could not be built on cheap wages in any section, and the *St. Louis Post-Dispatch* agreed that profits must not depend on starvation wages.[30] Generally, the bill's humanitarian objectives were recognized but its effect on industry and the economy was questioned. Clearly, faith in wage and hour regulation as panacea for purchasing-power recovery had diminished considerably since 1933.

House passage of the amended Black-Connery bill sent it back to the Senate. If the Senate simply rejected it, a House-Senate conference committee would be charged with working out a compromise. But if the Senate amended it in any way, the House would have to consent unanimously to send it to conference. Failing unanimous consent, it would go back to the Rules Committee and another petition would probably be required to extract it. In order to avoid having it returned to the Senate Labor Committee for possible amendment, Barkley worked out a last-minute agreement with southern senators. He assured them they could insist on differentials and would be properly represented on the conference committee. Hence, the Senate agreed to send the bill to conference and Barkley avoided a threatened filibuster.[31]

After reaching an agreement with Harrison, Byrd, and Byrnes, Barkley appointed only two southerners, Ellender and Pepper, to the seven-member Senate conference committee. But five of the conferees favored differentials. Pepper, Walsh, Chairman Elbert Thomas, James Murray of Montana, and LaFollette accepted flexible standards. Only Borah insisted on statutory rates, while Ellender wanted to postpone action for a year's study of regulation. Harrison mollified the southerners, calling Barkley's arrangement the best the South could get. Opponents of the bill, he promised, would have an opportunity to defeat the conference bill when it returned to the Senate floor. After the Senate was assured that the conference committee would work out a compromise within the bounds of the Black-Connery and Norton bills, the amended bill went to conference by unanimous consent.[32]

Speaker Bankhead appointed seven members of the House Labor Committee to the Conference Committee, which included only one southerner. In addition to Norton the northerners included Dunn, Keller, Randolph, and Republicans Welch and Hartley. Ramspeck, the only southerner, was committed to differentials, while the Democrats favored the escalator clause. When the Conference Committee began its deliberations, House conferees were allowed to win the first concessions. Senate conferees accepted the House child-labor sections, rather than the Wheeler-Johnson provisions.

The committee first accepted the basic 25-cent minimum, with a proviso that no agency could set a lower rate, but it reached an impasse on the escalator clause. Norton suggested a 30-cent minimum the second year and 2-cent increases thereafter for five years. Walsh was willing to accept a 3-cent increase over five years. Thomas proposed 2.5-cent increases for two years, with raises thereafter set by industry boards; but after seven years the 40-cent rate would be mandatory and the boards and administrative authority would be abolished. Randolph would allow the boards to set rates above the 30-cent rate after the second year. Because of the impasse over reaching the 40-cent rate in seven years, House and Senate conferees met separately to review their proposals, and a southern filibuster was threatened. Northern conferees backed the seven-year requirement because organized labor demanded the 40-hour-40-cent standard within a certain time. Southerners insisted on differentials and flexibility to avoid dislocating southern industry.[33]

After a canvass of the House indicated that the majority of members would compromise on flexible standards, agreement seemed possible. Although Norton and Welch remained committed to statutory increases above the 25-cent rate, the other five, led by Ramspeck, were willing to accept flexible rates set by industry boards above the basic rate. By a 4-to-3-vote the Senate conferees approved the Thomas plan to allow the boards to set rates above the 30-cent minimum after the second year and to reach the 40-cent limit as rapidly as possible without a time limit. Ramspeck supported it, and Norton said the House would accept it if the seven-year limit were retained. When Thomas suggested a ten-year limit, Ramspeak countered with a motion to reach the 40-cent limit in seven years, which the conferees approved by a 12 to 2 vote. The hours provision remained rigid: 44 the first year, 42 the second, and 40 thereafter. Ellender then caucused with seventeen southern senators who agreed to filibuster unless differentials were accepted.[34]

Faced with a filibuster, the conferees reopened consideration of differentials. Since southerners insisted on flexibility, the conferees agreed that the industry boards would consider the cost of living, prevailing wages and hours, and transportation costs, all of which would justify differentials. Exemptions would be granted to those industries guaranteeing annual wages and two thousand hours of employment yearly. Since southerners did not like Secretary Perkins, supervision would be in the hands of an independent administrator in a newly created Wage and Hour Division of the Labor Department. The compromise bill was accepted by a 10-to-4-vote, with Borah, Walsh, Welch, and Hartley opposed.[35] The conference bill was then returned to both houses for consideration.

Conferees of both houses claimed victory and threats of a filibuster ceased. Norton said the compromise retained the statutory 40-hour-40-cent standard after seven years and contained every principle incorporated in her substitute bill. Senate conferees claimed credit for obtaining flexible standards and exemptions, even though geographic differentials had not been written into the bill. Although Borah and Walsh said the bill did not recognize sectional differentials, Pepper and Ellender claimed the South was protected.[36]

Senate debate on the conference bill seemed pro forma. Senator Thomas described it as better than either the House or Senate versions. By accepting flexibility, arbitrary high statutory wage rates were avoided and industry would have time to adjust. Moreover, the requirement to reach the 40-hour-40-cent standard in seven years would guard against inertia. Although job classification was allowed, wage discrimination based on section, gender, or age was banned. In regard to constitutionality, administrative provisions were based on the model New York law, which had been praised by Chief Justice Hughes in the *Tipaldo* case. The bill had been drafted so that if the statutory standards were voided, the provisions for flexible rates would remain operative. Since Congress was not granting authority to any independent agency, Thomas deemed the bill constitutional. He also defined it as the most important measure considered by Congress since the Social Security Act.[37]

Not all opponents were convinced. Senator Bailey could not understand how the commerce power could give Congress the authority to regulate industry and agriculture; moreover, he could not see how hours and wages in any locality could be an obstacle to commerce requiring national regulation. Borah and Sherman Minton enlightened him, reminding him of the Supreme Court's acceptance of broad commerce power in the NLRB cases. During this exchange, there were cries for a vote, indicating that many senators considered the argument academic and wanted to go home. Anxious to approve a compromise bill upon which there was substantial agreement, and not wishing to embarrass members from either section, the Senate passed the bill by a voice vote, with but a few scattered nays.[38]

There was some ineffective opposition to the Fair Labor Standards Act on the other side of the Capitol during a mere hour's debate. All challenges questioning the conferees' authority to compromise were denied, the chair ruling that they had carte blanche to prepare provisions for wage and hour regulation. Hartley and Lambertson condemned regulation as unnecessary harassment of industry. Griswold regretted the House's surrender on differentials. They had been defeated in the House by an overwhelming vote, only to have a conference committee of fourteen surrender to seventeen southern senators because of a threatened filibuster. Very little, he regretted, had been accomplished out of so much hoped for. He stood ready to offer the Norton substitute again the next session. But Healey praised the bill as the culmination of a half-century struggle for humanitarian-labor standards, Ramspeck called it a victory for workers rather than sections, and even McReynolds said he would vote for it. Herbert S. Bigelow of Ohio was pleased to have Congress finally helping the poorest of the poor. If the worker received a scant increase, it was nonetheless a promise of a hope to come. The forgotten men and women of America, he declared, were finally being remembered. With such unprecedented support on both sides of the House, the bill easily passed by a 291-to-89 margin, thus concluding a fourteen-month legislative struggle on its behalf.[39]

That's that, said Roosevelt laconically, as he signed the Fair Labor Standards Act into law on June 27.[40] He was undoubtedly relieved to salvage something out of an otherwise unproductive legislative session. Success had finally crowned his efforts to carry out his party's pledge to enact a national wage and hour law. He succeeded in the spring of 1938 because he had worked much more closely with his congressional leaders in fashioning a satisfactory compromise. They in turn demonstrated greater skill in compromising the issue over statutory or flexible rates. He had also managed to win the support of the AFL, despite its ongoing feud with the CIO. Overcoming conflicting sectional interests among members of her committee, Norton secured a bill that satisfied a majority of House Democrats and many Republicans. Congressional backers were also aided by a more effective campaign on behalf of the bill and by the primary victories of New Dealers who supported wage and hour regulation.

Nevertheless, Representative Bigelow was accurate when he described the Fair Labor Standards Act as merely the promise of a hope to come.[41] Clearly, the law was far from the purchasing-power recovery measure originally introduced in 1937. Although the Fair Labor Standards Act title was retained, only oppressive wages and hours were banned. During the Roosevelt recession, Congress was more concerned about dislocating industry than guaranteeing wages and hours above the 40-hour-40-cent limit to enhance purchasing power.[42] Clearly, an annual $800-income would do little to help workers raise their standard of living.

Those who had anticipated a fight for higher fair standards in the House were quickly disillusioned. Under AFL pressure, Norton's committee readily abandoned a 35-hour-70-cent standard and purchasing-power recovery theory. It also gave up establishing the 40-hour-40-cent standard the first year. In order to overcome southern opposition, it was willing to accept a 44-hour-25-cent standard the first year and to achieve the 40-hour-40-cent rate after three years. Both the CIO and the AFL also abandoned the 40-hour-40-cent standard. By insisting on flexible rates, Senate conferees once again made it possible for some workers to achieve a 40-cent rate after the first year through industry committee action but made it mandatory after seven, rather than three years. Flexibility also meant differentials, and the bill's backers had no choice but to accept them. As southern senators undoubtedly understood when the Black-Connery Bill was introduced, it was either differentials or a filibuster and no law. Given the danger inherent in imposing a statutory 40-hour-40-cent standard on all industry immediately, the sliding scale was the sounder approach to regulation. The Labor Department was able to obtain industry-board regulation, which had been its objective since 1933. Eliminating the high fair-wage standard limited the scope of the FLSA but neverless, Congress finally accepted a law to end sweatshop labor, which had been the objective of humanitarian reformers for more than thirty years.

8

Out of the Jungle

Finally, the new order of things is accepted and becomes a part of our industrial folkways and at last the very interests that resisted most bitterly became not only reconciled but cooperative. And thus we emerge another step out of the jungle and in the end everybody is glad of it.

—Elmer F. Andrews

In a fireside chat in June, President Roosevelt called the Fair Labor Standards Act the most important social legislation passed by Congress since the Social Security Act. Making the most of his opportunity, he said it was the most far-reaching, far-sighted law adopted in any country for the benefit of workers. And yet it was only a start on the quest for better living standards and increased purchasing power. Do not let any "calamity-howling executive" whose employees were on relief, he cautioned, tell you that $11 weekly will have a destructive effect on industry. A good part of the public was inclined to agree. A poll the following month found 62 percent of those surveyed favoring the law, 28 percent disapproving, and the remainder with no opinion. But a Fortune poll of a select group found only 48.4 percent favored it.[1]

Press reaction to the FLSA was mixed and apprehensive. Southern editors wondered whether the law would actually benefit the South. Those who opposed differentials thought the low 25-cent hourly wage would do little for southern labor, while those who favored them doubted that they would be obtained. Northern and western editors looked upon the law with misgivings or as a victory for the South. They thought it would undermine labor's self-reliance and produce a false recovery; it was seen as a hopeless political approach to an economic problem and certainly no panacea for recovery; it was a complicated patchwork of exemptions that would do more harm than good. In short, outside of aiding the exploited, it was a dubious experiment,

131

an adventure into the unknown, and a dangerous expansion of federal regulation.[2]

Much of the concern about the FLSA stemmed from the uncertainty of its coverage. No systematic attempt had been made to determine the number of workers in interstate commerce or those producing goods for commerce who would be subject to its provisions. This uncertainty would remain until the administrator and the courts determined the workers completely exempted, exempted from the hours provisions only, or exempted by the seasonal 14-week provisions. Because of the numerous exemptions, many of the nation's lowest paid workers would not benefit. And most of an estimated forty million employees made more than the 25-cent minimum and worked less than 44 hours. Undoubtedly, southern workers in the textile, fertilizer, and sawmill industries would be the chief beneficiaries, but the law's effect on nonmanufacturing industries could not be estimated. The Bureau of Labor Statistics urgently compiled data on a dozen major industries in which the administrator would most likely appoint wage and hour committees. It also plotted employment curves in seasonal industries in order to enable the administrator to prepare a formula for exemptions. Both the AFL and CIO also created wage and hour agencies to gather data and to aid employees in securing their benefits under the law.[3]

Although the FLSA did not incorporate AFL standards, the federation thought it would eliminate sweatshops and benefit union workers. Initially, President Green accepted its guarantee of minimum standards as a foundation for collective bargaining. It gave unionized industries an advantage, he believed, since experienced union representatives "would know their industry and the need for equitable distribution of the returns for joint work." Union members would have the benefit of counsel, experienced negotiators, and statistical services. Green was nevertheless concerned about the administrator's authority to classify workers for fixing minimum rates. Such broad power, he warned, might lead to regimentation, and any tendency toward manipulation would have to be checked at once.[4]

If the AFL found some benefits in the FLSA, the National Association of Manufacturers (NAM) anticipated its failure. Despite its low minimum wage, Noel Sargent condemned purchasing-power recovery theory and anticipated more unemployment. The law, he argued, was based on the unsound theory that low purchasing power and underconsumption caused depressions. It was a reenactment of the old National Recovery Administration (NRA) purchasing-power experiment, which had failed. Wage and hour regulation, he warned, would lead to government planning in other areas of the economy, and once started, would be difficult to stop.[5]

Sargent thought the law would not help the majority of sweatshop workers in intrastate service industries and trades. He believed it would result in more unemployment, because marginal workers would be laid off. The higher the minimum, he warned, the greater the joblessness and loss of wages. Society, he believed, would have to decide whether it wanted marginal industries to employ marginal workers or wanted to support them on relief.[6]

Sargent also thought the FLSA would be impossible to administer. The administrator, he predicted, would find it impossible to consider all eleven factors in fixing differentials for the 625 job classifications listed by the U.S. Census of Occupations, much less the 6,300 used by the Employment Service. Playing on the fear of organized labor, he anticipated a decrease in the spread between skilled and unskilled wages. The minimum would become the maximum, and eventually all wages would be regulated. Dividing jobs among workers, he warned, would not raise living standards, which could only improved by increasing the production of goods.[7]

Congress had indeed created a difficult problem for the administrator. He was to fix wages above the statutory minimum to improve purchasing power without curtailing employment. But if he accepted rates that actually led to greater unemployment, he would foster the very evil the act sought to remedy. Congress created the dilemma when it simplified the law and authorized discretionary wage-fixing. The dilemma resulted from its effort to cope with a problem too complex to be solved by legislative enactment.[8]

Congress added to the uncertainty by allowing the administrator to decide whether workers were in occupations in interstate commerce or producing goods for interstate commerce. In addition, he would have to decide which workers were in management, professional occupations, agriculture, seasonal industries, or processing commodities and dairy products. Coverage would be extended if the administrator accepted a broad definition of production and goods for commerce which might include something other than handling goods and non-manufacturing occupations.[9]

The FLSA also allowed the administrator considerable flexibility in forming industry committees. Since Congress had not set qualifications for membership, he would be free to set them. Committees could be large or small, and a number of subordinate committees might be established for subdivisions of a large industry. It seemed unlikely that he would create as many as the 585 NRA code authorities, but if the committees were numerous, they might prove to be cumbersome and expensive. Much of their success would depend on their ability to act reasonably promptly in raising wages above the minimum. If they resisted pressure for such improvement in wages, labor might react against them and create problems for the administrator.[10]

Although the FLSA's child-labor provisions generally conformed to the guidelines of the National Child Labor Committee (NCLC), they were not entirely satisfactory. Since only a small number of children were employed in interstate industries, most of those working would not be covered. This weakness in coverage resulted from the reliance on the ban on goods produced by establishments employing children from entering commerce and by the failure of Congress to simply ban child labor. Of approximately 850,000 working children under sixteen years of age, only 6 percent, about 30,000 to 50,000, would be covered. Moreover, children were allowed to work in agricultural occupations while not in school, but if a state required only six months of schooling or failed to require attendance, nothing could be done to prevent them from working. Since 70 percent of those under sixteen were agricultural workers, the Children's Bureau would have a problem in granting exemptions based on school attendance laws. There was doubt as to whether children working in canneries and home industries would be covered. While the child-labor provisions were an advance in the protection of children, the NCLC nevertheless continued to urge the adoption of the Child Labor Amendment.[11]

In the middle of July, amid rumors that he was considering either Hillman or Donald M. Nelson, Roosevelt appointed New York State Industrial Commissioner Elmer F. Andrews administrator of the Wage and Hour Division. An experienced wage adjustor, Andrews had served as assistant commissioner under Perkins when Roosevelt was governor of New York. Governor Herbert Lehman had made him commissioner when Perkins moved to Washington in 1933. He had experience administering the New York minimum wage law for women, had been a consultant on the fair-labor standards bill, and was known to oppose differentials. Labor Commissioner Arthur L. Fletcher of North Carolina was made assistant administrator in charge of complaints. Paul Sifton, former New York state director of unemployment insurance, became deputy administrator, and Calvert Magruder, a National Labor Relations Board (NLRB) attorney, was made chief counsel. Beatrice McConnell of the Children's Bureau would administer the child-labor provisions. Andrews worked with a small staff, but much of the inspection work would be carried out by the existing personnel of state labor departments.[12]

Congress limited the scope of the Wage and Hour Division's activities by limiting its funds. Although the Labor Department asked for an initial appropriation of $500,000, Congress allowed only $400,000, of which $50,000 went to the Children's Bureau. Hence, when the FLSA became effective in October, the division had only 23 field inspectors. They were soon raised to 75 but fell far short of the 603 needed for effective administration. Although hampered by the shortage of inspectors, the division enjoyed something of a honeymoon over the initial six-month period because employers generally accepted the law's basic standards. The burden on the division was made easier because in no state was the average pay below $11 weekly and many employers made pay adjustments with only minor dislocations.[13]

Before Andrews assumed his duties in the middle of August, there were indications that 1.7 million more workers would be covered than Congress had anticipated. The higher estimate was based on several developments stemming from uncertainty about the FLSA's provisions. Initially, the Labor Department solicitor defined seasonal industries narrowly, exempting only those operating during a particular season and not those working throughout the year with peaks in certain months. In addition, since employers did not know whether all their employees in plants producing goods for interstate commerce were covered until the courts clarified the issue, those in the twilight zone of uncertainty were inclined to comply rather than risk penalties for violations. In regard to agricultural workers, Rufus Poole said the administrator could not decide which were included, and only the courts could make that determination. Disappointed agricultural workers soon learned that production of commodities was not covered because their work was considered to be intrastate activity.[14]

Upon taking office, Andrews set up the division and twelve regional offices, appointed field inspectors, issued interpretations of the law, and sought the cooperation of state labor departments. Because of labor pressure, he quickly established the first industry committee for the textile industry. He defined the industry broadly and included the manufacturing and finishing of cotton, silk, and rayon fabrics and yarn, but excluded the wool and hosiery industries and the chemical manufacturing of rayon fiber. He estimated that 1.3 million workers would be covered. He then created two tobacco-industry committees, one for the cigar-makers, and the other for the cigarette, smoking, and chewing-tobacco industries.[15]

Although they respected Andrews, conservative AFL leaders became concerned about his discretionary powers. They objected to his authority to classify workers on the basis of skill and his right to reject industry-committee wage recommendations. Vice President

Frey considered the administrator's authority to exempt learners and apprentices from the minimum-wage rate to be a threat to the federation's apprenticeship training program. Government officers, he complained, lacked experience and were incompetent to administer the law's provisions. He took a dim view of any agency of "college professors and theorists" preaching to workers. Since eight million remained unemployed, President Green revived the demand for a 30-hour week. Despite the warnings by economists about the effect of a shorter workweek on living standards, he insisted that productive efficiency justified a 30-hour week at the same pay for longer hours.[16]

Because of uncertainty about several important FLSA provisions, Andrews quickly issued a number of clarifying interpretations of the law. Workers in interstate commerce, he ruled, would include those in the transportation, telephone, telegraph, and radio industries. An employer was covered if he intended to have any part of his goods, no matter how small, move in interstate commerce. It was immaterial if the goods designated for commerce were produced at home or in factories. Piece workers must have compensation equal to that for the hourly minimum rate. All goods produced under substandard conditions after October 24, 1938 were "outlaw goods." Workers in the District of Columbia and the territories were covered, but not those in the Philippines.[17]

In regard to compensation, employers could not reduce rates when required to pay for overtime, and payment had to be at the rate for the job and not one and one-half of the minimum wage. If the employer provided board, lodging, or other services, they would have to be provided at "reasonable cost," and the total compensation could not be less than that required by the minimum wage. The "area of production" for the canning and dairy industries would be the area of first processing on the farm or in a local plant employing no more than seven employees. The coverage of local retail occupations would depend on the volume of interstate trade and gross income.[18]

Andrews also issued a long list of regulations, covering children, the disabled, and professional workers. The employment of children under the age of 16 was banned, except for those working for their parents in nonmining and manufacturing industries. Those between 14 and 16 could work outside school hours in nonmining and non-manufacturing occupations. Certificates were required for handicapped workers paid below minimum rates, but compensation would be based on their earning capacity. Certificates were also required for learners and messengers. Executives were those who exercised managerial or discretionary authority and earned at least $30 weekly. Professionals were those who had obtained intellectual and discretionary training and knowledge. Outside salesmen worked away from the home office and were regularly selling.[19] Inevitably, these rules and interpretations proved to be controversial, generated protests, and led to demands for amendment of the law.

For several months, Andrews enjoyed his honeymoon. He had the cooperation of the state agencies and organized labor. The American Bar Association urged employers to give the law a chance before resorting to the courts. Putting the 44-hour-25-cent standard into effect created no major problem. There were some reports of layoffs in the Arkansas lumber industry, but at the end of the year, Andrews detected increasing employment and no serious layoffs. An estimated 11 million workers were covered, but not 220,000 in establishments employing fewer than six workers. Approximately 300,000 had made less than the 25-cent minimum, 550,000 were below the 30-cent rate, and 1,418,000 were below the 40-cent rate. About 1,384,000 worked more than the 44-hour limit, 1,751,000 exceeded the 42-hour week, and 2,184,000 worked more than 40 hours. Hence, the FLSA initially benefitted 1,684,000 workers, but many in the lowest paid intrastate occupations were excluded. The increase in employment was attributed to the overtime-pay requirement.[20]

Down to the end of the year, the Wage and Hour Division made no attempt to punish violations. It received 5,294 complaints and was able to investigate about 700 of them. Of these, 40 percent revealed violations, 27 percent lacked sufficient information, 17 percent were made against employers not covered, and the remaining 16 percent were pending. Since some employers made honest mistakes and many agreed to compensate their employees, the division made no attempt to punish them. Andrews thought voluntary compliance was the most practical way standards could be established. He cautioned individual workers about taking their complaints to court. Nuisance suits, he warned, would bring the law into disrespect, but individual suits might be helpful where state and federal agencies were understaffed. When more adequate records became available in many establishments, more stringent enforcement would be possible, but it would require large additions to existing staffs.[21]

In his first six months, Andrews actuated only seven industry committees. He proceeded slowly because a rapid advance to the 40-hour-40-cent standard would have been disruptive and might have curtailed employment. Moreover, hours would be reduced and wages improved when the 42-hour-30-cent standard went into effect in October 1939. It was not until September of that year that he issued his first wage order, accepting a 32.5-cent rate for the seamless division of the hosiery industry and a 40-cent rate for the full-fashioned branch. The new rates would benefit 30,000 in the former and 16,000 in the latter division. Southern mills were most directly affected, but no curtailment of employment was expected. No differentials for southern mills were authorized because there was no evidence of any difference in costs which might justify them. There was little difference in costs of living, and freight-rate differentials were less than 1 percent of the value of the hose shipped. In the full-fashioned branch, improved efficiency and production offset a slight increase in costs.[22]

In October 1939, Andrews accepted the textile-industry committee's recommendation for a 32.5-cent rate for 175,000 of 650,000 employees. The woolen-textiles committee recommended a 36-cent rate, which would benefit only a small number of 149,000 workers. The apparel-industry committee recommended rates of 32.5, 35, and 37.5 cents according to the type of clothing produced, and approximately 200,000 of 650,000 workers were expected to benefit. The shoe-industry committee recommended a 35-cent rate and the millinery committee a 40-cent rate. Andrews acted cautiously and did not press the committees for the maximum rates because he accepted the FLSA as a labor-reform rather than as a pump-priming recovery measure.[23]

Despite an inadequate staff, the Wage and Hour Division's enforcement of the FLSA was outstanding. In the first nine months it received 7,500 complaints and investigated 1,254, of which 152 resulted in restitution of pay, 151 were without violations, 106 might result in prosecution, 787 were pending, and 58 were in industries not covered. In 61 prosecutions, the courts issued 46 decrees and denied enforcement only once. In 29 criminal suits, the Justice Department won 18 convictions. Through March 1941 the division handled 54,000 complaints and was successful in all but 2 of 1,657 civil cases and all but 2 of 122 criminal cases. During the first year, the division's work was made easier because of voluntary compliance with the basic standard. Complaints of violations came from only 1 in 500 workers. But more vigilant enforcement was necessary when the 42-hour-30-cent standard went into effect and when wage orders were issued.[24]

After a nationwide trip in January 1939, Andrews reported favorably on employer compliance. But he acknowledged problems in exempting workers from coverage and thought Congress would have to pass clarifying legislation. Representative Ramspeck criticized the inflexible-hours limitation and said Congress should exempt all employees in the higher-wage brackets. The American Farm Bureau Federation demanded an exemption for all farm workers. Given numerous problems in coverage and enforcement, the American Bar Association recommended clarifying amendments. Backers of the

FLSA faced a stiff fight in the House to prevent opponents from amending it to death.[25]

At least forty-three bills were offered for changes in the FLSA, many of which sought exemptions for occupations or from wage and hour provisions. Cigar makers, rural-telephone exchanges, white-collar employees, Alaskan placer miners, clerical employees, employees of weekly or semiweekly newspapers, and egg and poultry cooperatives wanted to be exempted from coverage. Several bills would exempt all employees in "areas of production" engaged in the packing, sorting, cleaning, canning, or processing of fruits, vegetables, tobacco, or cotton. Other proposals sought to freeze the 44-hour week for wholesale and distributing establishments, ban the importation of goods produced under conditions not in conformity with the FLSA, relax the "hot goods" penalty, freeze the 25-cent minimum for those processing commodities, and provide for special industry committees for Puerto Rico and the Virgin Islands. In order to cope with the flood of proposals, both the House and Senate committees worked closely with Andrews and Magruder to draft an omnibus amendment that would clarify ambiguities in the law and reduce administrative confusion without making concessions to opponents of wage and hour regulation.[26]

In late March the House Labor Committee introduced the omnibus Norton FLSA amendment. Unfortunately, the committee antagonized the farm bloc and powerful farm organizations by refusing to hold open hearings before reporting the amendment. A formidable group, including the National Grange, the American Farm Bureau Federation, the National Cooperative Council, the National Milk Producers' Federation, and other state organizations denounced the committee for denying them an opportunity to be heard on the question of coverage of employees processing farm commodities in "areas of production." They claimed that Andrews's ruling on the coverage of workers in such areas was burdensome and they wanted rigid wage and hour requirements for such workers eliminated. Such regulations, they argued, induced processors to compensate for higher costs by paying lower prices for farm products, which reduced farm income.[27]

Coverage of workers processing agricultural commodities in areas of production, Andrews explained, was a complex problem. The difficulty was defining an area without enhancing the competitive position of employers in the area over those in close proximity. Coverage, he believed, should not depend on the proximity of the processing operations to the source of the commodities. Since low wages in such areas depressed the income of all workers in such occupations, he recommended uniform standards for them all. He suggested eliminating the area of production provision, authorizing a seasonal work-week to meet the need of employers, and making the minimum wage applicable to all workers. But he would discourage excessive hours dangerous to the health and efficiency of workers by authorizing the overtime-pay penalty. His recommendations for the coverage of those processing farm commodities were incorporated in both Norton's and Senator Thomas's amendments.[28]

Since the 44-hour workweek imposed a burden on processors of agricultural commodities, and since the area-of-production provision created inequities among them, the House committee authorized a 60-hour week with overtime pay beyond the limit and eliminated the area provision. During the 14-week seasonal period, however, both the hours limitation and the overtime-pay requirement would be inoperable. The exemption was extended to fruit and vegetable canning and packing and to logging as well, but not to urban terminals receiving farm products. The extended workweek and coverage, the committee believed, would meet the needs of seasonal industries handling or processing perishable products.[29]

In addition, the Norton amendment authorized separate industry committees for Puerto Rico and the Virgin Islands; gave the administrator the right to make binding regulations; exempted salaried employees making $200 monthly and telephone exchanges with fewer than five-hundred stations; extended the hours exemption to refrigerator-car employees; provided for the employment of telegraph messengers at not less than the 25-cent rate; protected innocent purchasers of "hot goods"; and made it easier for workers to sue for unpaid wages. On the whole, the committee sought to eliminate ambiguities in the law, ease administrative burdens, and yet protect the benefits gained by hundreds of thousands of workers. Farm organizations, however, deemed the provisions covering the processing of commodities completely unsatisfactory.[30]

On behalf of the farm organizations, in April Graham A. Barden of North Carolina sponsored broad amendments to exempt numerous processing operations on agricultural products from the time they left the farm until they entered retail channels. His amendments went far beyond those accepted by the committees of either house. The hours exemption covering 933,000 workers would be expanded to cover 1,626,000 and the complete wage and hour exemption would be expanded from 268,000 to 1,129,000. Andrews denounced Barden's proposals as devoid of any economic or social justification. He thought they would burden administration and increase costs of enforcement. They would also deny benefits to hundreds of thousands of workers who had long been exploited. He was supported by Secretary of

Agriculture Henry Wallace, who agreed that processing activities off the farm were nonagricultural and should be covered. In some areas, Wallace said, workers processing commodities made 30 cents an hour under state law, and raising the minimum of those who did not would result in only a slight increase in costs, which would be no burden on processors, consumers, or farmers. Profit margins on farm products, he explained, were wide enough to absorb the increase.[31]

The Labor Committee rejected Barden's amendments, provoking the farm bloc and setting off another fight with the Rules Committee. Norton denied that her bill covered farmers or any farm operations at all. Over a million workers in canning, packing, and processing operations, she argued, were entitled to the same protection as other employees. Farm organizations should not seek to better their economic position at the expense of their workers. But since they objected to the provisions for processing operations in her bill, she offered to sponsor another without the controversial agricultural exemptions. The farm bloc was not appeased, however, and asked the Rules Committee for an open rule on the Norton bill so that it could be amended on the floor. But Norton insisted that it be brought up under a suspension of the rules so that the farm bloc would not have an opportunity to vitiate the FLSA by adding broad exemptions for workers processing agricultural commodities. Having refused to bring up the bill, Norton's committee tried to find a compromise on the processing exemptions.[32]

Early in June the Labor Committee altered the Norton amendment, accepting an hours exemption for workers canning perishable fruits and vegetables, but only during the seasonal harvesting period. It also granted a wage and hour exemption for workers in production areas engaged in cleaning and preparing farm products for market. And it accepted an hours exemption for employees of terminal establishments engaged in handling, preparing, freezing, and storing commodities. But it opposed all other wage and hour exemptions for employees engaged in cleaning, packing, and grading fruit, vegetables, and leaf tobacco. These concessions, however, failed to satisfy farm organizations or the farm bloc. The farm organizations sent telegrams opposing the amendment to all members, and the House refused to consider it under a suspension of the rules. Representative Cox, who led the drive for broad exemptions for agricultural workers, insisted on a full debate and the right to amend it. Norton said she would fight all efforts of the farm organizations to exempt processing occupations. She had the backing of Roosevelt, who said he would veto any bill accepting such exemptions.[33]

After efforts to compromise failed, Barden incorporated his amendments in a bill which was bottled up in the Labor Committee. In addition to his exemptions for workers processing farm products, his bill would provide a 56-hour week exemption for loggers, employees in terminal markets, and distributors of fruits and vegetables. It would also exempt salaried employees making as little as $150 monthly from the overtime pay requirement, as well as piece workers and home workers. Defending the broad exemptions, Barden said Andrews had based his estimate of the number of workers who would lose benefits on unreliable figures. Since Norton would not allow the farm bloc to amend her amendment, Barden asked the Rules Committee for a rule for his bill. But the farm bloc ran into stiff resistance from Rules Committee Chairman Sabath, an archenemy of the Barden amendments. Cox challenged him, warning him that no FLSA amendment would get a rule unless the Barden bill got one. Farm organization lobbyists, however, encountered countervailing pressure from the Emergency Committee for Preserving the Fair Labor Standards Act, which was backed by religious, consumer, and trade union groups. It was ready to fight any attempt of "reactionaries" to knife the act by amendment. Given the impasse, Ramspeck, temporary acting chairman of the Labor Committee in July, decided to try another compromise effort.[34]

Ramspeck appointed a subcommittee chaired by Keller to confer with Andrews and Barden on a compromise. But all hope quickly faded when Andrews abruptly reversed his support for the white-collar exemption. Organized labor opposed it, he explained, and since labor unions had helped him administer the FLSA, he could no longer in good conscience support the exemption. In his view, the Barden amendments were the "dime-an-hour bloc's proposal," which created differences impossible to resolve. It was clear, he said, that no carefully considered amendment for the benefit of workers, employers, and the public could be passed that session. The FLSA emergency committee agreed that no action should be taken until those affected could be heard. Keller suspended his efforts, and action shifted to the Rules Committee. Since the Labor Committee would not report the Barden bill and the Rules Committee would not allow the Norton bill to go to the House without an open rule, the latter invited Andrews and Barden to a hearing. In a boisterous session, Andrews told Cox he would not allow pressure groups to control his administration of the FLSA. Failing to reach agreement, the committee asked him to meet with Norton and Barden and to find a solution for the impasse.[35]

It took John L. Lewis to break the stalemate. The peppery labor leader told the Labor Committee to let amendments wait until the FLSA had a fair trial. During a denunciation of FLSA opponents, he said the source of reactionary opposition to the law was none other than Vice President John Nance Garner, "a labor-baiting, poker-playing, whiskey-drinking evil old man." His sensational attack on Garner produced unintended results. Not only did the entire Congress rally around the besieged sage of Uvalde, who remained eloquently noncommittal, but the Rules Committee immediately granted a rule for the Barden bill. Its action was also prompted by the Labor Committee, which offered a new bill without the controversial agricultural amendments. Cox had managed to restrain his colleagues in the hope that the Labor Committee would find a compromise, but the new Norton bill was unsatisfactory.[36]

Congress had a field day condemning Lewis, and Bankhead said he would not allow Norton to offer her new bill under a suspension of the rules. But Sabath could delay action on Barden's bill for seven days after the rule was granted. Since the Senate seemed unlikely to act on any FLSA amendment that session, one day before Congress adjourned Rayburn decided not to allow the House to consider the Barden bill. Just before Congress adjourned, however, it approved a minor change, exempting switchboard operators of telephone exchanges of fewer than five hundred stations. Thus House leaders defeated a strong effort by southern and western farm-bloc members to gut the FLSA.[37]

Although the farm-bloc's efforts failed, during the struggle Andrews lost congressional support and in October he resigned. Some of his rulings on processing operations and his denial of differentials to textile employers in the South antagonized southern congressmen. Organized labor was also critical of his slow pace in forming industry committees and in fixing wages above the basic standard. The CIO was displeased because he failed to crack down on employers violating the law. Many of these problems materialized because Congress refused to appropriate adequate funds for effective enforcement and an adequate staff. In an effort to please Congress, Roosevelt accepted his resignation and praised him for carrying out his responsibilities under such difficult circumstances. Deputy Administrator Paul Sifton also resigned in order to enable the new administrator to select his own deputy. Much to the dismay of organized labor, Roosevelt then appointed Colonel Philip Fleming of the Army Engineering Corps as administrator. The AFL objected strongly to having an army officer administering the FLSA. Pending congressional approval of Colonel Fleming's appointment to a civilian post, Perkins made Harold D. Jacobs, chief of the division's information section, assistant administrator.[38]

In October the new 42-hour-30-cent standard went into effect. Of

4.1 million workers in industries covered, the new standard raised the wages of 650,000 and lowered the hours of 2.4 million. The new wage rate improved the earnings of from 2 to 4 percent of those covered in the North and nearly 20 percent of those covered in the South. Approximately one-third of those benefiting from the new standard worked in southern textile, sawmill, cottonseed, and fertilizer industries. The new 32.5-cent minimum for the textile industry also became effective and improved workers' earnings by about 4 percent above the 25-cent rate and by 2.1 percent above the 30-cent minimum. Since it raised manufacturing costs by only 0.76 percent if based on the 30-cent rate, the new minimum for the textile industry was not expected to have a serious adverse effect on employment.[39]

Responding to labor criticism of the division's slow progress in raising wages, Fleming accelerated the organization of industry committees and wage-order recommendations. In addition to those for the hosiery and textile industries already in effect, from January through September 1940 he issued eight in rapid succession. Approximately 3,500 of 23,500 millinery workers' wages were raised to the 40-cent rate; 24,500 knitted-underwear and outwear workers benefited by a raise to 33.5 or 35 cents; 11,000 out of 140,000 wool-industry workers were raised to a 36-cent rate; 60,000 out of 240,000 shoe workers received 35 cents; 5,000 hat workers benefited from a 35- or 40-cent rate; and approximately 200,000 garment workers in nearly every state benefited from rates set at between 32.5 and 40 cents. Industry committees recommended rates between 33 and 40 cents for carpet and rug, luggage, and railroad workers. From September 1938 to August 1941 thirty-six industry committees were formed, and by November 1941 the administrator had issued thirty-one wage orders.[40]

Although the wages of thousands of workers were improved, nothing could be done for the lowest paid workers in intrastate occupations. When the FLSA was approved, Perkins, Beyer, and other reformers hoped the states would accept similar legislation to cover intrastate occupations. The Labor Department drafted a model bill for the states and urged them to incorporate federal standards. The CIO adopted a model bill almost identical with that of the department, but the AFL drafted one with a flat minimum and flexible hours. Backed by organized labor, forty-two bills were introduced in twenty-nine of the forty-four legislatures in session in 1939. The result of this campaign was discouraging. No state approved a model wage and hour bill, although several passed new laws for women and children, and Connecticut expanded the coverage of its law to include men. Moreover, not all state wage and hour laws were upheld by the state courts.[41]

The failure of the campaign for state legislation revealed that state legislatures could not be budged from their entrenched conservatism. Apparently many of them were reluctant to experiment with wage and hour laws and were content to accept the FLSA and to cooperate with federal officials in its enforcement. It also appears that while national AFL officers supported state action, many local union leaders were unenthusiastic about minimum-wage regulation. The CIO, however, seems to have supported the movement enthusiastically. But as Rufus Poole noted, the failure of the states to adopt such legislation left those workers suffering from the greatest abuse without protection. Moreover, many manufacturers in the garment, furniture, lumber, and sand and gravel industries were localizing their business on a state-by-state basis to escape FLSA coverage. Because of such "balkanization" of industry, he thought the FLSA should be amended to cover local processing. The Supreme Court allowed the ICC to regulate local railroad rates because they affected interstate rates and it might allow the FLSA to cover manufacturing for local consumption. But until such amendment could be obtained, employees in intrastate occupations, both male and female, would not be able to obtain living wages at even the lowest standard.[42]

Not only did the states decline to accept wage and hour laws, but the anticipated cooperation between state agencies and the Wage and Hour Division for FLSA enforcement also failed to develop. Congress authorized "cooperative federalism" to avoid confusion, conflict, waste, and duplication of effort, but serious impediments made such cooperation impossible. Great diversity of state standards, weak labor departments in many states, and the lack of trained personnel frustrated efforts to carry out the intent of Congress. Initially, the Wage and Hour Division relied on state agencies, which compiled lists of industries, distributed regulations to plants, referred complaints, and reported violations. The Labor Department also drafted a plan for cooperation and reviewed state policies, a necessary bureaucratic exercise that delayed implementation of the program. Finally, in November 1939 the North Carolina Department of Labor became the first state agency to be made responsible for cooperating with the division and with the Children's Bureau in enforcing the FLSA. The Minnesota Labor Department also signed a cooperative agreement, but no others followed.[43]

This experiment in cooperative federalism failed because of changes in the division, irresolute policy, inadequate state inspection staffs, and lack of funds. Because of labor pressure, the administrator preferred to use the funds available for the operation of industry committees rather than the reimbursement of those state agencies administering the law. The negotiation of state-enforcement agreements was a slow and tedious process, and congressional committees were indifferent to cooperative federalism.[44]

The inability of the administrator to develop effective cooperation with state agencies created serious enforcement problems. By late 1939 noncompliance with basic standards was reaching alarming proportions. The Wage and Hour Division received 33,000 complaints over the year, which came in at 1,000 a week by December. Employers failed to pay the minimum or overtime pay, employed children, failed to keep records, had employees take work home, and "balkanized" their production for the intrastate market to avoid coverage. In one notorious case, the Atlantic Coast Line Railroad paid black track workers as little as 5 cents an hour by providing "housing" in the form of abandoned box cars or charging them for transportation to the work site. In many cases workers were ignorant of violations or were afraid to complain. The division's enforcement was hopelessly inadequate because it lacked the funds to enable inspectors to make adequate inspection of employer records. In order to improve compliance, it asked for funds for 600 inspectors, but it needed 1,500 for effective administration.[45]

When challenges of the FLSA's constitutionality went to the courts, legal scholars deemed its chances of surviving a Supreme Court test to be highly favorable. The FLSA's standards were more definite than those of the National Industrial Recovery Act (NIRA), and it seemed unlikely that the law would be voided for delegating legislative power. Due process would be satisfied if the government could show a reasonable relationship between regulation and the protection of commerce from obstructions by maintaining fair-labor standards. The test was whether the activity regulated had a substantial effect on commerce. If Congress could use its power to protect commerce from the adverse effects of monopoly competition, surely Congress could protect it from competition in the form of sweatshops and child labor.[46]

Roosevelt also contributed to the probability that the FLSA would be sustained by adding sympathetic justices to the "Roosevelt Court." After his appointment of Hugo L. Black in 1937, he added Stanley Reed the following year, and Felix Frankfurter and William O. Douglas the year thereafter. In April 1939 only two of the anti-New Deal four horsemen, Pierce Butler and James C. McReynolds, remained to protest the expansion of national power when the majority upheld the Agriculture Adjustment Administration's tobacco-quota regulation in *Mulford* v. *Smith*. The Supreme Court said the quota did not regulate local production; it merely regulated the market at the "throat of commerce." Congress could regulate intrastate commerce when marketing conditions made it necessary for the effective regulation of interstate commerce. In order to protect commerce, the amount of tobacco transported could be limited, and the motive for the exercise of this power was irrelevant to the question of validity. Thus the Court abandoned the *Dagenhart* holding that it could inquire into the ulterior motive behind the legislation and void a law if it conflicted with the state police power.[47]

Despite the *Mulford* decision, the NAM claimed the Supreme Court might yet void the FLSA because of the indirect effect of local conditions on interstate commerce. It believed that regulation could be justified only if there was a clear and substantial relationship between interstate commerce and the law's objectives. Labor costs affected the marketplace only indirectly, and the connection was too remote to be direct and substantial. The commerce power, it insisted, would be destructive if used to control local activities merely because of temporary dislocations. But since the FLSA was based on the regulation of "production of goods for commerce," rather than "affecting commerce," legal scholars thought it provided a yardstick regardless of whether or not the effect was substantial. The *Mulford* decision convinced the Wage and Hour Division that the FLSA was constitutionally sound.[48]

Despite limited personnel and funds, in 1939 the division made a good start in prosecuting violations of the law. During the year it initiated 76 civil and 63 criminal cases and won consent decrees in 62 of the civil cases. When the Eastern Sugar Associates of Puerto Rico sought to enjoin the administrator from enforcing the minimum-wage rates in their sugar-refining plants, the district court said the FLSA was a valid exercise of the commerce power and did not violate the due process clause. Government attorneys won another important case when Montgomery Ward & Company challenged wage and hour regulation as an improper exercise of commerce power. The district court upheld the power of Congress to ban the transportation of goods produced in violation of the wage and hour standards. The standards, it said, had the quality of police regulations and were a proper exercise of police power.[49]

In 1940 several FLSA challenges reached the Supreme Court, and by the time it handed down its decisions, all of the four horsemen had retired. In *U.S.* v. *Darby* it unanimously rejected the lumber company's claim that Congress could not use its power to regulate intrastate activities affecting commerce. Congress, the Court held, could exclude from commerce whatever articles it deemed injurious to the public welfare. Congressional regulation was not an invasion of state power merely because it restricted use within the state of destination. The motive was a matter of congressional judgment and was constitutionally irrelevant. Production of goods for commerce covered products the employer intended to ship, even though all such goods might not enter commerce. The power of Congress extended to intrastate activities affecting commerce in such a way as to justify regulation. And Congress might adopt any reasonable means to achieve a permitted end, even by suppressing commerce. The *Dagenhart* decision was finally completely overruled. The Tenth Amendment did not limit the right of Congress to exercise an enumerated power, and the act did not violate Fifth Amendment due process.[50]

In the twin case, *Opp Cotton Mills* v. *Administrator*, the Supreme Court unanimously denied that Congress had delegated its authority to the administrator. Authority to classify industries, appoint committees, and approve recommended minimum wages was not an invalid exercise of legislative power. Administrative findings in conformity to legislative standards and congressional policy were made under its statutory command. The Wage and Hour Division was following procedures mandated by Congress, since it would be impossible for Congress to prescribe specific minimum wages for particular industries. The sole function of the administrator, the Court said, was to put into effect the policy adopted by Congress.[51]

By upholding the FLSA in the *Darby* and *Opp Cotton Mills* cases, the Roosevelt Court validated the decision of the law's framers to justify regulation on the ground that substandard-labor conditions caused obstructions to interstate commerce. Undoubtedly, the Court reflected the public's acceptance of the need to have the national government promote economic recovery and eliminate the evils of unbridled exploitation.

Although the FLSA restricted unbridled exploitation, neither its statutory rates or the eventual 40-hour-40-cent standard provided living wages at a subsistence level for those employees covered. If the average subsistence cost of living was $1,250 for a family of four in 1938, the basic 42-hour-30-cent rate provided only $630, or about half of what was needed; the 40-hour-40-cent standard provided $800, which was well below the subsistence standard. When the 40-hour-40-cent rate became mandatory after seven years, workers would have an income of one-third of the $2,500 needed to maintain a family at an American comfort standard, which would include rent, clothing, food, heat, electricity, health care, telephone, auto, and recreation.[52] Inadequate as the rates were, Congress had set the parameters to avoid destabilizing business, and Andrews and the Wage and Hour Division reflected its concern in administering the law.

Andrews was justly praised for his deliberate implementation of FLSA provisions. By proceeding cautiously, he avoided the mistakes made by Hugh Johnson in establishing the NRA. Congress was able to control his ability to implement the law by limiting his funds. Nevertheless, his slow progress in creating industry committees, issuing wage orders, and prosecuting violations antagonized organized labor. And his rulings on coverage and areas of production provoked the powerful farm bloc. Fortunately for hundreds of thousands of workers processing commodities off the farm, its effort to vitiate the law failed. But unfortunately, nothing could be done for hundreds of thousands of the lowest paid farm laborers. Congress excluded them from coverage, despite the movement of farm commodities into interstate commerce.[53] Because of the influence of powerful farm organizations in Congress, they remained among the most exploited workers in the country. And unfortunately for millions of female workers, they worked in intrastate occupations not subject to congressional control.

9

Goodness and Hope

The minimum wage may indeed cause a loss of some jobs, but its positive aspects outweigh this loss. A reasonable minimum wage reinforces the work ethic. Few would disagree that work should be more lucrative than welfare. Working is better for the individual's self-esteem and increases a poor person's chances of breaking out of the poverty cycle. Society also benefits from a drop in welfare costs and increased productivity.

—S.A. Levitan and Isaac Shapiro

EXPLAINING the success of the movement for national wage and hour regulation, Secretary Perkins emphasized the depression experience of the American people in the 1930s. Unemployment and the collapse of the economy, she said, induced them to accept regulation in order to raise purchasing power, stimulate recovery, and guarantee workers a reasonable standard of living. In regard to living wages, Calvin Magruder and Clara Beyer emphasized British trade-board and state industry-commission experience. Magruder noted the similarity between trade-board functions and those of state industry committees. The provisions of the Fair Labor Standard Act (FLSA) for industry committees and wage orders, he explained, were closely modeled on the New York minimum-wage law. Beyer believed that twenty-five years of experience with wage regulation for women had made national regulation acceptable. The depression, she believed, reinvigorated the state movement, and Congress took a step beyond state experience by covering men and providing for wage increases above the minimum.[1]

As Perkins and Beyer noted, national wage and hour regulation became possible because millions of Americans were no longer willing to accept labor as simply a commodity subject to the iron law of the marketplace. Competition based on stretching hours and chiseling wages was deemed a social and moral evil. In a rich nation blighted by a disintegrating economy, the degradation of jobless and poor workers

150

justified government intervention to ban sweatshop standards and guarantee workers at least a subsistence wage. The FLSA was clearly class legislation that sought to redress the balance between capital and labor in order to provide a more just distribution of wealth. Since regulation of the national marketplace was beyond state jurisdiction, the choice seemed to be either national regulation or continuing industrial disorder.[2]

Unfortunately for those New Deal reformers who sought to guarantee workers living wages, the NRA experiment in government-sponsored labor-management cooperation failed to establish the 40-hour-40-cent standard or eliminate unemployment and promote recovery. Its failure convinced many economists that wage and hour regulation had delayed recovery. The AFL was equally disillusioned with regulation by a government agency. Its support for the impractical 30-hour week and opposition to wage regulation proved to be the most difficult obstacle Roosevelt had to overcome. Roosevelt accepted the voluntary code plan with reluctance because of his concern about the return of sweatshop standards. Since the price for management cooperation in the voluntary program was the suspension of the antitrust laws, Roosevelt readily abandoned it. Labor Department officials had no illusions about the voluntary program and realized that its failure would undermine support for an enforceable wage and hour law.

The movement for living wages also suffered because economists were critical of the effect of wage and hour regulation on productivity. Technological efficiencies in production would not necessarily justify a shorter workweek if the overall increase in national production averaged only 1 percent per year. Moreover, a shorter week and higher wages would not result in higher purchasing power for all workers if higher prices resulted in lower consumption for those who were not covered. Higher minimum wages might also act as a brake on reemployment if production costs increased when employers were struggling to stay in business. And many marginal workers might be forced on relief rolls. These arguments not only undermined the AFL's demand for a 30-hour week and productivity wages, but also convinced many congressmen that regulation of high fair wages would have a dangerously distabilizing effect on the economy. Their concern was reflected in the Senate's decision to reduce the scope of the Fair Labor Standards Board's rate-setting authority.

Resistance to national wage and hour regulation was also enhanced by Roosevelt's attack on the Supreme Court. Although his Court-packing bill induced a majority of the justices to abandon liberty of contract and a narrow interpretation of the commerce power as limitations on social legislation, the fight over the Court bill undermined his prestige, angered congressional leaders, and united conservative southern Democrats and Republicans in opposition to any new experimental social legislation. Overconfident of his support, he miscalculated in thinking that the Black-Connery Bill would be a popular measure that would help reunite congressional Democrats. Instead, conservatives were encouraged by their success in killing the Court bill and were willing to defy the president again by opposing the Black-Connery Bill.

Roosevelt miscalculated again when he sent the controversial Black-Connery Bill to Congress and insisted on its immediate consideration. Cohen and Corcoran failed to resolve disagreements over the bill's scope of coverage and provisions for setting wage and hours. Omnibus coverage and the sweeping power of the Fair Labor Standards Board guaranteed opposition. Hostile congressmen knew the bill had not been drafted by the labor committee of either house. They also learned that it was not enthusiastically supported by the Labor Department. Well aware of disagreements over the bill, southern Democrats were able to defy the president on his "must legislation." Hence, even though Democratic leaders had commanding party majorities in both houses, they were unable to ram the Black-Connery Bill through Congress.

Because officials in the Labor Department favored industry-committee determination of nonoppressive wages and hours, the Labor Standards Board's authority was curtailed, the higher fair wage provisions were dropped, and the scope of coverage was narrowed. The Senate approved the 40-cent ceiling and thus abandoned regulation of high fair wages and purchasing-power recovery. The AFL then induced the House Labor Committee to reject the Wood high-wage standard and to accept the 40-hour-40-cent limit. But when loyal New Dealers joined conservatives in defeating the AFL bill, federation supporters joined the latter in killing the amended Black-Connery Bill. Conservative opponents outmaneuvered House leaders and it seemed that wage and hour regulation was dead.

Roosevelt, however, considered wage and hour regulation a party pledge and insisted on another fight. He accepted AFL demands for statutory standards, elimination of the Labor Standards Board, and a guarantee for collective bargaining. The AFL also compromised by accepting an initial 44-hour week and 25-cent minimum in the escalator standard. But statutory rates and the elimination of the board upset those southern senators who insisted on flexible wages and differentials. In the contest over wage and hour standards, Senator Thomas played a key role in avoiding a filibuster by devising a formula whereby the statutory 40-cent rate would be reached in seven years but flexible rates could be approved by an administrator after the first year. If the Thomas formula disappointed organized labor and House members, the conference-committee compromise prevented a filibuster and the FLSA became the law of the land.

Conservative opponents transformed the FLSA from a purchasing-power recovery measure into humanitarian social legislation. By accepting the 40-cent ceiling, the Senate reduced the annual-maximum income from $1,200 to $800; the House then reduced it to an initial $550, which was considered an emergency income. By approving the 25-cent-44-hour standard, Congress reduced the number of workers who would benefit under the initial standard. Proponents of living wages advocated rates that would maintain a family at a subsistence standard. But it is highly unlikely that even the poorest-of-the-poor in sections of the country with the lowest cost of living would consider $550 a living wage. As Representative Bigelow aptly noted, the forgotten men and women of America were being remembered by the promise of a living wage sometime in the future.

Despite the dire predictions of FLSA opponents, the regulation of wages and hours did not disrupt business or result in a large increase in unemployment. Economists found it difficult to evaluate the effect of statutory standards on the labor market because the economy was stimulated by the European war and by an increase in armaments production. Regulation caused a sharp division between steadily employed efficient workers and unskilled laborers who were permanently displaced. Sectional differentials seemed quite stable and enduring and were not due to the location of industry, the cost of living, or local business conditions alone. A dominant factor in persistent wage differentials among similar workers appeared to be imperfect mobility of labor and capital.[3]

Because Congress refused to provide adequate funding, FLSA administrators were unable to vigorously enforce the law's provisions. Those requiring the payment of minimum rates caused little trouble, but the overtime-pay requirement generated a large volume of litigation. Administrators had limited enforcement powers, but during the first ten years, they obtained 5,431 injunctions and settled 4,561 through consent decrees, securing $112 million for 3 million underpaid workers out of 22.6 million covered. They also expanded the number of workers covered by broadly defining occupations of employees engaged in commerce or in the production of goods for commerce. Employees were covered if a substantial part of their work was related to goods moving in interstate commerce or if they maintained buildings used for the production of goods intended for commerce. In approving these definitions, the Supreme Court construed the

FLSA's provisions broadly and recognized its humanitarian objectives.[4]

While enforcing the FLSA's child-labor provisions until 1946, the Children's Bureau tried to improve standards and to integrate state and federal activities. But because of variation in state laws, the protection of children against injuries and unsuitable employment was uneven and remained a distant goal. There were loopholes in the child-labor provisions, and some firms employing children held goods for more than thirty days to avoid coverage. But improvements in production technology eliminated some jobs and helped reduce the number of children in the workforce.[5]

After decades of experience, the effect of FLSA regulation on the labor market, employment, and the nation's economy remains a matter of controversy. Economists disagree on the effect that higher wage rates had on the efforts of businessmen to improve the productive efficiency of workers. They also question whether distortions in employment resulting from the displacement of workers offset the short-term advantages of higher wages. Although the income of some workers increased, such improvement would have come normally over a period of years. There were some business failures, but many workers who lost their jobs migrated to industries not covered. Some teenagers lost employment, mainly because they lacked the skills to make them more employable. But since the minimum wage remained well below other wages, economists agree that it was not dangerously destabilizing and did improve the income of the lowest paid. Overall, the minimum wage was neither as beneficial nor detrimental to the economy as many economists had anticipated.[6]

Economists also disagree on the effect of minimum wages on poverty. The relation between higher wages and the standard of living was blurred because family income depended on the number of members working, as well as nonwork incomes. As one critic noted, minimum wages had little effect on family poverty because the invisible hand did not necessarily direct earning gains to low paid workers from the poorest families. But other economists considered minimum wages as the most expedient means to cope with poverty. Since an estimated 60 percent of poverty was attributed to low wages, it seemed expedient to improve the income of those employed. Moreover, a minimum wage seemed to be the best way to reinforce the work ethic. Work was clearly better than welfare and the best way to raise the income of the poor without adding to the federal deficit.[7]

Since the FLSA did not eliminate unemployment and poverty or cover women, it was an ambiguous milestone. The AFL and the CIO continued to demand a shorter workweek and suggested doubling overtime pay to induce employers to hire more workers. Because these suggestions seemed impractical, others recommended early retirement and extended education as solutions for the unemployment problem. These latter suggestions have been adopted, but it is unlikely that they will solve the problem.[8]

Despite the failure of the FLSA to solve these problems, national wage and hour regulation seems strongly entrenched in the welfare state. Although the law had much less effect on purchasing power and living standards than its advocates desired, the American people have accepted regulation as a humanitarian limitation on the exploitation of unorganized workers.

Since living wages was defined as an income to support a worker and his family at a subsistence level, it is accurate to conclude that President Roosevelt was unsuccessful in his campaign to mandate living wages for the great majority of the forgotten men and women at the bottom of the economic pyramid. Living wages for the poorest workers as a remedy for poverty remains a visionary endeavor. Nevertheless, through a modest restraint of the invisible hand, the FLSA has enabled the nation to humanize capitalism and to adjust to industrial change with the least possible restriction of free enterprise. War and armaments production temporarily eliminated unemployment and brought about full recovery, but at a high cost in blood and treasure.

Notes

CHAPTER 1. BY THE SWEAT OF THY BROW

1. David J. O'Brien, *American Catholics and Social Reform: The New Deal Years* (New York, Oxford University Press, 1968), 1–10; Joseph Husslein, *Bible and Labor* (New York: Macmillan, 1924), 6, 7–11; Abraham Cronbach, *The Bible and Our Social Outlook* (Cincinnati: Union of American Hebrew Congregation, 1941), 120, 123–24; Philip Snowden, M.P., *The Living Wage* (London: Hodder and Stoughton, 1912), 3–8; Fr. John A. Ryan, *A Living Wage, Its Ethical and Economic Aspects* (New York: Arno Press, 1971), 43–46.

2. W. S. Woytinsky and Associates, *Employment and Wages in the United States* (New York, the Twentieth Century Fund, 1953), 3–6; Barbara N. Armstrong, *Insuring the Essentials, Minimum Wage Plus Social Insurance–A Living Wage Program* (New York: Macmillan Co., 1932), 17–40; Ryan, *Living Wage*, 23–32; Samuel Mencher, *Poor Law to Poverty Program, Economic Security Policy in Britain and the United States* (Pittsburgh: University of Pittsburgh Press, 1967), 34–35, 57–92.

3. O'Brien *American Catholics and Social Reform*, 13–16; Ryan, *Living Wage*, 32–35; Ryan, "The Catholic Church and Social Questions," *Annals of the American Academy of Political and Social Science* 165 (January 1933): 52–56; Ryan, *A Better Economic Order* (New York: Harper, 1935), 154–57; Patrick W. Gearty, *The Economic Thought of Monsignor John A. Ryan* (Washington, D.C.: Catholic University of America Press, 1953), 31–38; Michael P. Fogarty, *The Just Wage* (London: Geoffry Chapman, 1961), 257–99; Jerald C. Brauer, ed., *The Westminster Dictionary of Church History* (Philadelphia: Westminster Press, 1971), 523.

4. Snowden, *Living Wage*, 18–24; Dorothy Sells, *British Wage Boards, A Study in Industrial Democracy* (Washington, D.C.: Brookings Institution, 1939), 13, 16–19; Brian Bercusson, *Fair Wages Resolutions* (London: Mansell, 1978), 111–17.

5. Elizabeth L. Otey, *The Beginnings of Child Labor Legislation in Certain States, A Comparative Study*, vol. 6, *Report on Condition of Women and Child Wage-Earners in the United States*, S. Doc. 645, 61st Cong., 2d sess. (Washington, D.C., 1910), 73–128; Katharine D. Lumpkin and Dorothy W. Douglas, *Child Workers in America* (New York: Robert M. McBride and Co., 1937), 247–49; Marion C. Cahill, *Shorter Hours* (New York: AMS Press, 1968), 31–133.

6. John R. Commons and associates, *History of Labor in the United States, 1896–1932*, vol. 3 (New York: Macmillan, 1935), 51–57, 457–74; Foster R. Dulles, *Labor in America* (New York: Crowell, 1966), 180–83.

7. Armstrong, *Insuring the Essentials*, 58–60; Charles E. Hughes, *The Supreme Court of the United States* (New York: Columbia University Press, 1966), 184–99, 204–13.

8. Ryan, *Living Wage*, 129–32; Robert Bremner, *From the Depths* (New York: New York University Press, 1956), 140–63; Florence Kelley, "Thirty Years of the Consumers' League," *The Survey* 68 (November 1929): 210–12; James T. Patterson,

"Mary Dewson and the American Minimum Wage Movement," *Labor History* 5 (spring 1964): 139–40; Josephine Goldmark, *Impatient Crusader* (Westport, Conn.: Greenwood, 1976), 64–65, 134–35; Allis Rosenberg Wolfe, "Women, Consumerism, and the National Consumers' League in the Progressive Era, 1900–1923," *Labor History* 16, no. 3 (summer 1957): 378–87; Newel H. Comish, *The Standard of Living* (New York Macmillan Co., 1923), 62–66.

9. Frank H. Streightoff, *The Standard of Living Among the Industrial People of America* (Boston: Houghton, 1911), 159; James S. Youtsler, *Labor's Wage Policies in the Twentieth Century* (Saratoga Springs, N.Y.: Twayne Publications, Skidmore College, 1956), 36–37; Samuel Gompers, *Labor and the Common Welfare* (New York: Dutton, 1919), 17, 165.

10. Ryan, *Living Wage*, 129–38.

11. *Lochner v. New York*, 198 U.S. 45(1905); *Muller v. Oregon*, 208 U.S. 412(1908).

12. Harold U. Faulkner, *The Decline of Laissez Faire, 1897–1917* (New York: Harper, 1951), 284; Donald B. Johnson, ed., *National Party Platforms* (Urbana: University of Illinois Press, 1978), 1: 175–77; Commons and associates, *History of Labor in the United States*, 3: 501–2; Alice Kessler-Harris, *Out of Work: A History of Wage-Earning Women in the United States* (New York: Oxford University Press, 1982), 196–97; Ryan, *Distributive Justice* (New York: Macmillan, 1916), 417–18.

13. Commons and associates, *History of Labor in the United States*, 3: 503–5; *Stettler v. O'Hara*, 243 U.S. 629(1917); Judith Grunfel, "Regulation of Women's Work," in W. S. Woytinsky and associates, eds., *Employment and Wages in the United States*, 130–37.

14. *Bunting v. Oregon*, 243 U.S. 426(1917).

15. Gompers, *Labor and the Common Welfare*, 45–46, 55–56; William Green, *Labor and Democracy* (Princeton: Princeton University Press, 1939), 53; Dewey W. Grantham, "Government and Labor Before the New Deal," *Current History* 37 (September 1959): 134–37; Milton Derber, "Wage and Hour Policies in Historical Perspective," ibid., 36 (June 1959): 348–50; *Wilson v. New*, 243 U.S. 332(1917).

16. W. Jett Lauck and Claude S. Watts, *The Industrial Code* (New York: Funk, 1922), 32–41.

17. Ibid., 240–46.

18. Oscar A. Ornati, *Poverty and Affluence: A Report on a Research Project Carried Out at the New School for Social Research* (New York, the Twentieth Century Fund, 1966), 7–18, and Appendix 1 and 2, 141–47; Daniel Horowitz, *The Morality of Spending: Attitudes Towards the Consumer Society in America 1875–1940* (Baltimore, The Johns Hopkins Press: 1985), 120–23.

19. Lauck and Watts, *The Industrial Code*, 7–14, 23–27.

20. Ibid., 228–32, 326–64.

21. Gompers, "Labor, Its Grievances, Protests and Demands," *American Federationist* 27 (January 1920): 36, 64.

22. Lauck and Watts, *Industrial Code*, 493–94.

23. Ibid., 390–93.

24. Transportation Act of 1920, *U.S. Statutes at Large* 41/1, 456, 469–71; Harry E. Jones, *Railroad Wages and Labor Relations, 1900–1952* (New York: Bureau of Information of the Eastern Railways, 1953), 63–67.

25. Lauck and Watts, *Industrial Code*, 563–66; Melvin Dubofsky and Warren Van Tine, *John L. Lewis: A Biography* (New York: Quadrangle/New York Times Book Co., 1977), 80–90.

26. Charles N. Fay, *Labor in Politics, Or Class Versus Country* (Cambridge, Mass.:

University Press, 1920), 202–6, 239; Edward T. Layton, Jr., *The Revolt of the Engineers* (Cleveland: Press of Case Western Reserve University, 1971), 201–5.

27. John R. Commons, "Wage Theories and Wage Practices," *American Economic Review, Proceedings* 13 (1923): 114–15; George H. Soule, "The Productivity Factor in Wage Determination," ibid., 138–39; Herbert Feis, *The Settlement of Wage Disputes* (New York: Macmillan, 1921), 39, 181–96, 288; Joseph Dorfman, *The Economic Mind in American Civilization, Volume Four and Five, 1918–1923* (New York, Viking Press, 1949) IV, 377–80.

28. William F. Ogburn; "The Standard-of-Living Factor in Wages," *American Economic Review, Proceedings* 13 (1923): 118–28; Asher Achinstein, "Can Budget and Cost of Living Studies Be Used as Aids in Determining a Differential Wage?" *Journal of the American Statistical Association* 24 (March 1929): 29–39; Abraham Epstein, "Have American Wages Permitted an American Standard of Living?" *Annals of the American Academy of Political and Social Science* 97 (September 1921): 169–90; Paul H. Douglas, *Real Wages in the United States, 1890–1926* (New York: Augustus M. Kelly, 1966), 6–15; Dorfman, *The Economic Mind in American Civilization*, IV, 139–41.

29. Samuel A. Lewisohn, "Factors in Wage Determination-Discussion," *American Economic Review, Proceedings* 13 (1923): 143.

30. *Adkins v. Children's Hospital*, 261 U.S. 525(1923); Judith A. Baer, *Claims of Protection, The Judicial Response to Women's Labor Legislation* (Westport, Conn.: Greenwood, 1978), 93–94, 99.

31. Clarke A. Chambers, *Seedtime of Reform, American Social Services and Social Action, 1918–1933* (Minneapolis: University of Minnesota Press, 1963), 69–74; Egbert R. Nichols and Joseph H. Baccus, eds., *Selected Articles on Minimum Wages and Maximum Hours* (New York: H. W. Wilson Co., 1937), 132–39. See the National Consumers' League, *The Supreme Court and Minimum Wage Legislation* (New York: New Republic, 1925) for comments by the legal profession; and Commons and associates, *History of Labor in the United States*, 3: 504–5.

32. *Ribnik v. McBride*, 277 U.S. 350(1928); "New Jersey and the Ribnik Case," *The American Labor Legislation Review* 17 (September 1928): 279–80.

33. Commons and associates, *History of Labor in the United States*, 3: 522–39; Commons and John B. Andrews, *Principles of Labor Legislation* (New York: Augustus M. Kelley, 1967), 46–47; Frank T. de Vyver, "Regulation of Wages and Hours Prior to 1938," *Law and Contemporary Problems* 6 (summer 1939): 323–27.

34. Commons and associates, *History of Labor in the United States*, 3: 525–27; Commons and Andrews, *Principles of Labor Legislation*, 46–47; Valeska Bari, "From Minimum Wages to Mass Production," *Yale Review* 16 (October 1926): 68–71.

35. Commons and associates, *History of Labor in the United States*, 3: 82–86; W. Jett Lauck, *New Industrial Revolution and Wages* (New York: Funk-Wagnalls, 1929), 277–82; William J. Barber, *From New Era to New Deal: Herbert Hoover, the Economists, and American Economic Policy, 1921–33* (Cambridge, Cambridge University Press, 1985), 27, 42–64.

36. Green, *Labor and Democracy*, 100; Youtsler, *Labor's Wage Policies in the Twentieth Century*, 48; "Wages and Hours of Labor, A Basic Principle for Determining Wages–A Trade Union Viewpoint," *Monthly Labor Review* 22 (March 1926): 65–66; Louis Levine, *The Women's Garment Workers* (New York: B. W. Heubsch, 1924), 329–31, 423, 448.

37. Horowitz, *The Morality of Spending*, 158–64; Commons and associates, *History of Labor in the United States*, 3: 89–91; Roy Dickinson, *Wages and Wealth, This Business Roller-Coaster* (Princeton: Princeton University Press, 1931), 112, 114; "An

Employer's View of High Wages and Industrial Relations," *Monthly Labor Review* 25 (November 1927): 45–46.

38. Robert E. Lucey, "Industrial Life: Gains and Losses," *Proceedings of the National Conference of Social Work, 1929* (Chicago: University of Chicago Press, 1930), 329–36; Daisey Lee Worthington Worcester, "The Standard of Living," ibid., 337–53; Irving Bernstein, *The Lean Years* (Boston: Houghton, 1960), 10–11, 52–72.

39. Bernstein, *Lean Years*, 10–11.

40. Lauck, "Coal Labor Legislation: A Case," *Annals of the American Academy of Political and Social Science* 184 (March 1936), 130–37; Bernstein, *Lean Years*, 127–28, 132; U.S. Senate, *Bituminous Coal Commission, Hearing*, 70th Cong., 2d sess. (Washington, D.C., 1929).

41. Herbert Hoover, *Memoirs*, vol. 2 *The Cabinet and the Presidency, 1920–1933* (New York: Macmillan, 1952), 44–46, 101–8, 174–76, 259–66, 300–309, 312–19; Hoover, *American Individualism* (Garden City, N.Y.: Doubleday, Page & Co., 1922), 8–13, 44–45, 52–56; Arthur M. Schlesinger, *The Crisis of the Old Order* (Boston: Houghton, 1957), 89, 155; Albert U. Romasco, *The Poverty of Abundance* (New York: Oxford University Press, 1965), 6–20.

42. Hoover, *Memoirs*, vol. 3, *The Great Depression, 1929–1941*, 19–32, 42–46, 50–56, 97–100, 149–51; John K. Galbraith, *The Great Crash* (Boston: Houghton, 1961), 6, 74–79; Jordan A. Schwarz, *The Interregnum of Despair* (Urbana: University of Illinois Press, 1970), 8–16; Romasco, *Poverty of Abundance*, 30–38.

43. Schwarz, *Interregnum of Despair*, 17–21; Romasco, *Poverty of Abundance*, 74–80.

44. Schwarz, *Interregnum of Despair*, 23–42; Frank G. Dickinson, "Public Construction and Cyclical Unemployment," *Annals of the American Academy of Political and Social Science* 139 (September 1928): 175–209; Vernon A. Mund, "Prosperity Reserves of Public Works," ibid., 149 part 2 (May 1930): 8–12; Lester V. Chandler, *America's Greatest Depression, 1929–1941* (New York: Harper, 1970), 33–34, 49–52.

45. Charles A. Beard, "A 'Five Year Plan' for America," in Charles A. Beard, ed., *America Faces the Future* (Boston: Houghton, 1932), 117–40; Nathan B. Williams, "Advisory Councils to Government," *Annals of the American Academy of Political and Social Science* 147 (January 1930): 146–49; Sumner H. Slichter, "The Immediate Unemployment Problem," ibid., 165 (January 1933): 1–12; Evelyn C. Brooks and Lee M. Brooks, "A Decade of 'Planning' Literature," *Social Forces* 12 (March 1934): 427–64; Soule, "National Planning, The Problem of Creating a Brain for Our Economy," *New Republic* 66 (March 4, 1931): 61–65; Soule, "What Planning Might Do," ibid. (March 11, 1931): 88–91; Lewis L. Lorwin, "A Federal Economic Council," ibid. (April 29, 1931): 294–297; Romasco, *Poverty of Abundance*, 217–19; Wesley C. Mitchell, "The Economic Basis for Social Progress," *Proceedings of the National Conference of Social Work, 1930* (Chicago: University of Chicago Press, 1931), 35–49.

46. George G. Higgins, *Voluntarism in Organized Labor in the United States, 1930–1940* (New York: Arno Press, 1969), 59–72; Milton L. Farber, "Changing Attitudes of the American Federation of Labor Towards Business and Government, 1929–1933" (Ph.D. diss., Ohio State University, 1959), 63–83, 89–108; Philip Taft, *The A.F. of L., From the Death of Gompers to the Merger* (New York: Harper, 1959), 1–2, 6–8, 15–21, 29–37; William Green, "Six-Hour Day," *American Federationist* 39 (July 1932): 733–34; Green, "Five-Day Week," ibid. (August 1932): 863–64; Green, "Why Eight Hours?" ibid. (December 1932): 1341–42; ; J. E. Myer, "The Present Economic Situation and the 5-Day Week," ibid. (November 1932): 1246–47; "American Industry and the Five-Day Week," *Congressional Digest* 11, no. 10 (1932): 225–48; National Industrial Conference Board, *The Five-Day Week in Manufacturing Industries*

(New York: National Industrial Conference Board, 1929), 1–8, 15–22, 25–36; Ronald Radosh, "The Corporate Ideology of American Labor Leaders from Gompers to Hillman," *Studies on the Left* 6 (November-December, 1966): 72–74.

47. Samuel I. Rosenman, ed., *The Public Papers and Addresses of Franklin D. Roosevelt, The Genesis of the New Deal, 1928–1932* (New York: Random, 1938), 1: 852; Rexford G. Tugwell, *In Search of Roosevelt* (Cambridge, Mass.: Harvard University Press, 1972), 105–7; Tugwell, "The Progressive Orthodoxy of Franklin D. Roosevelt," in Bernard Sternsher, ed., *The New Deal, Doctrines and Democracy* (Boston: Allyn, 1966), 65–99.

48. *Congressional Record*, 72d Cong., 2d sess., 820, 1435, 1711; Elizabeth Brandeis, "Organized Labor and Protective Labor Legislation," in Milton Derber and Edwin Young, eds., *Labor and the New Deal* (Madison: University of Wisconsin Press, 1957), 199–202; John P. Frank, *Mr. Justice Black, The Man and His Opinions* (New York: Knopf, 1949), 88–91; Virginia Hamilton, *Hugo Black, The Alabama Years* (Baton Rouge: Louisiana State University Press, 1972), 215; Norman L. Zucker, *George W. Norris* (Urbana: University of Illinois Press, 1966), 51–52; *Hammer v. Dagenhart*, 247 U.S. 251(1918); Louis Galambos, *Competition and Cooperation: The Emergence of a National Trade Association* (Baltimore: Johns Hopkins University Press, 1966) 175 n. 12.

49. U.S. Senate, *Thirty-Hour Work Week, Hearings*, 72d Cong., 2d sess. (Washington, D.C., 1933), 1–21, 47–51, 85, 133, 142, 272, 283, 413–19; *New York Times*, January 6, 1933.

50. U.S. Senate, *Thirty-Hour Work Week, Hearings*, 39–40, 67–83, 147–63, 186, 189–234, 311–16, 330, 371–82; *Employers' Liability Cases*, 207 U.S. 463 (1908), 494–503; *New State Ice Co. v. Liebmann*, 285 U.S. 262(1932), 306–11.

51. U.S. Senate, *Thirty-Hour Work Week, Hearings*, 117–30, 167, 234, 327, 357–69, 519–25, 584, 607.

52. *Congressional Record*, 72 Cong., 2d sess., 4304–5, 4311–15, 14096; U.S. House of Representatives, *Six-Hour Day-Five-Day Week, Hearings*, 72d Cong., 2d sess. (Washington, D.C., 1933), 198, 239–43; U.S. House of Representatives, *Prevent Interstate Commerce in Industrial Activities In Which Persons Are Employed More than Five Days Per Week or Six Hours Per Day*, H. Rept. 1999, 72d Cong., 2d sess. (Washington, D.C., 1933), 1–5; Thomas George Karis, "Congressional Behavior at Constitutional Frontiers, From 1906, The Beveridge Child Labor Bill, to 1938, The Fair Labor Standards Act" (Ph.D. diss., Columbia University , 1951), 210–13; E. Pendleton Herring, "Second Session of the Seventy-second Congress," *The American Political Science Review* 27 (June 1933): 421–22.

53. U.S. Senate, *National Income, 1929–32*, S. Doc. 124, 73rd Cong., 2d sess. (Washington, D.C., 1934), 13–18; Horst Mendenshausen, *Changes in Income Distribution During the Great Depression* (New York: National Bureau of Economic Research, 1946), 114–16; U.S. Department of Labor, *Twentieth Annual Report of the Secretary of Labor, 1932* (Washington, D.C., 1932), 16–17; and *Twenty-First Annual Report of the Secretary of Labor, 1933* (Washington, D.C., 1934), 67.

54. O'Brien, *American Catholics and Social Reform*, 17–21; "Social Justice," *The American Labor Legislation Review* 22 (December 1932): 115; Paul K. Conkin, *FDR and the Origins of the Welfare State* (New York: Crowell, 1967), 24; Franklin D. Roosevelt, *Looking Forward* (New York: John Day Co., 1933), 34–36; Nicholas Rescher, *Distributive Justice, A Constructive Critique of the Utilitarian Theory of Distribution* (Indianapolis: Bobbs, 1966), 98–100; "Testing the Adequacy of Wages," *Monthly Labor Review* 32 (May 1931): 146–50; Dorothea D. Kittredge, "Determining a Living Wage," Thomas D. Eliot, ed., *American Standards and Planes of Living* (Boston:

Ginn and Co., 1931), 280–84; Edward S. Corwin, "Social Planning Under the Constitution," Alpheus T. Mason and Gerald Garvey, eds., *American Constitutional History, Essays by Edward S. Corwin* (New York: Harper, 1964), 125; "Economic Statistics, What Is a Living Wage?" *American Federationist* 37 (May 1930): 591–94.

CHAPTER 2. WAGE AND HOUR REGULATION ON TRIAL

1. William E. Leuchtenburg, *Franklin D. Roosevelt and the New Deal, 1932–1940* (New York: Harper, 1963), 31–33; Rexford G. Tugwell, *The Democratic Roosevelt* (Garden City, N.Y.: Doubleday, 1957), 32–34, 47, 52–55; Frank Freidel, *F.D.R. and the South* (Baton Rouge: Louisiana State University Press, 1965), 40, 42, 45; Otis L. Graham, *An Encore for Reform, The Old Progressives and the New Deal* (New York: Oxford University Press, 1967), 3–23; Esmond Wright, "The Roosevelt Revolution of 1933–38," *History Today* 12 (December 1962): 826; Bernard Sternsher, "The New Deal 'Revolution'," *Social Studies* 57 (April 1966): 157–61.

2. Freidel, *Franklin D. Roosevelt, Launching the New Deal* (Boston: Little, Brown, 1973) 4: 60–82; Charles Michelson, *The Ghost Talks* (New York: Putnam, 1944), 186–87; James A. Farley, *Behind the Ballots* (New York: Harcourt, 1938), 348, 355; Sternsher, "Tugwell's Appraisal of F.D.R.," *Western Political Quarterly* 15 (March 1962): 70–76.

3. Daniel R. Fusfield, *The Economic Thought of Franklin D. Roosevelt and the Origins of the New Deal* (New York: Columbia University Press, 1956), 200, 206–22; Sternsher, *Rexford Tugwell and the New Deal* (New Brunswick: Rutgers University Press, 1964), 39–50; Tugwell, *The Brain Trust* (New York: Viking, 1968), 73–82; Raymond Moley, *After Seven Years* (New York: Harper, 1939), 5–24; Theodore Rosenoff, *Dogma, Depression, and the New Deal* (Port Washington, N.Y.: Kennikat Press, 1975), 20–42; Arthur B. Adams, *Trend of Business, Yesterday-Today-Tomorrow* (New York: Harper, 1932), 34, 39, 45–48, 59; Ellis W. Hawley, "The Discovery and Study of 'Corporate Liberalism'," *Business History Review,* 52 (Autumn 1977), 309–17.

4. Alfred B. Rollins, "Franklin Roosevelt's Introduction to Labor," *Labor History* 3 (winter 1962): 3–4, 10–18; Gerald D. Nash, "Franklin D. Roosevelt and Labor: The World War Origins of Early New Deal Policy," ibid., 1 (winter 1960): 39–52; Murray Edelman, "New Deal Sensitivity to Labor Interests," in Milton Derber and Edwin Young, eds. *Labor and the New Deal* (Madison: University of Wisconsin Press, 1957), 177–80; Stanley High, *Roosevelt—And Then?* (New York: Harper, 1937), 178, 182–85; Jerold S. Auerbach, "The Influence of The New Deal," *Current History* 48 (June 1965): 334; Sidney Fine, "Government and Labor Relations During the New Deal," ibid., 37 (September 1959): 139–40; Dorfman, *The Economic Mind in American Civilization,* 5, 504–5.

5. James R. Anderson, "The New Deal Career of Frances Perkins, Secretary of Labor, 1933–1939" (Ph.D. diss., Case Western Reserve University, 1968), 1–32, 82, 100, 151–60, 203–6; Isador Lubin, *The Reminiscences of Isador Lubin,* Columbia University Oral History Collection, 1957, 65, 67, 111; George Martin, *Madam Secretary, Frances Perkins* (Boston: Houghton, 1976), 3–4, 18–19, 233–47, 251–56, 292–305; Frances Perkins, *The Roosevelt I Knew* (New York: Viking, 1946), 15–52, 303; Elliot Roosevelt, ed., *F.D.R.: His Personal Letters, 1928–1945* (New York: Duel, Sloan and Pearce, 1950), 3: 316; Kenneth G. Crawford, *The Pressure Boys* (New York: Julian Messner, 1939), 275.

6. Anderson, "New Deal Career of Frances Perkins," 82; High, *Roosevelt–And Then?* 182; Dorfman, *The Economic Mind in American Civilization*, 5, 534.

7. Anderson, "New Deal Career of Frances Perkins," 94, 100; Frances Perkins, *People at Work* (New York: John Day Co., 1934), 125–26.

8. Anderson, "New Deal Career of Frances Perkins," 151; Charles K. McFarland, *Roosevelt, Lewis, and the New Deal, 1933–1940* (Fort Worth: Texas Christian University Press, 1970), 11–13.

9. Walter I. Trattner, *Crusade for the Children, A History of the National Child Labor Committee and Child Labor Reform in America* (Chicago: Quadrangle Books, 1970), 190–212; Donald Murtha, "Wage-Hour and Child Labor Legislation in the Roosevelt Administration," *Lawyers Guild Review* 5 no. 3 (May-June 1945): 185–91.

10. Trattner, *Crusade for the Children*, 45–186; *Bailey v. Drexel Furniture Company*, 259 U.S. 20(1922).

11. Lucy Randolph Mason, "Progress and Administration of Minimum Wage Laws in 1933," *Proceedings of the National Conference of Social Work, 1933* (Chicago: University of Chicago Press, 1933), 379–81; Bernstein, *Lean Years*, 312–22; Commons and Associates, *History of Labor in the United States*, 3: 92–96; Dorfman, *The Economic Mind in American Civilization*, 5, 643–44.

12. Mason, "Progress and Administration of Minimum Wage Laws in 1933," 378–81; Irene O. Andrews, "Minimum Wage Comes Back!" *The American Labor Legislative Review* 23 (June 1933): 103–5; Louis W. Koenig, *The Invisible Presidency* (New York: Reinhart & Co., 1960), 256.

13. Benjamin V. Cohen, "Constitutional Aspects of the New Standard Minimum Wage Bill," *Proceedings of the National Conference of Social Work, 1933* (Chicago: University of Chicago Press, 1933), 372–75; Mason, "Progress and Administration of Minimum Wage Laws in 1933," ibid., 381–82; *Highland v. Russell Car Co.*, 279 U.S. 253(1929), 261.

14. Cohen, "Constitutional Aspects of the New Standard Minimum Wage Bill," 375.

15. Ibid., 375–77; Mason, "Progress and Administration of Minimum Wage Laws in 1933," 382–86.

16. Black to Roosevelt, March 10, 1933, Official File 372, Franklin D. Roosevelt Papers, Franklin D. Roosevelt Library, Hyde Park, N.Y.; hereafter cited as FDR Papers with the Official File, Personal File, or Secretary's File number; Max Freedman, *Roosevelt and Frankfurter, Their Correspondence, 1928–1945* (Boston: Little, Brown, 1967), 125–26; "Minimum Wage Legislation in the United States," *Monthly Labor Review* 37 (December 1933): 1344–54.

17. Frances Perkins, *Reminiscences of Frances Perkins*, Columbia University Oral History Collection, part 3, 439–47; Moley, *After Seven Years*, 186–88; Robert F. Himmelberg, *The Origins of the National Recovery Administration* (New York: Fordham University Press, 1976), 190–92; Irving Bernstein, *The New Deal Collective Bargaining Policy* (Berkeley: University of California Press, 1950), 29–30; John Culter to Roosevelt, April 10, 1933, White House File, Secretary Frances Perkins General Subject File, 1933–1944, Records of the Department of Labor, 1933–1945, RG 174, National Archives, Washington, D.C.; hereafter cited as Secretary Perkins Records with the file location.

18. Hillman to Perkins, December 21, 1932; Harry A. Millis to Perkins, April 6, 1933; and Perkins to the editor of the *Washington Post*, April 20, 1933, Frances Perkins Papers, Butler Library, Columbia University; hereafter cited as Perkins Correspondence; Perkins, *The Roosevelt I Knew*, 192–96; Perkins, *Reminiscences of Frances Perkins*, 439–42; Perkins, *People at Work*, 132–36; George Soule, *Sidney*

Hillman, Labor Statesman (New York: Macmillan, 1939), 164–66; Sidney Hillman, "A Shorter Working Day and a Minimum Wage," *Harvard Business Review*, 11 (July 1933), 457–61; Steven Fraser, "Dress Rehearsal for the New Deal: Shop Floor Insurgents, Political Elites, and Industrial Democracy in the Amalgamated Clothing Workers," Michael H. Frisch and Daniel J. Walkowitz, eds., *Working Class America, Labor, Community, and American Society* (Urbana, University of Illinois Press, 1983), 212–55.

19. Benjamin K. Hunnicutt, *Work Without End: Abandoning Shorter Hours for the Right to Work* (Philadelphia, Temple University Press, 1988), 151–58; Perkins, *Reminiscences of Frances Perkins*, 450; Karis, "Congressional Behavior at Constitutional Frontiers," 214–17.

20. Karis, "Congressional Behavior at Constitutional Frontiers," 218–21; *New State Ice Co.* v. *Liebman*, 285 U.S. 262(1932).

21. Karis, "Congressional Behavior at Constitutional Frontiers," 223–43.

22. Ibid.

23. U.S. House of Representatives, *To Prevent Interstate Commerce in Industrial Activities in Which Persons Are Employed More than 5 Days Per Week or 6 Hours Per Day*, H. Rept. 24, 73rd Cong., 1st sess. (Washington, D.C., 1933), 1–6; John Ryan to Perkins, April 7, 1933; Frankfurter to Perkins, April 15, 1933; and Frankfurter to Dewson, February 27, 1933, Perkins Correspondence; Perkins, *The Roosevelt I Knew*, 193–95.

24. Robert Szold, two acts to regulate interstate commerce (n.d.), Perkins Correspondence.

25. Swope to Perkins, April 21, 1933; Harriman to Perkins, April 11, 1933; Dickinson to Perkins, April 21, 1933; and Wyzanski to Perkins, April 24, 1933, ibid.

26. Perkins to the *Washington Post*, April 20, 1933; and Wyzanski to Perkins, April 24, 1933, ibid.; *New York Times*, April 18, 19, 1933; Steven Fraser, *Labor Will Rule, Sidney Hillman and the Rise of American Labor* (New York, The Free Press, 1991), 285–86.

27. Wyzanski to Perkins, April 24, 1933, Enclosure: Informal Memorandum on Redrafting the Black Bill, Perkins Correspondence.

28. James O. Morris, *Conflict Within the AFL, A Study of Craft versus Industrial Unionism, 1901–1938* (Ithaca: Cornell University Press, 1958), 142; Moley, *After Seven Years*, 186–88; *New York Times*, May 2, 1933.

29. Turner W. Battle to Perkins, May 5, 1933; and Perkins to Dickinson, May 5, 1933, Perkins Correspondence; Dewson to Roosevelt, Dickinson, Wagner, and Johnson, May 11, 1933; and Dickinson to Dewson, May 15, 1933, Papers of the National Consumers' League, Library of Congress, Washington, D.C.; U.S. House of Representatives, *Thirty-Hour Week Bill*, H. Rept. 124, 73rd Cong., 1st sess. (Washington, D.C., 1933), 1–6; Karis, "Congressional Behavior at Constitutional Frontiers," 252–57.

30. Perkins to Connery, May 10, 1933, Perkins Correspondence.

31. Himmelburg, *Origins of the National Recovery Administration*, 204–9; Ellis W. Hawley, *The New Deal and the Problem of Monopoly* (Princeton: Princeton University Press, 1966), 22–42; Charles F. Roos, *NRA Economic Planning* (New York: DeCapo Press, 1971), 36–41; Samuel I. Rosenman, ed., *The Public Papers and Addresses of Franklin D. Roosevelt*, vol. 2, *The Year of Crisis, 1933*, 202–6, 246–48, 251–56; Saul Alinsky, *John L. Lewis, An Unauthorized Biography* (New York: Putnam, 1949), 66–67.

32. Wyzanski to Wagner, May 23, 1933; and Wilcox to Perkins, May 23, 1933,

Perkins Correspondence; "Are the Provisions of the National Recovery Act Constitutional?" *Congressional Digest* 12 (1933): 289–315.

33. Leuchtenburg, *Franklin D. Roosevelt and the New Deal*, 57–58; *The Public Papers and Addresses of Franklin D. Roosevelt*, vol. 2, *The Year of Crisis, 1933*, 275–79, 308–12; "The Industrial Recovery Bill and the Antitrust Laws," *Congressional Digest* 12 (1933): 165–67.

34. Grace Abbott to Perkins, January 17, 1934, White House File, Secretary Perkins Records; Roos, *NRA Economic Planning*, 88–93.

35. Lucy R. Mason to Martha Adamson, September 4, 1933; and to Hattie Horn, December 20, 1934, and Proposed Principles for Labor Provisions of NRA Codes, December 1, 1933, Papers of the National Consumers' League; *AFL Weekly News Service*, October 2, 1933; "Convention of the American Federation of Labor, 1933," *Monthly Labor Review* 37 (November 1933): 1120–21; James P. Johnson, "Drafting the NRA Code of Fair Competition for the Bituminous Coal Industry," *Journal of American History* 53 (December 1966): 532–33.

36. Thomas Eliot to Perkins, January 25, 1934, Perkins Correspondence; U.S. House of Representatives, *Thirty-Hour Week for Industry*, H. Rept. 889, 73rd Cong., 2d sess. (Washington, D.C. 1934), 1–5; *Franklin D. Roosevelt Papers, 3, The Advance of Recovery and Reform, 1934*, 127–28.

37. Eliot to Perkins, March 8, 1934, and Black to Perkins, June 30, 1934, Perkins Correspondence; "National Recovery Program," *Monthly Labor Review* 38 (April 1934): 800–803; Witt Bowden, "Employment, Hours, Earnings and Production Under the N.R.A.," ibid. (May 1934): 1013–31; Douglas V. Brown, "Helping Labor," in Douglas v. Brown, et al., *The Economics of the Recovery Program* (New York, McGraw-Hill Book Co., 1934), 69–75; Edward Chamberlin, "Purchasing Power," ibid., 32–37; Overton Taylor, "Economics Versus Politics," ibid., 167–88.

38. Leverett S. Lyon et al., *The National Recovery Administration, An Analysis and an Appraisal* (Washington, D.C.: Brookings Institution, 1935), 830–36; National Industrial Conference Board, *The Thirty-Hour Work Week* (New York: National Industrial Conference Board, 1935), 1–3, 20; John L. Lewis, "Labor and the National Recovery Administration," *Annals of the American Academy of Political and Social Science* 72 (March 1934): 58–63; Sidney Hillman, "The NRA, Labor and Recovery," ibid., 70–75; Dudley Cates, "A Current Appraisal of the National Recovery Administration," ibid., 138; Leo Wolman, "Accomplishments of the NRA in Labor Legislation," *American Labor Legislation Review* 25 (March 1935): 39–44; William Green, "What Labor Wants," *American Federationist* 42 (March 1935): 248–50; Henry Weiss, "The Enforcement of Federal Wage and Hour Regulations," ibid., 43 (September 1936): 930–37; Mauritz A. Hallgren, *The Gay Reformer* (New York: Knopf, 1935), 182–200.

39. U.S. Senate, *Thirty-Hour Work Week*, S. Rept. 367, 74th Cong., 1st sess. (Washington, D.C., 1935), 1–6; U.S. Senate, *Thirty-Hour Work Week, Hearings*, 74th Cong., 1st sess. (Washington, D.C., 1935); William Green, "30 Hours," *American Federationist* 42 (January 1935): 13.

40. *Panama Refining Co. v. Ryan*, 293 U. S. 388, 414(1935); Robert H. Jackson, *The Struggle for Judicial Supremacy* (New York: Random, 1941), 86–95; Carl B. Swisher, ed., *Selected Papers of Homer Cummings* (New York: Scribner, 1939), 98–99; Harrison J. Barrett, "Is There a National Police Power: If So, What Is Its Relation to the Recent Federal Statutes Affecting Industry and Trade Generally, Particularly the 'National Industrial Recovery Act'?" *Boston University Law Review* 14 (April 1934): 281; Robert L. Stern, "That Commerce Which Concerns More States Than One," *Harvard Law Review* 47 (June 1934): 1340, 1351–54; Cornelius W.

Wickersham, "The NIRA From the Employers' Viewpoint," ibid., 48 (April 1935): 967–77.

41. Jackson, *Struggle for Judicial Supremacy*, 113; Robert E. Cushman, "Constitutional Law in 1934–35," *American Political Science Review* 30 (February 1936): 58–62; Donald B. Richberg, *My Hero* (New York: Putnam, 1954), 185–89; Charles P. Curtis, *Lions Under the Throne* (Boston: Houghton, 1947), 116–21; James M. Burns, *Roosevelt: The Lion and the Fox* (New York: Harcourt, 1956), 193.

42. *A.L.A. Schechter Poultry Corp.* v. *United States*, 295 U.S. 495(1935), 528–30, 537–39, 542–48; Felix Frankfurter and Henry M. Hart, "The Business of the Supreme Court at October Term, 1934," *Harvard Law Review* 49, no. 2 (November 1935): 99–105; Thomas Reed Powell, "Commerce, Pensions, and Codes, II," ibid. (December 1935), 197–237; Edward S. Corwin, "The Schechter Case-Landmark Or What?" *New York University Law Quarterly Review* 13 (January 1936): 152–53, 189.

43. "Cost of Living," *Monthly Labor Review* 40 (May 1935): 1386; Paul H. Douglas, *Controlling Depressions* (New York: Norton, 1935), 211, 214, 226; Donald S. Howard, *The WPA and Federal Relief Policy* (New York: Russel Sage Foundation, 1943), 160–61, 175–76.

CHAPTER 3. HORSE AND BUGGY DAYS

1. *New York Times*, January 14, 16, 18, 1935.

2. Richberg to Perkins, January 23, February 7, 1935, Perkins Correspondence; Richberg to Roosevelt, June 13, 1935, Memorandum for the President Concerning Future of NRA, and Confidential Draft, A Bill to Amend Title I of the National Recovery Act, Donald Richberg Papers, Library of Congress; *New York Times*, January 16, 23, 1935.

3. *Franklin D. Roosevelt Papers, The Court Disapproves, 1935*, 4: 80–84; *New York Times*, February 21, 1935.

4. U.S. House of Representatives, *Extension of National Industrial Recovery Act, Hearings*, 74th Cong., 1st sess. (Washington, D.C., 1935); U.S. House of Representatives, *Extension of National Industrial Recovery Act*, H. Rept. 1115, 74th Cong., 1st sess. (Washington, D.C., 1935); U.S. House of Representatives, *Hearings, H. Joint Res. 295*, 74th Cong., 1st sess. (Washington, D.C., 1935).

5. U.S. Senate, *Investigation of the National Recovery Administration, Hearings*, 74th Cong., 1st sess. (Washington, D.C., 1935); U.S. Senate, *Extension of National Recovery Act*, S. Rept. 570, 74th Cong., 1st sess. (Washington, D.C., 1935); Bernard Bellush, *The Failure of the NRA* (New York: Norton, 1975), 66–71, 149, 165–67; *New York Times*, April 27, May 11, 15, 30, June 8, 1935; "Washington Notes," *The New Republic* 83 (May 22, 1935): 46, and ibid. (June 5, 1935): 100; "The Week," ibid. (June 5, 1935): 85.

6. *New York Times*, June 8, 1935; Moley, *After Seven Years*, 306–7; Rinehart J. Swenson, "The Chamber of Commerce and the New Deal," *Annals of the American Academy of Political and Social Science* 179 (May 1935): 138–39.

7. Perkins, *The Roosevelt I Knew*, 254.

8. Lubin to Perkins, May 29, 1935; and Thomas Eliot to Perkins, Memo, Proposed Plan for Dealing With the NRA Emergency (n.d.), Perkins Correspondence; Leverett S. Lyon et. al., *National Recovery Administration*, 11–12.

9. *New York Times*, June 8, 9, 1935.

10. *U.S. Statutes at Large*, 49, part 1, 375; "National Recovery Program, Extension

of National Industrial Recovery Act," *Monthly Labor Review* 41 (August 1935): 354–55.

11. "National Recovery Program, Extension of National Industrial Recovery Act," 354–55; *New York Times*, June 18, 20, 22, 1935.

12. *New York Times*, June 18, 20, 1935.

13. Ibid. July 3, 4, 23, 27, 1935; Miss Jay to Perkins, August 5, 1935, White House File, Secretary Perkins Records; "FTC Ready to Go," *Business Week* (July 13, 1935): 16.

14. Wyzanski to Perkins, October 30, 1935; and Beyer to Perkins, August 9, November 1, 1935, Perkins Correspondence; Cummings to Perkins, August 26, 1935, White House File, Secretary Perkins Records.

15. Cummings to Roosevelt, August 13, 1935, Official File 466, FDR Papers.

16. Cummings to Roosevelt, August 23, 1935; Roosevelt to McIntyre, August 26, 1935; Reed to Roosevelt, August 30, 1935; McIntyre to E. L. Davis; August 31, 1935, Official File 2452; Martin to Roosevelt, August 27, 1935, Official File 466, ibid.

17. Berry to Roosevelt, August 29, 1935; Reed to Roosevelt, August 30, 1935; Berry to McIntyre, and September 13, 1935; Official File 2452; McClintock to T. Corcoran, November 15, 1935; Personal File 6721, ibid.; Frey to Appleton, September 9, 1935, John P. Frey Papers, Library of Congress, Washington, D.C.; *Report of the Proceedings of the Fifty-Fifth Annual Convention of the American Federation of Labor, 1935* (Washington, D.C., Judd & Detwiler 1935), 373; G. L. Berry, "Voluntary Codes," *American Federationist* 42 (November 1935): 1176–77; "Coordinator for Industrial Cooperation," *Monthly Labor Review* 41 (November 1935): 1203; *New York Times*, August 25, 27, September 26, November 13, 20, 1935.

18. Martin to Reed, September 6, 1935, Reed to Roosevelt, September 7, 1935, Official File 2452, FDR Papers; *Annual Report of the Federal Trade Commission for the Fiscal Year Ending June 30, 1935* (Washington, D.C., 1935), 7–8; David A. McCabe, "The American Federation of Labor and the NIRA," *Annals of the American Academy of Political and Social Science*, 179 (May 1935): 144–47; *New York Times*, November 1, 1935.

19. Eliot to Perkins, June 19, 1935, Perkins Correspondence; James R. Anderson, "The New Deal Career of Frances Perkins, Secretary of Labor, 1933–1939" (Ph.D., Case Western Reserve University, 1968), 122–24; Lauck, "Coal Labor Legislation," 134–35; Irving Bernstein, *Turbulent Years* (Boston: Houghton, 1970), 324–49.

20. Altmeyer to Perkins, April 25, 1935, Perkins Correspondence; Lubell, *Future of American Politics*, 53; "Works Program Under Relief Act of 1935," *Monthly Labor Review* 41 (August 1935): 343–45; "Wage Determination for Government Contracts," ibid., 45 (September 1937), 694.

21. U.S. House of Representatives, *Thirty-Hour Week Bill*, H. Rept. 1550, 74th Cong., 1st sess. (Washington, D.C., 1935), 1–5; Karis, "Congressional Behavior at Constitutional Frontiers," 266, 289, 298; William Green, "Minimum Wages," *American Federationist* 43 (April 1936): 354; William Green, "Cut Hours and Maintain Wages," ibid. (May 1936): 465.

22. Perkins to Roosevelt, June 15, 1935, White House File, Secretary Perkins Records; Eleanor Roosevelt to Perkins, September 16, 1935, Perkins Correspondence; U.S. Senate, *Cotton Textile Industry*, S. Doc. 126, 74th Cong., 1st sess. (Washington, D.C., 1935), 20–21; *Franklin D. Roosevelt Papers, The Court Disapproves, 1935*, 4: 334–36; Thomas L. Stokes, *Chip Off My Shoulder* (Princeton: Princeton University Press, 1940), 508–10; "Departures from N.R.A. Standards by Manufacturing Industries," *Monthly Labor Review* 42 (May 1936): 1234.

23. E. G. Draper to Roper, November 5, 1935; McIntyre to Roosevelt, November

6, 1935; and Berry to Roosevelt, November 21, December 11, 1935, Official File 2452, FDR Papers; Green to Roosevelt, February 14, 1935, American Federation of Labor File, Secretary Perkins Records; *New York Times*, November 1, December 1, 6, 8, 1935.

24. Wyzanski to Perkins, October 30, November 8, 1935, Beyer to Perkins, November 1, 1935, Perkins Correspondence; "NRA in No Man's Land," *Business Week* (November 23, 1935): 12; "Termination of the National Recovery Administration," *Monthly Labor Review* 42 (February 1936): 334.

25. Berry to Roosevelt, March 14, 1936; and Berry to McIntyre, March 18, 1936, Official File 2452, FDR Papers; Coordinator for Industrial Cooperation, Council for Industrial Progress, *Reports of Committees and Resolutions Adopted, March 12, 1936* (Washington, D.C., 1936); "Meeting of the Council for Industrial Cooperation," *Monthly Labor Review* 42 (February 1936): 335; "Council for Industrial Progress Adopts Committee Reports," ibid. (April 1936): 932–33; "Continuation of Office of Coordinator for Industrial Cooperation," ibid. (May 1936): 1234; "Creation of Committee to Complete Summary of N.R.A. Accomplishments," ibid; Hawley, *New Deal and the Problem of Monopoly*, 161–62.

26. Karis, "Congressional Behavior at Constitutional Frontiers," 323–25; James A. Hodges, *The New Deal Labor Policy and the Southern Cotton Textile Industry* (Knoxville, University of Tennessee Press, 1986), 135; O. R. Altman, "Second Session of the Seventy-Fourth Congress, January 3, 1936 to June 20, 1936," *American Political Science Review* 30 (December 1936): 1095; Burns, *Roosevelt*, 229, 269.

27. Reilly to Perkins, January 10, 1936; and Reilly to Sen. David I. Walsh, April 23, 1936, Miscellaneous Bills-1936 File, Secretary Perkins Records.

28. *Carter v. Carter Coal Company*, 298 U.S. 238(1936) 295–97, 307–10(1936); *Morehead v. New York ex rel. Tipaldo*, 298 U.S. 587(1936) 609–10(1936); Jackson, *Struggle for Judicial Supremacy*, 160–65, 170–75; Curtis, *Lions Under the Throne*, 130–53.

29. Frankfurter and Adrian S. Fisher, "The Business of the Supreme Court at the October Terms, 1935 and 1936," *Harvard Law Review* 51 (February 1938): 634–35; Nichols and Baccus, *Minimum Wages and Maximum Hours*, 204–24, 231–33, 249–58, 278–84; John W. Hester, "How the Supreme Court Has Dealt With the 'New Deal'," *Congressional Digest* 14 (1935): 300–301; "Should Congress Be Empowered to Override Supreme Court Decisions?" ibid., 302–17; "The Question of Fixing a Minimum Wage for American Industry," ibid., 15 (November 1936): 257–88; Victor S. Yarros, "Progress and the Supreme Court," *American Federationist* 43 (June 1936): 616–19; William Green, "Is It Stalemate?" ibid. (July 1936): 685–86; Ethel M. Johnson, "Minimum Wage Legislation," ibid., 692–99; "Helpless in No Man's Land," *Christian Century* 53 (June 1936): 862–64; Freedman, *Roosevelt and Frankfurter*, 272–74.

30. Cummings to Roosevelt, January 20, 1936, Secretary's File 74, FDR Papers; Jackson, *Struggle for Judicial Supremacy*, 176–77; Edward S. Corwin, *The Commerce Power versus States Rights* (Princeton: Princeton University Press, 1936), 172, 208–9, 262–63, 265; Charles A. Beard, "Rendezvous With the Supreme Court," *New Republic* 88 (September 1936): 92–94; Fredrick Rudolph, "The American Liberty League, 1934–1940," *American Historical Review* 56 (October 1950): 19–29; George Wolfskill, *The Revolt of the Conservatives* (Boston: Houghton, 1962), 56–79; Raoul E. Desvernine, *Democratic Despotism* (New York: Dodd, 1936), 92–95, 124–27, 131, 139.

31. Roosevelt to Berry, August 3, 1936, Official File 15, FDR Papers, *Franklin D. Roosevelt Papers*, vol. 5 *The People Approve, 1936*, 280–81; Morris, *Conflict Within the AFL*, 212–43; Taft, *A.F. of L. From the Death of Gompers to the Merger*, 140–48;

John L. Lewis, "Labor and the Future," Labor Day address, September 7, 1936, John L. Lewis Papers, State Historical Society of Wisconsin, Madison, Wis.

32. R. W. Johnson to McIntyre, November 5, 1936, Official File 2452; Ogburn to Roosevelt, November 4, 13, 1936, Personal File 3794; National Association of Manufacturers, Report of the Committee on Employment Relations, December, 1936, Official File 264; Perkins to Roosevelt, November 21, 1936; Roosevelt to Perkins, December 2, 1936, Official File 15, FDR Papers; Hadley Cantril, *Public Opinion, 1935–1946* (Princeton: Princeton University Press, 1951), 97, 290, 1018, 1021; Lubin, *Reminiscences of Isador Lubin*, 164.

33. Gregory to Perkins, November 6, December 18, 1936, Perkins Correspondence.

34. Berry to Cosgrove, November 20, 1936, Records of the Coordinator for Industrial Cooperation, Council for Industrial Progress, Records of the National Recovery Administration, RG 9, National Archives, Washington, D.C.; hereafter cited as Records of the Coordinator; Gregory to Perkins, December 16, 1936, Council for Industrial Progress File, Secretary Perkins Records; *Report of the Proceedings of the Fifty-Sixth Annual Convention of the American Federation of Labor, 1936*, (Washington, D.C.: Judd & Detwiler 1936) 331–32.

35. Report of the Committee on a Maximum Work Week, General Wage, and Child Labor, December 11, 1936, Records of the Coordinator; Gregory to Perkins, December 16, 1936, Council for Industrial Progress File, Secretary Perkins Records.

36. Ogburn to Roosevelt, December 23, 1936, Personal File 3794, FDR Papers; Berry to Congressman Michael J. Brady, December 22, 1936; E. J. Tracy to William Green, December 31, 1936; and Tracy to Richberg, December 31, 1936, Records of the Coordinator; Perkins to Cummings, December 29, Attorney General File, Secretary Perkins Records; *Franklin D. Roosevelt Papers*, vol. 5, *The People Approve, 1936*, 624–25; Swisher, *Selected Papers of Homer Cummings*, 100; *Washington Evening Star*, December 15, 1936.

37. Stern, "The Commerce Clause and the National Economy, 1933–1946," *Harvard Law Review* 59 (May 1946): 651–52.

38. Lenroot to Perkins, December 31, 1936, Perkins Correspondence; *Report of the Proceedings of the Fifty-Sixth Convention of the American Federation of Labor, 1936*, 137; Lumpkin and Douglas, *Child Workers in America*, 113.

39. T. N. Carver, "The Theory of the Shortened Working Week," *American Economic Review* 26 (September 1936): 44–62; *Report of the Proceedings of the Fifty-Sixth Annual Convention of the American Federation of Labor, 1936*, 143–44.

Chapter 4. Ghost of the NRA

1. *Franklin D. Roosevelt Papers*, vol. 5, *The People Approve, 1936*, 634–40, 657; ibid., vol. 6, *The Constitution Prevails, 1937*, 1–9.

2. Karis, "Congressional Behavior at Constitutional Frontiers," 354–55; *New York Times*, January 10, 1937.

3. Berry to Siegfried Hartman, January 8, 1937; Ogburn to Berry, January 14, 1937; and Minutes of the Correlating and Legal Advisory committees, January 11, 1937, Hartman, Memorandum Re Annexed Bill, and Hartman, A Bill to Prohibit and Prevent Unfair Competition and to Amend the Anti-Trust Acts, Records of the Coordinator; Gregory to Perkins, January 18, 1937, Solicitor's Office, 1937–1938 File, Secretary Perkins Records; Walter L. Pope to Reed, Report on Legislative Drafting Project (n.d.), Records of Pope, Special Assistant to the Attorney General,

File 143–01–236–144, August, 1938, Justice Department Records, Washington, D.C.; hereafter cited as Pope File, Justice Department Records; Coordinator for Industrial Cooperation, *Recommendation and Representation of the Council for Industrial Progress* (Washington, D.C., 1938), 53, 55–56; "Legislative Program Endorsed by Council for Industrial Progress," *Monthly Labor Review* 44 (February 1937): 374–75.

4. Ogburn to Roosevelt, December 30, 1936; February 6, 1937; March 3, 1937; and May 21, 1937, Personal File 3794, FDR Papers; Perkins to Black, February 16, 1937, Perkins Correspondence; Perkins to Copeland, March 3, 1937; Reilly to Perkins, March 25, 1937; and Perkins to Black, February 17, 1937, Miscellaneous Bills-1937 File, Secretary Perkins Records.

5. Beyer to Perkins, January 5, 1937, Perkins Correspondence; Lucy R. Mason to Hugh W. Ransom, January 29, 1937; and Louise Stitt to Mason, General Secretary, National Consumers' League, March 1, 1937, National Consumers' League Papers.

6. Gregory to Perkins, February 12, 1937, Memo: Proposed National Labor Standards Act, Perkins Correspondence.

7. Cummings to Roosevelt, January 22, 1937, Official File 10, Memo, January 22, 1937, Official File 372, FDR Papers; High, *Roosevelt-And Then?* 31–32, 44–48; Schlesinger, *The Politics of Upheaval* (Boston: Houghton, 1960), 226–29; Alva Johnson, "White House Tommy," *Saturday Evening Post* 210 (July 31, 1937): 5–7; "Necks In: Irishman and Jew Keep Quiet Behind Today's Rooseveltian Brain Trust," *Literary Digest* 123 (May 22, 1937): 7–8; Bruce Allen Murphy, *The Brandeis/Frankfurter Connection, The Secret Political Activities of Two Supreme Court Justices* (New York: Oxford University Press, 1982), 132; Jerold S. Auerback, "Lawyers and Social Change in the Depression Decade," John Braeman, Robert N. Bremner, and David Brody, eds., *The New Deal*, I, *The National Level* (Columbus, Ohio State University Press, 1975), 133–69.

8. *New York Times*, February 2, 3, 8, 1937; Richberg to Roosevelt, February 19, 1937; and Roper to Roosevelt, March 18, 1937, Official File 372; Roosevelt to James Roosevelt, February 1, 1937, Official File 2452, FDR Papers.

9. *Franklin D. Roosevelt Papers*, vol. 6, *The Constitution Prevails, 1937*, 35–66; Joseph Alsop and Turner Catledge, *The 168 Days* (Garden City, N.Y.: Doubleday, Doran & Co., 1938), 17–49, 54–64; William E. Borah, "Our Supreme Judicial Tribunal," *Vital Speeches* 3 (February 1937): 258–61; Elmo Roper, *You and Your Leaders* (New York: Morrow, 1957), 29, 31.

10. John L. Lewis, "Labor and the Supreme Court," radio address, May 14, 1937, John L. Lewis Papers; AFL *Weekly News Service*, February 20, 1937; Alsop and Catledge, *168 Days*, 67–74, 87–96, 102–5, 164–75, 178–82; Richard Polenberg, "The National Committee to Uphold Constitutional Government, 1937–1941," *Journal of American History* 52 (December 1965): 582; Murphy, *Brandeis/Frankfurter Connection*, 178–84.

11. W. W. Gardner, February 20, 1937, memo, in Pope to Reed, Report on Legislative Project, Pope to Hartman, March 30, 1937; and Pope to Robert Jackson, April 5, 1937, Pope File, Justice Department Records.

12. Pope to Reed, Report on Legislative Drafting Project, Pope File, Justice Department Records; Reilly to Perkins, March 8, 1937, Solicitor's Office, 1937–1938 File, Secretary Perkins Records.

13. Reilly to Perkins, March 8, 1937, Solicitor's Office 1937–1938 File, Secretary Perkins Records; *Kentucky Whip & Collar Co.* v. *Illinois Central Railroad Co.*, 299 U.S. 334(1937), 345–53; Jackson, *Struggle for Judicial Supremacy*, 197, 202–3.

14. *Franklin D. Roosevelt Papers,* vol. 6, *The Constitution Prevails, 1937,* 118–19, 122–23; *West Coast Hotel Co.* v. *Parrish,* 300 U.S. 379(1937), 391, 393–94, 397–99, 404; Swisher, *Selected Papers of Homer Cummings,* 155–56; Mary Anderson to Perkins, April 9, 1937, Memo, State Minimum Wage Legislation, Women's Bureau File, Secretary Perkins Records; Olin L. Browder, "Constitutional Law-Due Process Clause-Validity of Washington Minimum Wage Law," *Illinois Bar Journal* 25 (April 1937): 285–86; J. Kennard Cheadle, "The Parrish Case: Minimum Wages for Women and, Perhaps, for Men," *University of Cincinnati Law Review* 11 (May 1937): 314–15, 319; Andrew K. Black, "Wages and Hours Laws in the Courts," *University of Pittsburgh Law Review* 5 (May 1939): 231–32, 243; Jackson, *Struggle for Judicial Supremacy,* 206–12.

15. *National Labor Relations Board* v. *Jones & Laughlin Steel Corp.,* 301 U.S. 1–3, 31–41(1937), 76; Richard C. Cortner, *The Jones & Laughlin Case* (New York: Knopf, 1970), 78–96, 125–66; Cushman, "Constitutional Law in 1936–37," *American Political Science Review* 32 (April 1938): 283–84; Arthur Selwyn Miller, "Toward a Concept of Constitutional Duty," in Arthur Selwyn Miller, ed., *Social Change and Fundamental Law, America's Evolving Constitution* (Westport, Conn.: Greenwood, 1979), 110–11, 137–38, 348; Eugene C. Gerhart, *America's Advocate, Robert H. Jackson* (Indianapolis: Bobbs, 1958), 95.

16. Pope to Reed, Report on Legislative Drafting Project, Pope File, Justice Department Records; Reilly to Perkins, May 1, 1937, Perkins Correspondence.

17. Pope to Reed, Report on Legislative Drafting Project, Pope File, Justice Department Records; Corcoran to Roosevelt, Memo, April 27, 1937, Official File 1560, FDR Papers; Trattner, *Crusade for the Children,* 203–4; Joseph P. Lash, *Dealers and Dreamers: A New Look at the New Deal* (New York: Doubleday, 1988), 334–39; Jonathan Grossman, "Fair Labor Standards Act of 1938: Maximum Struggle for a Minimum Wage," *Monthly Labor Review,* 101: 6 (1978), 22, 25.

18. Confidential Revised Draft, April 30, 1937, Fair Labor Standards Bill File, Secretary Perkins Records.

19. Ibid., Sections 2 and 4.

20. Ibid., Sections 4 and 6.

21. Pope to Reed, Report on Legislative Drafting Project, Pope File, Justice Department Records; Hartman to Pope, May 5, 1937, ibid.; Hartman to Jones, May 5, 1937; and Jones to Robert Cook, May 5, 15, 1937, Records of the Coordinator; Reilly to Perkins, May 5, 1937, Perkins Correspondence.

22. Confidential Revised Draft, May 12, 1937, Fair Labor Standards Bill File, Secretary Perkins Records.

23. Pope to Cohen, May 15, 1937; and Cohen to Pope, May 17, 1937, Pope File, Justice Department Records.

24. Reilly to Perkins, May 5, 10, 1937, Perkins Correspondence; Perkins to Roosevelt, May 13, 1937, Official File 1560, FDR Papers; Perkins to Roosevelt, May 17, 1937, White House File; Perkins to Black, July 31, 1937, Miscellaneous Bills-1937 File, Secretary Perkins Records; U.S. Senate, *Regulating the Products of Child Labor,* S. Rept. 726, 75th Cong., 1st sess. (Washington, D.C., 1937).

25. Connery to James Roosevelt, April 22, 1937, James Roosevelt Papers, Franklin D. Roosevelt Library, Hyde Park, N.Y.; *Franklin D. Roosevelt Papers,* vol. 6, *The Constitution Prevails, 1937,* 205; O. R. Altman, "Second and Third Sessions of the Seventy-Fifth Congress, 1937–1938," *American Political Science Review* 32 (December 1938): 1099, 1102; *New York Times,* May 14, 15, 17, 1937.

26. Confidential Revised Draft, May 20, 1937, Fair Labor Standards Bill File,

Secretary Perkins Records; Benjamin Cohen, The Proposed Fair Labor Standards Act of 1937, Pope File, Justice Department Records.

27. Cohen, The Proposed Fair Labor Standards Act of 1937, Pope File, Justice Department Records.

28. F. G. Grimes to Sullivan Jones and E. J. Tracy, March 3, 1937; Pope to Cohen, May 24, 1937; Hartman to Pope, May 24, 1937; and Pope to Reed, May 21, 1937, Report on Legislative Drafting Project, ibid; Ogburn to Roosevelt, May 21, 1937; and Roosevelt to James Roosevelt, Memo, May 24, 1937, Personal File 3794, FDR Papers.

29. Reilly to Perkins, June 1, 1937, Solicitor's Office, 1937–1938 File, Secretary Perkins Records; Jeremy P. Felt, "The Child Labor Provisions of the Fair Labor Standards Act," *Labor History* 11, no. 4 (fall 1970): 475–77.

30. Beyer to Perkins, May 28, 1937, Perkins Correspondence.

31. Reilly to Perkins, June 1, 1937, Solicitor's Office, 1937–1938 File, Secretary Perkins Records.

32. *New York Times*, May 5, 22, 23, 24, 25, 27, 30, 1937; Fraser, *Labor Will Rule*, 629, note 10.

CHAPTER 5. THE SENATE ABANDONS LIVING WAGES

1. *Franklin D. Roosevelt Papers*, vol. 6, *The Constitution Prevails, 1937*, 209–14.

2. *Washington Evening Star*, May 25, 1937; *New York Times*, May 25, 1937.

3. *Washington Evening Star*, May 28, 1937; *New York Times*, May 25, 29, 30, 1937.

4. *Report of the Proceedings of the Fifty-Seventh Annual Convention of the American Federation of Labor, 1937*, (Washington, D.C.: Judd & Detwiler, 1937) 501–2; *Washington Evening Star*, May 22, 27, 29, 1937; *New York Times*, May 29, 1937.

5. Blackwell Smith to Reilly, June 14, 1937, Perkins Correspondence.

6. Beyer to Perkins, May 28, 1937; and Lenroot to Perkins, June 1, 1937, ibid.; Beyer to Perkins, June 4, 1937. Fair Labor Standards Bill-1937 File, Secretary Perkins Records.

7. Sells to Perkins, Memo, June 1, 1937, Fair Labor Standards Bill-1937 File, Secretary Perkins Records.

8. U.S. House of Representatives, *To Regulate the Textile Industry, Hearing*, 75th Cong., 1st sess. (Washington, D.C., 1937), 550–62.

9. Ibid.; M. Ada Beney, *National Industrial Conference Board Studies, No. 238, Differentials in Industrial Wages and Hours in the United States* (New York, National Industrial Conference Board, 1938), 1–5.

10. U.S. Congress, *Fair Labor Standards Act of 1937, Joint Hearings Before the Committee on Education and Labor, U.S. Senate, and Committee on Labor, House of Representatives, on S. 2475 and H.R. 7200*, 75th Cong., 1st sess. (Washington, D.C., 1937), 1–25, 39, 42, 54, 65–67.

11. Reilly to Perkins, June 1, 1937, Perkins Correspondence.

12. U.S. Congress, *Fair Labor Standards Act of 1937, Joint Hearings*, 173–74.

13. Ibid., 175–78.

14. Ibid., 179–80.

15. Ibid., 181–86.

16. Ibid.

17. Ibid., 186, 193, 207.

18. Ibid., 309–10, 316–17, 323–24, 338–43.

19. Ibid., 155–71; Witt Bowden, "Hours and Earnings Before and After the NRA," *Monthly Labor Review*, 44 (January 1937): 13–36.

20. U.S. Congress, *Fair Labor Standards Act of 1937, Joint Hearings*, 623–45, 645–64, 848, 935.

21. Ibid., 91–104, 126–32.

22. W. L. Pope Memo on Proposed Amendments of William Green, n.d., Pope File, Justice Department Records; U.S. Congress, *Fair Labor Standards Act of 1937, Joint Hearings*, 219–36.

23. U.S. Congress, *Fair Labor Standards Act of 1937, Joint Hearings*, 262–68, 271–88, 943–57.

24. Ibid., 262–68.

25. Ibid., 390–93, 396; *New York Times*, June 9, 1937.

26. U.S. Congress, *Fair Labor Standards Act of 1937, Joint Hearings*, 1018–96.

27. John R. Moore, "Senator Josiah W. Bailey and the 'Conservative Manifesto' of 1937," *Journal of Southern History* 31 (February 1965): 21–25; John R. Moore, *Senator Josiah William Bailey of North Carolina* (Durham, N.C.: Duke University Press, 1968), 96, 140; James T. Patterson, *Congressional Conservatism and the New Deal* (Lexington: University of Kentucky Press, 1967), 149–50; *Washington Evening Star*, June 15, 16, 17, 1937.

28. David I. Walsh Press Release, July 8, 1937, David I. Walsh Papers, Dinand Library, Holy Cross College, Worcester, Mass.; U.S. Senate, *Fair Labor Standards Act*, S. Rept. 884, 75th Cong., 1st sess. (Washington, D.C., 1937), 4–9; Hamilton, *Hugo Black*, 264–67; *New York Times*, July 8, 9, 1937; Gerald T. Dunne, *Hugo Black and the Judicial Revolution* (New York: Simon & Schuster, 1977), 170–72.

29. Walsh Press Release, July 8, 1937, David I. Walsh Papers.

30. U.S. Senate, *Fair Labor Standards Act*, 4–5.

31. Reilly to Perkins, July 9, 1937, Perkins Correspondence.

32. C. C. Gilbert to James Farley, July 27, 1937, Official File 2730, FDR Papers; Polenberg, "National Committee to Uphold Constitutional Government, 1937–41," 584; *New York Times*, July 6, 16, 24, 26, 27, 1937.

33. John P. Frey to W. A. Appleton, September 25, 1937, Frey Papers; *Report of the Proceedings of the Fifty-Seventh Annual Convention of the American Federation of Labor, 1937*, 164–65; Charles Madison, "Boss of the 'Fighting Carpenters', William L. Hutchison," *American Scholar* 18 (spring 1949): 164–66; *New York Times*, July 24, 30, 1937.

34. UMW petitions, Senate Committee on Education and Labor Records, National Archives, Washington, D.C.; *Proceedings of the Thirty-Fifth Constitutional Convention of the United Mine Workers of America, January–February, 1938;* 310; *New York Times*, July 18, 28, 29, 30, 1937.

35. Memo on tariff provisions in the Black Wage and Hours Bill (n.d.), Fair Labor Standards Bill-1937 File, Secretary Perkins Records; Perkins to Black, July 24, 1937, Perkins Correspondence; Perkins to Roosevelt, July 25, 1937, Official File 2730, FDR Papers.

36. Cummings to Roosevelt, July 26, 1937, Secretary's File 74, FDR Papers; Alsop and Catledge, *168 Days*, 266–76; Patterson, *Congressional Conservatism and the New Deal*, 145–48; John Forsythe, "Legislative History of the Fair Labor Standards Act," *Law and Contemporary Problems*, 6 (summer 1939): 465, 469–70.

37. Farley to Roosevelt, August 3, 1937, Official File 2730, FDR Papers; *Washington Evening Star*, July 22, 23, 25, 28, 1937.

38. *Congressional Record*, 75th Cong., 1st sess., 7746, 7778–94, 7802–6, 7813, 7878–79, 7921, 7954–57; *New York Times*, July 28, 29, 30, 31, August 1, 1937.

39. *Congressional Record*, 75th Cong., 1st sess., 7778–94, 7809.

40. Ibid., 7746–47.

41. Ibid., 7793, 7801.

42. Ibid., 7940; *New York Times*, August 10, 1937; Roos, *NRA Economic Planning*, 153, 192–94; John A. Zellers, "Wage and Hour Legislation," *Vital Speeches* 3 (October 1937): 762–64.

43. *Congressional Record*, 75th Cong., 1st sess., 7954.

44. Patterson, *Congressional Conservatism and the New Deal*, 152–54; Jerry Voorhis, *Confessions of a Congressman* (Garden City, N.Y.: Doubleday, 1948), 90.

45. *Congressional Record*, 75th Cong., 1st sess., 7890; "Employment Conditions and Unemployment Relief," *Monthly Labor Review* 44 (February 1937): 363–71.

CHAPTER 6. NO RULE IN THE HOUSE

1. Mary T. Norton, "Madam Congressman," 134–40, Mary T. Norton Papers, Alexander Library, Rutgers University, New Brunswick, N.J.; Thomas H. Coode, "Georgia Congressmen and the New Deal, 1933–1938" (Ph.d. diss, University of Georgia, 1966), 22; *Washington Evening Star*, June 18, July 14, 1937.

2. *Washington Evening Star*, July 11, 16, 28, 29, 1937; Voorhis, *Confessions of a Congressman*, 91.

3. *Report of the Proceedings of the Fifty-Seventh Annual Convention of the American Federation of Labor, 1937*, 165–66; *Washington Evening Star*, August 3, 4, 1937; *New York Times*, August 4, 5, 1937; James M. Burns, *Congress on Trial* (New York: Harper, 1949), 73; Katie Louchheim, ed. *The Making of the New Deal, The Insiders Speak* (Cambridge, Mass.: Harvard University Press, 1983), 172.

4. *Report of the Proceedings of the Fifty-Seventh Annual Convention of the American Federation of Labor, 1937*, 166.

5. U.S. House of Representatives, *Fair Labor Standard Act*, H. Rept. 1452, 75th Cong., 1st sess. (Washington, D.C., 1937), 2–3, 5, 10–11, 13, 15–16, 18–20.

6. Farley to Roosevelt, August 3, 1937, Official File 2730, FDR Papers; Lawrence Lewis Diary, August 8, 9, 1937, Lawrence Lewis Papers, State Historical Society of Colorado, Denver Colo.; Zellers, "Wage and Hour Legislation," 762–64; *Washington Evening Star*, August 5, 6, 11, 1937; *New York Times*, August 7, 10, 11, 12, 1937; William Gellerman, *Martin Dies* (New York: John Day Co., 1944), 36–39, 42.

7. Lawrence Lewis Diary, August 11, 13, 1937; Patterson, *Congressional Conservatism and the New Deal*, 179–82; *Washington Evening Star*, August 11, 1937; *New York Times*, August 10, 12, 1937; Altman, "First Session of the Seventy-Fifth Congress, January 5, 1937 to August 21, 1937," *American Political Science Review* 31 (December 1937): 1081–82.

8. Lawrence Lewis Diary, August 10, 11, 13, 14, 27, 1937; Patterson, *Congressional Conservatism and the New Deal*, 182–83; *Washington Evening Star*, August 6, 11, 13, 20, 21, 1937.

9. Lawrence Lewis Diary, August 27, 1937; *Washington Evening Star*, August 19, 21, 22, 23, 1937; *New York Times*, August 21, 22, 25, 1937.

10. *Washington Evening Star*, August 19, 21, 22, 23, 1937; *New York Times*, August 21, 22, 25, 1937.

11. *Franklin D. Roosevelt Papers* vol. 6, *The Constitution Prevails, 1937*, 332–33, 361, 404–5, 429, 435; W. D. McFarlane to Roosevelt, September 9, 1937, Official

File 419, FDR Papers; *Washington Evening Star*, August 28, 29, September 24, 25, 28, October 4, 6, 13, 1937.

12. Cantril, *Public Opinion*, 290, 1019, 1021.

13. National Industrial Conference Board, *Machinery, Employment and Purchasing Power* (New York: National Industrial Conference Board, 1935), 26–28, 101.

14. Harold G. Moulton, "In Defense of the Longer Week," *Annals of the American Academy of Political and Social Science* 184 (March 1936): 68–71; Moulton, *Income and Economic Progress* (Washington, D.C.: Brookings Institution, 1935), 64–67, 102, 111; Moulton et al., *The Recovery Problem in the United States* (Washington, D.C.: Brookings Institution, 1936), 167–76.

15. Paul H. Douglas, "The Economic Theory of Wage Regulation," *University of Chicago Law Review* 5 (February 1938): 184–209.

16. Douglas, *The Theory of Wages* (New York: Augustus M. Kelley, 1964), 67, 94–95.

17. Carroll R. Daugherty, "Wage Policies," *American Economic Review* 28 (March 1938): 155–56; Wolman, "Wage Rates," ibid, 128–30.

18. *Report of the Proceedings of the Fifty-Seventh Annual Convention of the American Federation of Labor, 1937*, 364–65, 501–02; Lubin to Perkins, November 6, 1937, Perkins Correspondence.

19. Berry to Roosevelt, October 26, 1937, Fair Labor Standards Bill-1937 File, Secretary Perkins Records; Roosevelt to Berry, November 5, 1937 (not sent), White House File, ibid.

20. Reilly to Perkins, August 25, 1937; and Mary La Dame to Perkins, November 3, 1937, Perkins Correspondence.

21. Merle D. Vincent to Roosevelt, September 10, 1937, Official File 2730, Perkins to James Roosevelt, Jr., October 23, 1937, Secretary's File 75, FDR Papers; La Dame to Perkins, November 3, 1937, Perkins Correspondence; Beyer to Perkins, October 22, 1937, Secretary Perkins Records; "National Conference on Labor Legislation, 1937," *Monthly Labor Review* 45 (November 1937): 1159–60.

22. Abbott to Perkins, November 4, 1937, Perkins Correspondence.

23. La Dame to Perkins, November 3, 1937, Green to Norton, November 22, 1937, ibid.

24. La Dame to Perkins, November 22, 1937, ibid.

25. National Labor Standards Bill, Fair Labor Standards Bill-1937 File, Secretary Perkins Records; Louchheim, *Making of the New Deal*, 172.

26. National Labor Standards Bill, Fair Labor Standards Bill-1937 File, Secretary Perkins Records.

27. *Franklin D. Roosevelt Papers*, vol. 6, *The Constitution Prevails, 1937*, 490–97.

28. John W. McCormack to Roosevelt, August 23, 1937, Official File 2730, FDR Papers; Norton to Perkins, November 17, 1937, Perkins to Norton, November 22, 1937, Perkins Correspondence; *Washington Evening Star*, November 19, 23, 1937; *New York Times*, November 11, 12, 13, 15, 17, 19, 23, 1937.

29. Green to Norton, November 22, 1937, Perkins Correspondence.

30. Lawrence Lewis Diary, November 19, 29, December 1, 1937; *Washington Evening Star*, November 26, 1937.

31. Lawrence Lewis Diary, November 23, 24, December 2, 1937; Hopkins to McIntyre, December 2, 1937, Official File, 2730, FDR Papers; *Documentary History of the Amalgamated Clothing Workers of America, 1936–1938*, (New York: Herald-Nathan Press, 1938) 241–42; Patterson, *Congressional Conservatism and the New Deal*, 194; *New York Times*, November 19, 20, 23, 26, 29, 30, December 1, 1937.

32. Dewey W. Johnson to Roosevelt, December 15, 1937; American Retail Federa-

tion, ser. 23, Bulletin H, November 24, 1937, Official File 2730, FDR Papers; *Congressional Record*, 75th Cong., 2d sess., 20, 102, 103, 800, 868, 1519; *New York Times*, November 16, 1937.

33. Green to Claude A. Fuller, December 10, 1937; and Green to Hamilton Fish, December 7, 1937, *Congressional Record, Appendix*, 75th Cong., 2d sess., 347, 427; AFL, *Weekly News Service*, December 4, 11, 1937; *Washington Evening Star*, December 4, 5, 6, 10, 11, 1937; *New York Times*, December 4, 5, 7, 1937.

34. Norton Amendment, December 14, 1937, *Congressional Record, Appendix*, 75th Cong., 2d sess., 1511; *Washington Evening Star*, December 9, 10, 11, 1937; *New York Times*, December 9, 10, 12, 13, 1937; Fred A. Hartley, "Wages and Hours," December 3, 1937, *Vital Speeches* 4 (January 1938): 185–86.

35. *Congressional Record*, 75th Cong., 2d sess., 1385–93, 1511–16.

36. Ibid., *Appendix*, 452.

37. *Congressional Record*, 75th Cong., 2d sess., 1395–1415, 1463, 1478, 1483, 1485, 1494, 1497, 1505; *New York Times*, December 15, 16, 1937; "National Minimum for Labor," *New Republic* 93 (December 1, 1937): 88.

38. *Congressional Record*, 75th Cong., 2d sess., 1570–1604, 1664–99; *Washington Evening Star*, December 15, 16, 17, 1937; *New York Times*, December 16, 1937.

39. *Congressional Record*, 75th Cong., 2d sess., 1772–1835; *Washington Evening Star*, December 17, 18, 1937; *New York Times*, December 18, 1937.

40. Norton, "Madam Congressman," Norton Papers, 149–50; *Washington Evening Star*, December 18, 1937; *New York Times*, December 18, 1937.

41. Patterson, *Congressional Conservatism and the New Deal*, 196–97.

42. Editorial, *Washington News*, December 20, 1937, *Congressional Record, Appendix*, 75th Cong., 2d sess., 568; *Washington Evening Star*, December 19, 22, 1937; *New York Times*, December 19, 22, 1937.

43. *Report of the Proceedings of the Fifty-Eighth Annual Convention of the American Federation of Labor, 1938*, (Washington, D.C.: Judd & Detwiler, 1938) 153; *Proceedings of the Thirty-Fifth Constitutional Convention of the United Mine Workers of America, January–February, 1938*, 60–61, 311–12; *Washington Evening Star*, December 19, 1937; *New York Times*, December 19, 22, 1937.

44. Harold Ickes, *Secret Diary*, vol. 2, *Inside Struggle, 1936–39* (New York: Simon & Schuster, 1953), 256, 260, 264; James A. Farley, *Jim Farley's Story* (New York: McGraw-Hill, 1948), 116; Milton Plesur, "The Republican Congressional Comeback of 1938," *Review of Politics* 24 (October 1962): 538–40; Patterson, "The Failure of Party Realignment in the South, 1937–1939," *Journal of Politics* 27 (August 1965): 602–4; *New York Times*, December 21, 1937.

45. *New York Times*, December 19, 1937.

CHAPTER 7. THOU SHALT EAT BREAD

1. *Franklin D. Roosevelt Papers*, vol. 7, *The Continuing Struggle for Liberalism, 1938*, 5–7; Perkins to Gertrude Ely, January 4, 1938, Perkins Correspondence; Maverick to Roosevelt, January 6, 1938, Official File 2730, FDR Papers; *New York Times*, January 4, 1938; *Washington Evening Star*, January 4, 1938; Richard B. Henderson, *Maury Maverick* (Austin: University of Texas Press, 1970), 166.

2. *New York Times*, January 8, 1938; *Washington Evening Star*, January 8, 1938; Senator Claude Pepper to James Roosevelt, February 11, 1938, James Roosevelt Papers; Robert A. Lively, "The South and Freight Rates: Political Settlement of an

Economic Argument," *The Journal of Southern History* 14, no. 3 (August 1948): 357–63, 368.

3. Dies to Roosevelt, January 11, 1938; and Roosevelt to McIntyre, January 13, 1938, Official File 2730, FDR Papers; *New York Times*, January 8, 1938; *Washington Evening Star*, January 8, 1938.

4. Lenroot to Perkins, December 22, 1937; Altmeyer to Perkins, December 23, 1937; La Dame to Perkins, December 29, 1937 and April 7, 1938; Reilly to Perkins, January 5, 1938; and Beyer to Perkins, January 15, 1938, Perkins Correspondence; Beyer to Perkins, January 17, 1938, Special File: Wage and Hour Bill: 1937, Secretary Perkins Records; Harry Haskel, *A Leader of the Garment Workers, The Biography of Isadore Nagler* (New York: Shulsinger Bros., 1950), 214–15.

5. Reilly to Perkins, January 5, 1938, Perkins Correspondence; Perkins to Senator Elbert Thomas, December 10, 1937, Bills: Miscellaneous File, Secretary Perkins Records; Norton, "Madam Congressman," 153–54, Norton Papers; *New York Times*, January 13, 1938; *Washington Evening Star*, January 12, 1938.

6. Perkins to Roosevelt, February 9, 1938, Official File 2730, FDR Papers; Elizabeth Brandeis to Beyer, March 31, 1938, Box 3, Folder 51, Clara M. Beyer Papers, Schlesinger Library, Radcliffe College, Cambridge, Mass.; *New York Times*, February 6, 1938.

7. Cantril, *Public Opinion*, 404, 1032; Beyer to Brandeis, April 5, 1938, Beyer Papers; *New York Times*, February 16, 1938; *Washington Evening Star*, February 16, 1938.

8. *Bill for Wages and Hours Recommended by the American Federation of Labor (Together with an Analysis Thereof)*, Wages and Hours File, John O'Connor Papers, Manuscripts Department, Lilly Library, Indiana University, Bloomington, Ind.; hereafter cited as O'Connor Papers.

9. O'Connor, press release, March 5, 1938, ibid.

10. *New York Times*, February 24, 25, 26, March 2, 1938; *Washington Evening Star*, February 26, 28, March 1, 1938.

11. Perkins to Roosevelt, March 10, 1938, Official File 2730, FDR Papers; Perkins to Representative Bruce Barton, January 26, and 30, February 14, 1938, Perkins Correspondence; Perkins to Barton, February 14, 1938, Wage and Hour Bill: 1937, Secretary Perkins Records; O'Connor press release, March 5, 1938, Wages and Hours File, O'Connor Papers; *New York Times*, March 2, 3, 11, 17, 1938; *Washington Evening Star*, March 7, 8, 25, 1938.

12. Poole to Perkins, March 24, 1938, Perkins Correspondence; Alexander Printz, chairman, National Coat and Suit Industry Recovery Board, to Roosevelt, February 3, 1938; and Vincent to O'Connor, February 16, 1938, Wages and Hours File, O'Connor Papers; *New York Times*, March 23, 24, 26, 1938; *Washington Evening Star*, March 26, 27, 1938.

13. John L. Lewis, radio address, March 15, 1938, *Congressional Record, Appendix*, 75th Cong., 3d sess., 1074–75; John W. Edelman to Roosevelt, March 23, 1938, AFL File, Secretary Perkins Records; Oliver to all House members, March 3, 1938; Vincent to O'Connor, February 16, 1938; Alexander Racolin, American Labor Party, to O'Connor, March 10, 1938; and O'Connor, to J. David Stern, March 8, 1938, Wages and Hours File, O'Connor Papers; *New York Times*, April 4, 1938; *Washington Evening Star*, April 4, 1938.

14. *New York Times*, April 7, 1938; *Washington Evening Star*, April 6, 1938.

15. Frey to Appleton, April 13, 1938, Frey Papers; Poole to Perkins (n.d.), Special File, Wage and Hour Bill: 1937, Secretary Perkins Records; Oliver to Norton, April

7, 1938, Wages and Hours File, O'Connor Papers; *New York Times*, April 12, 13, 1938.

16. Norton to Roosevelt, April 13, 1938, Official File 2730, FDR Papers; *New York Times*, April 14, 1938; *Washington Evening Star*, April 14, 1938; Norton, "Wage and Hour Legislation," *Vital Speeches*, 4 (June 1, 1938), 485–86.

17. U.S. House of Representatives, *Fair Labor Standards Act of 1938*, H. Rept. 2182, 75th Cong., 3d sess. (Washington, D.C., 1938), 1–15; Lambertson, "Wages and Hours Legislation," May 15, 1938, *Congressional Record, Appendix*, 75th Cong., 3d sess., 1993–94; *New York Times*, April 15, 1938; *Washington Evening Star*, April 15, 1938.

18. Poole to Freda Miller, New York State Labor Department, April 21, 1938, Perkins Correspondence; *New York Times*, April 21, 1938; *Washington Evening Star*, April 22, 1938.

19. O'Connor to Sabath, April 15, 1938; and Norton to O'Connor, April 25, 1938, Wages and Hours File, O'Connor Papers; Norton to Perkins, April 22, 1938, Perkins Correspondence.

20. Perkins to Dies, April 26, 28, 1938, Perkins Correspondence.

21. Lawrence Lewis Diary, April 28, 29, 1938; Norton to Roosevelt, April 29, 1938; and Roosevelt to Norton, April 30, 1938; Norton Papers; William C. Hushing, AFL Legislative Representative, to O'Connor, April 29, 1938, Wages and Hours File, O'Connor Papers; *New York Times*, April 28, 1938; *Washington Evening Star*, April 28, 29, 1938.

22. Alexander Rose, American Labor Party, to O'Connor, April 18, 1938; and Oliver to O'Connor, April 19, 1938, Wages and Hours File, O'Connor Papers; *Documentary History of the Amalgamated Clothing Workers of America, 1936–1938*, 241–43; *New York Times*, May 1, 2, 3, 4, 5, 1938; Matthew Josephson, *Sidney Hillman, Statesman of American Labor* (Garden City, N.Y.: Doubleday, 1952), 440, 446–47.

23. Norton, "Madam Congressman," 156, Norton Papers; Perkins to Healey and Mead, May 12, 1938, Perkins Correspondence; *New York Times*, May 7, 1938; *Washington Evening Star*, May 5, 6, 1938.

24. Lawrence Lewis Diary, May 11, 1938; Norton to Perkins, May 17, 1938, Perkins Correspondence; Dies Amendments, May 16, 1938, *Congressional Record, Appendix*, 75th Cong., 3d sess., 2001–2; National Grange letter, May 5, 1938, ibid., 1879–80; Thomas address, May 30, 1938, ibid., 2235–37; *New York Times*, May 10, 11, 1938; *Washington Evening Star*, May 18, 1938.

25. *Congressional Record*, 75th Cong., 3d sess., 7274–79; *New York Times*, May 24, 1938; *Washington Evening Star*, May 23, 1938.

26. *Congressional Record*, 75th Cong., 3d sess., 7286, 7291, 7297, 7298, 7307.

27. Ibid., 7286–87, 7293, 7299, 7387.

28. Ibid., 7389, 7399, 7415–16, 7419.

29. Ibid., 7449; *New York Times*, May 25, 26, 1938; *Washington Evening Star*, May 25, 1938; Patterson, *Congressional Conservatism and the New Deal*, 245.

30. *Congressional Record*, 75th Cong., 3d sess., 7303–4; ibid., *Appendix*, 2024, 2042, 2131.

31. *New York Times*, May 26, 27, 1938; *Washington Evening Star*, May 26, 27, 1938.

32. Thomas address, May 30, 1938, *Congressional Record, Appendix*, 75th Cong., 3d sess., 2235–37; *New York Times*, May 27, 1938; *Washington Evening Star*, May 27, 1938.

33. Reilly to Jay, June 7, 1938, Solicitor's Office File, Secretary Perkins Records; Ellender address, June 5, 1938, *Congressional Record, Appendix*, 75th Cong., 3d sess., 2451–52; Abraham C. Weinfeld, "The Legal Aspects of the Child-Labor Provisions

of the Senate and House Wage-Hour Bill," ibid., 2466–69; *New York Times*, June 3, 4, 5, 7, 1938; *Washington Evening Star*, June 1, 2, 3, 4, 5, 6, 1938.

34. McIntyre to Roosevelt, June 7, 1938, Official File 2730, FDR Papers; Reilly to Jay, June 7, 1938, Solicitor's Office File, Secretary Perkins Records; *New York Times*, June 7, 8, 9, 1938; *Washington Evening Star*, June 7, 8, 9, 1938.

35. U.S. House of Representatives, *Fair Labor Standards Act of 1938*, H. Rept. 2738, 75th Cong., 3d sess. (Washington, D.C.: 1938); *New York Times*, June 10, 11, 12, 1938; *Washington Evening Star*, June 10, 11, 12, 1938; "Fair Labor Standards Act of 1938," sections 4, 5, 6, 7, 8, vol. 52, *Statutes at Large*, 1060–69.

36. *New York Times*, June 11, 12, 13, 1938; *Washington Evening Star*, June 12, 1938.

37. *Congressional Record*, 75th Cong., 3d sess., 9158, 9164–66; *New York Times*, June 13, 1938, *Washington Evening Star*, June 13, 1938.

38. *Congressional Record*, 75th Cong., 3d sess., 9166–78; *New York Times*, June 14, 15, 16, 1938.

39. *Congressional Record*, 75th Cong., 3d sess., 9246, 9255–66; ibid., *Appendix*, 2731, 2883–85.

40. *Washington Evening Star*, June 27, 1938.

41. *Congressional Record*, *Appendix*, 75th Cong., 3d sess., 2731.

42. Albert D. Romasco, *The Politics of Recovery: Roosevelt's New Deal* (New York: Oxford University Press, 1983), 226–30.

CHAPTER 8. OUT OF THE JUNGLE

1. *Franklin D. Roosevelt Papers*, vol. 7, *The Continuing Struggle for Liberalism, 1938*, 391–92, 404; Cantril, *Public Opinion*, 1022.

2. "Wages and Hours," *Commonweal* 29 (November 4, 1938): 46–47; *New York Times*, June 14, 19, 1938.

3. Harry Weiss, "Administering 'Fair Labor Standards'," *American Labor Legislation Review* 28 (September 1938): 133–35; Otto Nathan, "Favorable Economic Implications of the Fair Labor Standards Act," *Law and Contemporary Problems*, 6 (Summer 1939), 416–21; *New York Times*, June 18, 21, 1938.

4. William Green, "Wages and Hours Act," *American Federationist* 45 (July 1938): 689–90; Green, "Wages and Hours Law," ibid., (August 1938): 807.

5. Noel Sargent, "Economic Hazards in the Fair Labor Standards Act," *Law and Contemporary Problems*, 6 (Summer 1939): 422–24.

6. Ibid.

7. Ibid., 425–28.

8. Samuel Herman, "The Administration and Enforcement of the Fair Labor Standards Act," ibid., 371–73.

9. Frank E. Cooper, "The Coverage of the Fair Labor Standards Act and Other Problems in Its Interpretation," ibid., 333–52.

10. Z. Clark Dickinson, "The Organization and Functioning of Industry Committees Under the Fair Labor Standard Act," ibid., 353–64; Calvert Magruder, "Administrative Procedures Under the Fair Labor Standards Act," *American Bar Association Journal* 25 (August 1939): 694.

11. Katharine D. Lumpkin, "The Child Labor Provisions of the Fair Labor Standards Act," *Law and Contemporary Problems* 6 (summer 1939): 393–405.

12. "The Wage and Hour Law," *American Federationist* 45 (October 1938): 1102–3.

13. Herman, "Administration and Enforcement of the Fair Labor Standards Act,"

369–70, 377, 384; Elmer F. Andrews, "Making the Wage-Hour Law Work," *American Labor Legislation Review* 29 (June 1939): 53–61.

14. *New York Times*, August 14, 1938.

15. U.S. Senate, *The First Annual Report of the Administrator of the Wage and Hour Division, United States Department of Labor, 1939*, S. Doc. 142, 76th Cong., 3d sess. (Washington, D.C., 1940), 8.

16. Boris Shishkin, "Wage-Hour Law Administration from Labor's Viewpoint," *American Labor Legislation Review* 29 (June 1939): 64–71; William Green, "Thirty Hour Week," *American Federationist* 45 (November 1938): 1176; *New York Times*, August 24, September 13, 15, 27, 1938.

17. "Interpretations and Regulations Under Fair Labor Standards Act, 1938," *Monthly Labor Review* 48 (January 1939): 152–53.

18. Ibid., 154–61; "Wage and Hour Administration, Area of Production," *American Federationist* 46 (April 1939): 407–9.

19. "Interpretations and Regulations Under Fair Labor Standards Act, 1938," 154–61.

20. "Operation of Wage and Hour Law, 1938," *Monthly Labor Review*, 48 (March 1939): 657–59; Daugherty, "The Economic Coverage of the Fair Labor Standards Act: A Statistical Study," *Law and Contemporary Problems* 6 (summer 1939): 406–7; S. Harold Shefelman, "Fair Labor Standards Act of 1938," *Washington Law Review* 14 (January 1939): 66: Andrews, "The Administration of the Fair Labor Standards Act in the United States," *International Labor Review* 40 (November 1939): 616–40.

21. Andrews, "Making the Wage-Hour Law Work," 59–61; Leon Despres, "Wage and Hour Act," *The John Marshall Law Quarterly* 4 (December 1938), 314–22.

22. "Minimum Wages in the Hosiery Industry Under Wage and Hour Act," *Monthly Labor Review* 49 (October 1939): 912–15.

23. Ibid.; Harold November, "Industry Committees Under the Fair Labor Standards Act," *American Federationist* 47 (March 1940): 271–80.

24. American Federation of Labor, *Report of the Proceedings of the Fifty-Ninth Annual Convention of the American Federation of Labor, 1939*, (Washington, D.C.: Judd & Detwiler, 1939) 178–80.

25. *New York Times*, December 1, 9, 10, 15, 16, 1938, January 22, March 16, 1939.

26. U.S. Senate, *First Annual Report of the Administrator of the Wage and Hour Division, 1939*, 160–61.

27. *Congressional Record, Appendix*, 76th Cong., 1st sess., 1585–86, 3618; *New York Times*, March 29, 30, 1939.

28. Andrews to Norton, April 19, 1939, *Congressional Record, Appendix*, 76th Cong., 1st sess., 1567–68.

29. U.S. House of Representatives, *Amendments to the Fair Labor Standard Act of 1938*, H. Rept. 522, 76th Cong., 1st sess. (Washington, D.C., 1939), 6–7.

30. Ibid.

31. Andrews to Norton, July 15, 1939, *Congressional Record, Appendix*, 76th Cong., 1st sess., 3270–74.

32. Norton letter, May 13, 1939, ibid., 2078–80; *New York Times*, April 26, May 14, 16, 1939.

33. *Congressional Record*, 76th Cong., 1st sess., 6622; *New York Times*, June 2, 6, 1939.

34. *Congressional Record, Appendix*, 76th Cong., 1st sess., 3114–5, 3576; *New York Times*, July 12, 14, 19, 1939.

35. *New York Times*, July 21, 22, 23, 26, 1939.

36. Ibid., July 28, 29, 30, August 3, 4, 1939; *Congressional Record*, 76th Cong.,

1st sess., 10257; ibid., *Appendix*, 3649–50; U.S. House of Representatives, *Amendments to Fair Labor Standards Act of 1938*, H. Rept. 1376, 76th Cong., 1st sess. (Washington, D.C., 1939), 1–7.

37. *Congressional Record, Appendix*, 76th Cong., 1st sess., 1892; U.S. House of Representatives, *Amendments to the Fair Labor Standards Act of 1938*, H. Rept. 1448, 76th Cong., 1st sess. (Washington, D.C., 1939).

38. *Congressional Record, Appendix*, 76th Cong., 1st sess., 3820; *New York Times*, October 18, 19, 1939.

39. "Second Year of the Wage and Hour Act," *Monthly Labor Review*, 49 (December 1939): 1439–42; "Minimum Wage for Cotton Industry Under Wage and Hour Act," ibid., 1446–47; *New York Times*, October 23, 1939.

40. "Millinery Wage Under Fair Labor Standards Act," *Monthly Labor Review* 50 (February 1940): 399; "Recent Wage Orders Under Fair Labor Standards Act," ibid. (May 1940): 1194–95; "Wool Industry Wage Under Wage and Hour Law," ibid. (June 1940): 1461; "Garment Workers' Wages Fixed Under Wage and Hour Law," ibid., 1458–61; "Wages in the Hat Industry Under Wage and Hour Law," ibid., 51 (July 1940): 157; "Two Years of the Fair Labor Standards Act," ibid. (September 1940): 554–55; John J. Kolehmainen and John C. Shinn, "Labor and Public Representation on Industry Committees," *American Labor Legislation Review* 31 (December 1941): 175–77.

41. "Fifth National Conference on Labor Legislation," *Monthly Labor Review* 48 (January 1939): 131; "State Wage and Hour Legislation," *American Federationist* 46 (January 1939): 78; Rufus G. Poole, "Relationship of State and Federal Wage and Hour Legislation," *American Labor Legislation Review* 31 (March 1941): 18–21; Clara M. Beyer, "Wage-Hour Inspection, A Federal Program," ibid. (June 1941): 86; Louise Stitt, "State Fair Labor Standards Legislation," *Law and Contemporary Problems* 6 (summer 1939): 455, 458–59, 462–63; Alice S. Cheyney, "The Course of Minimum Wage Legislation in the United States," *International Labor Review* 38 (July 1938): 42–43; Charles C. Rohlfing et al., *Business and Government* (Chicago: Foundation Press, 1941), 610–11, 615.

42. Patterson, "The New Deal and the States," *American Historical Review* 73, no. 1 (October 1967): 70; Poole, "Relationship of State and Federal Wage and Hour Legislation," 18–19.

43. John B. Andrews, "A Southern State Pioneers in Federal Cooperation, Labor Law Administration in North Carolina," *American Labor Legislation Review* 30 (September 1940): 132–33; Virginia G. Cook, "State Cooperation in Enforcement of the Federal Wage-Hour Law," *American Political Science Review* 48 (September 1954): 721–37.

44. Cook, "State Cooperation in Enforcement of the Federal Wage-Hour Law," 734.

45. November, "Enforcement of the Wage and Hour Law," *American Federationist* 47 (February 1940): 144–50.

46. Henry Epstein, "The 'Fair Labor Standard Act of 1938'," *American Bar Association Journal* 14 (December 1938): 965–69; "Wages, Hours, and the Constitution," *Illinois Law Review* 33 (December 1938): 450–58; M. M. Caplin, "The Fair Labor Standards Act: Evils and Burdens in Interstate Commerce," *Virginia Law Review* 15 (January 1939): 341–51; Walter D. Murphy, "The Fair Labor Standards Act of 1938," *Georgetown Law Journal* 27 (February 1939): 470–75; "The Fair Labor Standards Act," *New York University Law Quarterly* 16 (March 1939): 457–58.

47. Henry J. Abraham, *Justices and Presidents, A Political History of Appointments to the Supreme Court* (New York: Oxford University Press, 1985), 209–10, 216,

219–20, 222–23; *Mulford v. Smith,* 307 U.S. 38 (1939), 38–39, 47, 51; "The Federal Wages and Hours Act," *Harvard Law Review* 52 (February 1939): 647; "Interstate Commerce-Federal Regulation of Tobacco Marketing Held Constitutional," ibid. (June 1939): 1364–65.

48. R. S. Smethurst, "How the Supreme Court May View the Fair Labor Standards Act, An Opinion Holding the Act Unconstitutional," *Law and Contemporary Problems* 6 (summer 1939): 445–53; Robert L. Stern, "How the Supreme Court May View the Fair Labor Standards Act: An Opinion Holding the Act Constitutional," ibid., 433–34, 436, 440–41; C. Moxley Featherston, "The Commerce Clause and the Fair Labor Standards Act," *George Washington Law Review* 8 (November 1939): 72–80; J. Lee Rankin, "Federal Wages and Hours Act," *Nebraska Law Bulletin* 18 (December 1939): 162–63.

49. U.S. Senate, *First Annual Report of the Administrator of the Wage and Hour Division, 1939,* 61–68; Irving J. Levy, "A Year of Wage-Hour Litigation," *The Law Society Journal* 8 (November 1939): 740–41.

50. *United States v. Darby,* 312 U.S. 100 (1941), 100–101, 113–26; Paul R. Benson, *The Supreme Court and the Commerce Clause, 1937–1970* (New York: Dunellen Publishing Co., 1970), 86–95; Paul R. Barron, "Constitutional Law-Commerce Clause-Constitutionality of the Fair Labor Standards Act," *Boston University Law Review* 21 (April 1941): 339–43; William T. Pegues and Benjamin B. Taylor, "The Wage and Hour Law in the Supreme Court," *Louisiana Law Review* 3 (March 1941): 605–07.

51. *Opp Cotton Mills, Inc. v. Administrator of the Wage and Hour Division of the Department of Labor,* 312 U.S. 126 (1941), 126–27, 142–44; John A. Wright, "Fair Labor Standards Act," *The John Marshall Law Quarterly* 6 (March 1941): 457–58.

52. "Estimated Differences in Costs of Living, September 15, 1940," *Monthly Labor Review* 51 (December 1940): 1563, table 7; "Minimum Wage Determination for Manufacture of Work Clothing, Under Public Contracts Law," ibid., 44 (March 1937): 686–87; "Income, Family Size, and the Economic Level of the Family," ibid., 50 (January 1940): 115–17; *Congressional Record, Appendix,* 76th Cong., 1st sess., 2822–23; Mordecai Ezekiel, *$2500 a Year, From Scarcity to Abundance* (New York: Harcourt, 1936), 4.

53. James R. Wason, "Legislative History of the Exclusion of Agricultural Employees from the National Labor Relations Act, 1935, and the Fair Labor Standards Act, 1938," Congressional Research Service, Library of Congress (Washington, D.C., 1966), 2–4, 11, 17–18.

CHAPTER 9. GOODNESS AND HOPE

1. Perkins to Frankfurter, June 7, 1945 and Beyer to Perkins, November 1938, Perkins Correspondence; Magruder, "Administrative Procedures Under the Fair Labor Standards Act," 693.

2. W. S. Woytinsky, "The Institutional Setting of the Labor Market," in W. S. Woytinsky and Associates, *Employment and Wages in the United States* (New York: Twentieth Century Fund, 1953), 105–6; Walton H. Hamilton and Douglas Adair, *The Power to Govern* (New York: DeCapo Press, 1972), 17; Orme W. Phelps, "The Legislative Background of the Fair Labor Standards Act," *Journal of Business,* 12 (April 1939): *Supplement,* part 2, 4.

3. Paul H. Douglas, "Are There Laws of Production?" *American Economic Review* 38, no. 1 (March 1948): 4–5; Paul Webbink, "Unemployment in the United States, 1930–1940," *American Economic Review* 30, no. 1 (February 1941): 253;

Dorothea Tuney, "Ten Years Operations Under Fair Labor Standards Act," *Monthly Labor Review* 67 (September 1948): 272; Carrie Glasser, *Wage Differentials, The Case of the Unskilled* (New York: AMS Press, 1968), 155–64.

4. William S. Tyson, "The Fair Labor Standards Act of 1938: A Survey and Evaluation of the First Eleven Years," *Labor Law Journal* 1 (January 1950): 282; Stefan A. Riesenfeld and Richard C. Maxwell, *Modern Social Legislation* (Brooklyn: Foundation Press, 1950), 604–05, 614, 631, 659, 662, 667.

5. Grunfel, "Regulation of Child Labor," in Woytinsky and Associates, *Employment and Wages in the United States*, 122–29; Ella Arviela Merritt and Floy Hendricks, "Trend in Child Labor, 1940–44," *Monthly Labor Review* 60 (April 1945): 757.

6. Vivian Hart, "Minimum Wage Policy and Constitutional Inequality: The Paradox of the Fair Labor Standards Act of 1938," *Journal of Policy History*, 1:3 (1984), 319–43; Yale Brozen, "The Effect of Statutory Minimum Wage Increases on Teen-Age Employment," *Journal of Law and Economics* 12 (April 1969): 109–27; Edward M. Gramlich, "Impact of Minimum Wages on Other Wages, Employment, and Family Incomes," *Brookings Papers on Economic Activity, 1976*, no. 2 (Washington, D.C.: Brookings Institution, 1976), 409, 450–51; John M. Peterson, "Employment Effects of Minimum Wages, 1938–1950," *Journal of Political Economy*, 65 (October 1957): 413, 430; Jacob J. Kaufman and Terry G. Foran, "The Minimum Wage and Poverty," in Sar A. Levitan, Wilbur J. Cohen, and Robert J. Lampman, eds., *Towards Freedom from Want* (Madison, Wis.: Industrial Relations Research Association, 1968), 192–94, 211–15.

7. George T. Stigler, "The Economics of Minimum Wage Legislation," *American Economic Review* 36 (June 1946): 358, 361–63; Lloyd G. Reynolds, "Cutthroat Competition," ibid., 30: 4 (December 1940), 736–47; Gramlich, "Impact of Minimum Wages on Other Wages, Employment and Family Incomes," 458; Finis Welch, *Minimum Wages: Issues and Evidence* (Washington, D.C.: Enterprise Institute, 1987), 1, 44–45; Donald O. Parsons, *Poverty and the Minimum Wage* (Washington, D.C.: American Enterprise Institute for Public Policy Research, 1980), 56–57, 62; Woytinsky, "Wage Theories," in Woytinsky and Associates, *Employment and Wages in the United States*, 548–49, note 1; Leon H. Keyserling, *The Role of Wages in a Great Society, Stressing Minimum-Wage Gains to Help the Working Poor* (Washington, D.C.: Conference on Economic Progress, 1966), 7, 14, 16–17; Allen G. King, "Minimum Wages and the Secondary Labor Market," *Southern Economic Journal* 41 (October 1974): 215, 218; Levitan, *Shorter Hours, Shorter Weeks, Spreading the Work to Reduce Unemployment* (Baltimore: Johns Hopkins University Press, 1977), 28–29; Levitan and Richard S. Belous, *More Than Subsistence: Minimum Wages for the Working Poor* (Baltimore: Johns Hopkins University Press, 1979), 20–23, 52–53, 55–57; *New York Times*, January 16, March 30, 1986.

8. Levitan, *Reducing Worktime as a Means to Combat Unemployment* (Kalamazoo, Mich.: W. E. Upjohn Institute for Employment Research, 1964), 4–9, 12–13; Levitan, *Shorter Hours*, 2–29.

Bibliography

GOVERNMENT & ARCHIVES

Commerce Department. Coordinator for Industrial Cooperation, Council for Industrial Progress. Records of the National Recovery Administration. Record Group 9. National Archives. Washington, D.C.

Justice Department. Walter L. Pope File. Solicitor General's Office. Records of the Department of Justice. Washington, D.C.

Labor Department. Secretary Frances Perkins. General Subject File, 1933–44. Records of the Department of Labor, 1933–45. Record Group 174. National Archives. Washington, D.C.

United States Senate. Labor Committee Records. National Archives. Washington, D.C.

MANUSCRIPT COLLECTIONS

Beyer, Clara M. Papers. Schlesinger Library. Radcliffe College. Cambridge, Mass.

Frey, John P. Papers. Library of Congress, Manuscripts Division. Washington, D.C.

Lewis, John L. Papers. State Historical Society of Wisconsin. Madison, Wis.

Lewis, Lawrence. Papers. State Historical Society of Colorado. Denver, Colo.

National Consumers' League. Papers. Library of Congress, Manuscripts Division. Washington, D.C.

Norton, Mary T. Papers. Alexander Library, Manuscripts Division. Rutgers University. New Brunswick, N.J.

O'Connor, John J. Papers. Lilly Library, Manuscripts Division. Indiana University. Bloomington, Ind.

Perkins, Frances. Papers. Butler Library, Manuscripts Division. Columbia University. New York, N.Y.

Richberg, Donald. Papers. Library of Congress, Manuscripts Division. Washington, D.C.

Roosevelt, Franklin D. Papers. Franklin D. Roosevelt Library. Hyde Park, N.Y.

Roosevelt, James. Papers. Franklin D. Roosevelt Library. Hyde Park, N.Y.

Walsh, David I. Papers. Dinand Library, Manuscriptions Division. Holy Cross College. Worcester, Mass.

GOVERNMENT PUBLICATIONS

Annual Report of the Federal Trade Commission for the Fiscal Year Ending June 30, 1935. Washington, D.C., 1935.

Chin, Felix, "Minimum Wage: Selected References, 1978–87." Congressional Research Service, Library of Congress. Washington, D.C., 1966.

Coordinator for Industrial Cooperation, Council for Industrial Progress. *Recommendations and Representation of the Council for Industrial Progress.* Washington, D.C., 1937.

————. *Reports of Committees and Resolutions Adopted, March 12, 1936.* Washington, D.C., 1936.

Fritsch, Conrad F., and Steven E. Connell. "Evolution of Wage and Hour Laws in the United States." *Report of the Minimum Wage Study Commission.* 7 vols. Washington, D.C., 1981, Vol. 2.

Otey, Elizabeth L. *The Beginnings of Child Labor Legislation in Certain States, A Comparative Study.* Vol. 6, *Report on Condition of Women and Child Wage-Earners in the United States.* S. Doc. No. 645, 61st Cong., 2d sess. Washington, D.C., 1910.

Stewart, William J. *The Era of Franklin D. Roosevelt, A Selected Bibliography of Periodical and Dissertation Literature, 1945–1966.* Government Service Administration, National Archives and Record Center, Franklin D. Roosevelt Library, Hyde Park, N.Y., 1967.

U.S. Congress. *Fair Labor Standards Act of 1937. Joint Hearings Before the Committee on Education and Labor, U.S. Senate, and Committee on Labor, House of Representatives, on S. 2475 and H.R. 7200,* 75th Cong., 1st sess. Washington, D.C., 1937.

U.S. *Congressional Record,* 76–85 (1933–39).

U.S. Department of Labor. *Twentieth Annual Report of the Secretary of Labor, 1932.* Washington, D.C., 1932.

————. *Twenty-First Annual Report of the Secretary of Labor, 1933.* Washington, D.C., 1934.

————. U.S. Department of Labor, Bureau of Labor Statistics. *Monthly Labor Review.*

"An Employer's View of High Wages and Industrial Relations." 25 (November 1927).

Bowden, Witt. "Employment, Hours, Earnings and Production Under the N.R.A.) 37 (May 1934).

"Continuation of Office of Coordinator for Industrial Cooperation." 42 (May 1936).

"Convention of the American Federation of Labor, 1933." 37 (November 1933).

"Coordinator for Industrial Cooperation." 41 (November 1935).

"Cost of Living." 40 (May 1935).

"Council for Industrial Progress Adopts Committee Reports." 42 (April 1936).

"Creation of Committee to Complete Summary of N.R.A. Accomplishments." 42 (May 1936).

"Departures from N.R.A. Standards by Manufacturing Industries." 42 (May 1936).

Elder, Peyton K., and Heidi D. Miller. "The Fair Labor Standards Act: Changes of Four Decades." 102 (July 1979).

"Employment Conditions and Unemployment Relief." 44 (February 1937).

"Estimated Differences in Costs of Living, September 15, 1940." 51 (December 1940).

"Fifth National Conference on Labor Legislation." 48 (January 1939).

"Garment Workers' Wages Fixed Under Wage and Hour Law." 50 (June 1940).

Grossman, Jonathan. "Fair Labor Standards Act of 1938: Maximum Struggle for a Minimum Wage." 101 (June 1978).

"Income, Family Size, and the Economic Level of the Family." 50 (January 1940).

"Interpretations and Regulations Under Fair Labor Standards Act, 1938." 48 (January 1939).

"Legislative Program Endorsed by Council for Industrial Progress." 44 (February 1937).

"Meeting of the Council for Industrial Cooperation." 42 (February 1936).

Merritt, Ella Arvilla, and Floy Hendricks. "Trend in Child Labor, 1940–44." 60 (April 1945).

"Millinery Wage Under Fair Labor Standards Act." 50 (February 1940).

"Minimum Wage Determination for Manufacture of Work Clothing, Under Public Contracts Law." 44 (March 1937).

"Minimum Wage for Cotton Industry Under Wage and Hour Act." 49 (December 1939).

"Minimum Wages in the Hosiery Industry Under Wage and Hour Act." 49 (October 1939).

"Minimum Wage Legislation in the United States." 37 (December 1933).

"National Conference on Labor Legislation, 1937." 45 (November 1937).

"National Income, 1936." 45 (August 1937).

"National Recovery Program." 38 (April 1934).

"National Recovery Program, Extension of National Industrial Recovery Act." 41 (August 1935).

"Operation of Wage and Hour Law, 1938." 48 (March 1939).

"Recent Wage Orders Under Fair Labor Standards Act." 50 (May 1940).

"Second Year of the Wage and Hour Act." 49 (December 1939).

"Termination of National Recovery Administration." 42 (February 1936).

"Testing the Adequacy of Wages." 32 (May 1931).

Tuney, Dorothea. "Ten Years Operations Under Fair Labor Standards Act." 67 (September 1948).

"Two Years of the Fair Labor Standards Act." 51 (September 1940).

"Wage Determinations for Garment Contracts," 45 (September 1937).

"Wages and Hours of Labor, A Basic Principle for Determining Wages—A Trade-Union Viewpoint." 22 (March 1926).

"Wages in the Hat Industry Under Wage and Hour Law." 51 (July 1940).

"Wool Industry Wage Under Wage and Hour Law." 50 (June 1940).

"Works Program Under Relief Act of 1935." 41 (August 1935).

U.S. House of Representatives. *Amendment to the Fair Labor Standards Act of 1938.* H. Rept. 1448. 76th Cong., 1st sess., 1939.

———. *Amendments to Fair Labor Standards Act of 1938.* H. Rept. 1376. 76th Cong., 1st sess., 1939.

———. *Amendments to the Fair Labor Standards Act of 1938.* H. Rept. 522. 76th Cong., 1st sess., 1939.

———. *Extension of National Industrial Recovery Act.* H. Rept. 1115. 74th Cong., 1st sess., 1935.

———. *Extension of National Industrial Recovery Act, Hearings.* 74th Cong., 1st sess. 1935.

———. *Fair Labor Standards Act.* H. Rept. 1452. 75th Cong., 1st sess., 1937.

———. *Fair Labor Standards Act of 1938.* H. Rept. 2182. 75th Cong., 3d sess., 1938.

———. *Fair Labor Standards Act of 1938.* H. Rept. 2738. 75th Cong., 3d sess., 1938.

———. *Hearings, H. Joint Resolution 295.* 74th Cong., 1st sess., 1935.

———. *Prevent Interstate Commerce in Industrial Activities in Which Persons Are Employed More than Five Days Per Week or Six Hours Per Day.* H. Rept. 1999. 72d Cong., 2d sess., 1933.

———. *Six-Hour Day Five-Day Week, Hearings.* 72d Cong., 2d sess., 1933.

———. *Thirty-Hour Week Bill.* H. Rept. 124, 73d Cong., 1st sess., 1933.

———. *Thirty-Hour Week Bill.* H. Rept. 1550. 74th Cong., 1st sess., 1935.

———. *Thirty-Hour Week for Industry.* H. Rept. 889. 73d Cong., 2d sess., 1934.

———. *To Prevent Interstate Commerce in Industrial Activities In Which Persons Are Employed More than 5 Days Per Week or 6 Hours Per day.* H. Rept. 24. 73d Cong., 1st sess., 1933.

———. *To Regulate the Textile Industry, Hearing.* 75th Cong., 1st sess., 1937.

U.S. Senate. *Bituminous Coal Commission, Hearing.* 70th Cong., 2d sess., 1929.

———. *Cotton Textile Industry.* S. Doc. 126. 74th Cong., 1st sess., 1935.

———. *Extension of National Recovery Act.* S. Rept. 570. 74th Cong., 1st sess., 1935.

———. *Fair Labor Standards Act.* S. Rept. 884. 75th Cong., 1st sess., 1937.

———. *The First Annual Report of the Administrator of the Wage and Hour Division, . . . United States Department of Labor. 1939.* S. Doc. 142. 76th Cong., 3d sess., 1940.

———. *Investigation of the National Recovery Administration, Hearings.* 74th Cong., 1st sess., 1935.

———. *National Income, 1929–32.* S. Doc. 124. 73d Cong., 2d sess., 1934.

———. *Regulating the Products of Child Labor.* S. Rept. 726. 75th Cong., 1st sess., 1937.

———. *Thirty-Hour Work Week.* S. Rept. 367. 74th Cong., 1st sess., 1935.

———. *Thirty-Hour Work Week, Hearings.* 72d Cong., 2d sess., 1933.

———. *Thirty-Hour Work Week, Hearings.* 74th Cong., 1st sess., 1935.

U.S. *Statutes at Large:*

Fair Labor Standards Act of 1938. Vol. 52.

National Industrial Recovery Act. Vol. 48.

National Industrial Recovery Act, Duration of Act. Vol. 49.

Transportation Act of 1920. Vol. 41.

Wason, James R. "Legislative History of the Exclusion of Agricultural Employees from the National Labor Relations Act, 1935, and the Fair Labor Standards Act, 1938." Congressional Research Service, Library of Congress Washington, D.C., 1966.

Supreme Court Cases

Adkins v. *Children's Hospital*, 261 U.S. 525(1923).

A.L.A. Schechter Poultry Corp. v. *United States*, 259 U.S. 495(1935).

Bailey v. *Drexel Furniture Company*, 259 U.S. 20(1922).

Bunting v. *Oregon*, 243 U.S. 426(1917).

Carter v. *Carter Coal Company*, 298 U.S. 238(1936).

Employers' Liability Cases, 207 U.S. 463(1908).

Hammer v. *Dagenhart*, 247 U.S. 251(1918).

Highland v. *Russell Car Co.*, 279 U.S. 253(1929).

Kentucky Whip & Collar Co. v. *Illinois Central Railroad Co.*, 299 U.S. 334(1937).

Lochner v. *New York*, 198 U.S. 45(1905).

Morehead v. *New York ex rel. Tipaldo*, 298 U.S. 587(1936).

Mulford v. *Smith*, 307 U.S. 38(1939).

Muller v. *Oregon*, 208 U.S. 412(1908).

National Labor Relations Board v. *Jones & Laughlin Steel Corp.*, 301 U.S. 1(1937).

New State Ice Co. v. *Liebmann*, 285 U.S. 262(1932).

Opp Cotton Mills, Inc. et al. v. *Administrator of the Wage and Hour Division of the Department of Labor*, 312 U.S. 126(1941).

Panama Refining Co. v. *Ryan*, 293 U.S. 388, 414(1935).

Ribnik v. *McBride*, 277 U.S. 350(1928).

Sonzinsky v. *United States*, 300 U.S. 506(1937).

Stettler v. *O'Hara*, 243 U.S. 629(1917).

United States v. *Darby*, 312 U.S. 100(1941).

West Coast Hotel Co. v. *Parrish*, 300 U.S. 379(1937).

Wilson v. *New*, 243 U.S. 332(1917).

SECONDARY SOURCES

Abraham, Henry J. *Justices and Presidents, A Political History of Appointments to the Supreme Court*. New York: Oxford University Press, 1985.

Adams, Arthur B. *Trend of Business, Yesterday–Today–Tomorrow*. New York: Harper & Bros., 1932.

Akin, William E. *Technocracy and the American Dream: The Technocratic Movement, 1900–41*. Berkeley, University of California Press, 1977.

Alinsky, Saul. *John L. Lewis, An Unauthorized Biography*. New York, G. P. Putnam's Sons., 1949.

Alsop, Joseph, and Turner Catledge. *The 168 Days*. Garden City, N.Y.: Doubleday, Doran & Co., 1938.

Amalgamated Clothing Workers Union. *Documentary History of the Amalgamated Clothing Workers of America, 1936–1938*. New York: Herald Nathan Press, 1938.

American Federation of Labor. *Report of the Proceedings of the Fifty-Fifth Annual Convention of the American Federation of Labor, 1935*.

———. *Report of the Proceedings of the Fifty-Sixth Annual Convention of the American Federation of Labor, 1936*.

———. *Report of the Proceedings of the Fifty-Seventh Annual Convention of the American Federation of Labor, 1937*.

———. *Report of the Proceedings of the Fifty-Eighth Annual Convention of the American Federation of Labor, 1938*.

————. *Report of the Proceedings of the Fifty-Ninth Annual Convention of the American Federation of Labor, 1939.*

Anderson, James R. "The New Deal Career of Frances Perkins, Secretary of Labor, 1933–1939," diss., Case Western Reserve University, 1968.

Armstrong, Barbara N. *Insuring the Essentials, Minimum Wage Plus Social Insurance— A Living Wage Program.* New York: Macmillan Co., 1932.

Baer, Judith A. *Chains of Protection, The Judicial Response to Women's Labor Legislation.* Westport, Conn.: Greenwood Press, 1978.

Barber, William J. *From New Era to New Deal: Hoover, the Economists, and American Economic Policy, 1921–33.* Cambridge, Cambridge University Press, 1985.

Beard, Charles A., ed. *America Faces the Future.* Boston: Houghton Mifflin Co., 1932.

Bellush, Bernard. *The Failure of the NRA.* New York, W. W. Norton & Co., 1975.

Beney, M. Ada. *National Industrial Conference Board Studies, No. 238, Differentials in Industrial Wages and Hours in the United States.* New York, 1938.

Benson, Paul R. *The Supreme Court and the Commerce Clause, 1937–1970.* New York: Dunellen Publishing Co., 1970.

Bercusson, Brian. *Fair Wages Resolutions.* London: Mansell, 1978.

Bernstein, Irving. *A Caring Society. The New Deal, The Worker, and the Great Depression.* Boston: Houghton Mifflin Co., 1985.

————. *The Lean Years.* Boston: Houghton Mifflin Co., 1960.

————. *The New Deal Collective Bargaining Policy.* Berkeley: University of California Press, 1950.

————. *Turbulent Years.* Boston: Houghton Mifflin Co., 1970.

Braeman, John, Robert Bremner, and David Brody, eds. *The New Deal, I, The National Period.* Columbus, Ohio State University Press, 1975.

Brauer, Jerald C., ed. *The Westminster Dictionary of Church History.* Philadelphia: Westminster Press, 1971.

Bremner, Robert. *From the Depths.* New York: New York University Press, 1956.

Brown, Douglas V. et al. *The Economics of the Recovery Program.* New York: McGraw-Hill Co., 1934.

Burns, James M. *Congress on Trial.* New York: Harper & Bros., 1949.

————. *Roosevelt: The Lion and the Fox.* New York: Harcourt, Brace & Co., 1956.

Cahill, Marion C. *Shorter Hours.* New York: AMS Press, 1968.

Cantril, Hadley. *Public Opinion, 1935–1946.* Princeton: Princeton University Press, 1951.

Chambers, Clarke A. *Seedtime of Reform, American Social Service and Social Action, 1918–1933.* Minneapolis: University of Minnesota Press, 1963.

Chandler, Lester V. *America's Greatest Depression, 1929–1941.* New York: Harper & Row, Publishers, 1970.

Comish, Newel H. *The Standard of Living.* New York: Macmillan Co., 1923.

Commons, John R. and associates. *History of Labor in the United States, 1896–1932.* Vol. 3. New York: Macmillan Co., 1935.

————, and John B. Andrews. *Principles of Labor Legislation.* New York: Augustus M. Kelley, 1967.

Conkin, Paul K. *FDR and the Origins of the Welfare State.* New York: Thomas Y. Crowell Co., 1967.

Coode, Thomas H. "Georgia Congressmen and the New Deal, 1933–1938." Ph.D. diss., University of Georgia, 1966.

Cortner, Richard C. *The Jones & Laughlin Case.* New York: Alfred A. Knopf, 1970.

Corwin, Edward S. *The Commerce Power versus States Rights.* Princeton: Princeton University Press, 1936.

Crawford, Kenneth G. *The Pressure Boys.* New York: Julian Messner, 1939.

Critchlow, Donald T. *The Brookings Institution, 1916–1952, Expertise and the Public Interest in a Democratic Society.* DeKalb: Northern Illinois University Press, 1985.

Cronbach, Abraham. *The Bible and Our Social Outlook.* Cincinnati: Union of American Hebrew Congregations, 1941.

Curtis, Charles P. *Lions Under the Throne.* Boston: Houghton Mifflin Co., 1947.

Dawson, Nelson L. *Lewis D. Brandeis, Felix Frankfurter and the New Deal.* Hamden, Conn.: Archon Books/The Shoe String Press, 1980.

Dearing, Charles L. et al. *The ABC of the NRA.* Washington, D.C.: Brookings Institution, 1934.

Derber, Milton, and Edwin Young, eds. *Labor and the New Deal.* Madison: University of Wisconsin Press, 1957.

Desvernine, Raoul E. *Democratic Despotism.* New York: Dodd Mead and Co., 1936.

Dickinson, Roy. *Wages and Wealth, This Business Roller-Coaster.* Princeton: Princeton University Press, 1931.

Dorfman, Joseph. *The Economic Mind in American Civilization, 1918–1933.* Vols. 4, 5. New York: Viking Press, 1959.

Douglas, Paul H. *Controlling Depressions.* New York: W. W. Norton Co., 1935.

———. *Real Wages in the United States, 1890–1926.* New York: Augustus M. Kelley, 1966.

———. *The Theory of Wages.* New York: Augustus M. Kelley, 1964.

Dubofsky, Melvin, and Warren Van Tine. *John L. Lewis: A Biography.* New York: Quadrangle/New York Times Book Co., 1977.

Dulles, Foster F. *Labor in America.* New York: Thomas Y. Crowell Co., 1966.

Dunne, Gerald T. *Hugo Black and the Judicial Revolution.* New York: Simon & Schuster, 1977.

Eliot, Thomas D., ed. *American Standards and Planes of Living.* Boston: Ginn & Co., 1931.

Ezekiel, Mordecai. *$2500 a Year, from Scarcity to Abundance.* New York: Harcourt, Brace & Co., 1936.

Farber, Milton L. "Changing Attitudes of the American Federation of Labor Toward Business and Government." Ph.D. diss., Ohio State University, 1959.

Farley, James A. *Behind the Ballots.* New York: Harcourt Brace and Co., 1938.

———. *Jim Farley's Story.* New York: McGraw-Hill Co., 1948.

Faulkner, Harold U. *The Decline of Laissez Faire, 1897–1917.* New York: Harper & Row, Publishers, 1951.

Fay, Charles N. *Labor in Politics, Or Class Versus Country* Cambridge, Mass.: University Press, 1920.

Feis, Herbert. *The Settlement of Wage Disputes.* New York: Macmillan Co., 1921.

Fogarty, Michael P. *The Just Wage.* London: Geoffrey Chapman, 1961.

Frank, John P. *Mr. Justice Black, The Man and His Opinions*. New York: Alfred A. Knopf, 1949.

Fraser, Steven. *Labor Will Rule: Sidney Hillman and the Rise of American Labor*. New York, The Free Press, 1991.

Freedman, Max. *Roosevelt and the Frankfurter, Their Correspondence, 1928-1945*. Boston: Little, Brown and Co., 1967.

Freidel, Frank. *F.D.R. and the South*. Baton Rouge: Louisiana State University Press, 1965.

———. *Franklin D. Roosevelt, Launching the New Deal*. Boston: Little, Brown and Co., 1973.

Frish, Michael H. and David J. Walkowitz. eds. *Working Class America: Labor, Community, and American Society*. Urbana, University of Illinois Press, 1983.

Fusfield, Daniel R. *The Economic Thought of Franklin D. Roosevelt and the Origins of the New Deal*. New York: Columbia University Press, 1956.

Galambos, Louis. *Competition & Cooperation, The Emergence of a National Trade Association*. Baltimore: Johns Hopkins University Press, 1966.

Galbraith, John K. *American Capitalism, The Concept of Countervailing Power*. Boston: Houghton Mifflin Co., 1962.

———. *The Great Crash*. Boston: Houghton Mifflin Co., 1961.

Garraty, John A. *Unemployment in History*. New York: Harper & Row, Publishers, 1978.

Gearty, Patrick W. *The Economic Thought of Monsignor John A. Ryan*. Washington, D.C.: Catholic University of America Press, 1953.

Gellerman, William. *Martin Dies*. New York: John Day Co., 1944.

Gerhart, Eugene C. *America's Advocate, Robert H. Jackson*. Indianapolis: Bobbs-Merrill Co., 1958.

Glasser, Carrie. *Wage Differentials, The Case of the Unskilled*. New York: AMS Press, 1968.

Goldmark, Josephine. *Impatient Crusader*. Westport, Conn.: Greenwood Press, 1976.

Gompers, Samuel. *Labor and the Common Welfare*. New York: E. P. Dutton & Co., 1919.

Graham, Otis L. *An Encore for Reform, The Old Progressives and the New Deal*. New York: Oxford University Press, 1967.

Green, William. *Labor and Democracy*. Princeton: Princeton University Press, 1939.

Hallgren, Mauritz A. *The Gay Reformer*. New York: Alfred A. Knopf, 1935.

Hamilton, Virginia V. *Hugo Black, The Alabama Years*. Baton Rouge: Louisiana State University, 1972.

Hamilton, Walton H., and Douglas Adair. *The Power to Govern*. New York: DeCapo Press, 1972.

Haskel, Harry. *A Leader of the Garment Workers, The Biography of Isadore Nagler*. New York: Shulsinger Bros. Co., 1950.

Henderson, Richard B. *Maury Maverick*. Austin: University of Texas Press, 1970.

Hawley, Ellis W. *The New Deal and the Problem of Monopoly*. Princeton: Princeton University Press, 1966.

Higgins, George G. *Voluntarism in Organized Labor in the United States, 1930-1940*. New York: Arno Press, 1969.

High, Stanley. *Roosevelt—And Then?* New York: Harper & Bros., 1937.

Himmelberg, Robert F. *The Origins of the National Recovery Administration.* New York: Fordham University Press, 1976.

Hodges, James A. *New Deal Labor Policy and the Southern Cotton Textile Industry.* Knoxville, University of Tennessee Press, 1986.

Hoover, Herbert. *American Individualism.* Garden City, N.Y.: Doubleday, Page & Co., 1922.

———. *Memoirs.* Vol. 2, *The Cabinet and the Presidency, 1920–1933.* New York: Macmillan Co., 1952.

———. *Memoirs.* Vol. 3, *The Great Depression, 1929–1941.* New York: Macmillan Co., 1952.

Horowitz, Daniel. *The Morality of Spending: Attitudes Towards the Consumer Society in America, 1875–1940.* Baltimore, The Johns Hopkins Press, 1985.

Howard, Donald S. *The WPA and Federal Relief Policy.* New York: Russell Sage Foundation, 1943.

Hughes, Charles E. *The Supreme Court of the United States.* New York: Columbia University Press, 1966.

Hunnicutt, Benjamin K. *Work Without End: Abandoning Shorter Hours for the Right to Work.* Philadelphia, Temple University Press, 1988.

Husslein, Joseph. *Bible and Labor.* New York: Macmillan Co., 1924.

Huthmacher, J. Joseph. *Senator Robert F. Wagner and the Rise of Urban Liberalism.* New York, Atheneum Publishers, 1968.

Ickes, Harold. *Secret Diary.* Vol. 1, *The First Thousand Days, 1933–36.* New York, Simon & Schuster, 1953.

———. *Secret Diary.* Vol. 2, *Inside Struggle, 1936–39.* New York: Simon & Schuster, 1953.

Jackson, Robert H. *The Struggle for Judicial Supremacy.* New York: Random House, 1941.

Johnson, Donald B., ed. *National Party Platforms.* Urbana: University of Illinois Press, 1978.

Jones, Harry E. *Railroad Wages and Labor Relations, 1900–1952.* New York: Bureau of Information of the Eastern Railways, 1953.

Josephson, Matthew. *Sidney Hillman, Statesman of American Labor.* Garden City, N.Y.: Doubleday & Co., 1952.

Karis, Thomas G. "Congressional Behavior at Constitutional Frontiers, From 1906, The Beveridge Child Labor Bill, to 1938, The Fair Labor Standards Act." Ph.D. diss., Columbia University, 1951.

Kaun, David E. "Economics of the Minimum Wage: The Effects of the Fair Labor Standards Act, 1945–1964." Ph.D. diss., Stanford, 1964.

Keir, Malcolm. *Labor's Search for More.* New York: Ronald Press Co., 1937.

Kessler-Harris, Alice. *Out of Work: A History of Wage-Earning Women in the United States.* New York: Oxford University Press, 1982.

Keyserling, Leon H. *The Role of Wages in a Great Society, Stressing Minimum-Wage Gains to Help the Working Poor.* Washington, D.C.: Conference on Economic Progress, 1966.

Koenig, Louis W. *The Invisible Presidency.* New York: Rinehart & Co., 1960.

Lash, Joseph P. *Dealers and Dreamers, A New Look at the New Deal.* New York: Doubleday & Company, 1988.

Lauck, W. Jett. *The New Industrial Revolution and Wages.* New York: Funk & Wagnalls Co., 1929.

———, and Claude S. Watts. *The Industrial Code.* New York: Funk & Wagnalls Co., 1922.

Layton, Edward T., Jr. *The Revolt of the Engineers.* Cleveland: Press of Case Western Reserve University, 1971.

Leuchtenburg, William E. *Franklin D. Roosevelt and the New Deal, 1932–1940.* New York: Harper & Row, Publishers, 1963.

Levine, Louis. *The Women's Garment Workers.* New York: B. W. Heubsch, 1924.

Levitan, Sar A. *Reducing Worktime as a Means to Combat Unemployment:* Kalamazoo, Mich.: W. E. Upjohn Institute for Employment Research, 1964.

———. *Shorter Hours, Shorter Weeks, Spreading the Work to Reduce Unemployment.* Baltimore: Johns Hopkins University Press, 1977.

———, and Richard S. Belous. *More Than Subsistence: Minimum Wages for the Working Poor.* Baltimore: Johns Hopkins University Press, 1979.

———, Wilbur J. Cohen, and Robert J. Lampman. eds. *Towards Freedom From Want.* Madison, Wis.: Industrial Relations Research Assn., 1968.

Louchheim, Katie, ed. *The Making of the New Deal: The Insiders Speak.* Cambridge, Mass.: Harvard University Press, 1983.

Lubell, Samuel. *The Future of American Politics.* New York: Harper & Bros., 1952.

Lubin, Isador. *The Reminiscences of Isador Lubin.* Columbia University Oral History Collection, N.Y., 1957.

Lumpkin, Katharine D., and Dorothy W. Douglas. *Child Workers in America.* New York: Robert M. McBride and Co., 1937.

Lyon, Leverett S. et al. *The National Recovery Administration, An Analysis and Appraisal.* Washington, D.C.: Brookings Institution, 1935.

Martin, George. *Madam Secretary, Frances Perkins.* Boston: Houghton Mifflin Co., 1976.

Martin, Joe. *My First Fifty Years in Politics.* New York: McGraw-Hill Book Company, 1960.

Mason, Alpheus T., and Gerald Garvey, eds. *American Constitutional History, Essays by Edward S. Corwin.* New York: Harper & Row, Publishers; 1964.

McFarland, Charles K. *Roosevelt, Lewis, and the New Deal, 1933–1940.* Fort Worth: Texas Christian University Press, 1970.

Mencher, Samuel. *Poor Law to Poverty Program, Economic Security Policy in Britain and the United States.* Pittsburgh: University of Pittsburgh Press, 1967.

Mendenshausen, Horst. *Changes in Income Distribution During the Great Depression.* New York: National Bureau of Economic Research, 1946.

Michelson, Charles. *The Ghost Talks.* New York: G. P. Putnam's Sons, 1944.

Miller, Arthur Selwyn, ed. *Social Change and Fundamental Law, America's Evolving Constitution.* Westport, Conn.: Greenwood Press, 1979.

Moley, Raymond. *After Seven Years.* New York: Harper & Bros., 1939.

Moore, John R. *Senator Josiah William Bailey of North Carolina.* Durham, N.C.: Duke University Press, 1968.

Morris, James O. *Conflict Within the AFL, A Study of Craft Versus Industrial Unionism, 1901–1938.* Ithaca: Cornell University Press, 1958.

Moulton, Harold J. *Income and Economic Progress.* Washington, D.C., Brookings Institution, 1935.

———. *The Recovery Problem in the United States.* Washington, D.C., Brookings Institution, 1936.

Murphy, Bruce Allen. *The Brandeis/Frankfurter Connection, The Secret Political Activities of Two Supreme Court Justices.* New York: Oxford University Press, 1982.

National Consumers' League. *The Supreme Court and Minimum Wage Legislation.* New York: New Republic, 1925.

National Industrial Conference Board. *Machinery, Employment, and Purchasing Power.* New York: National Industrial Conference Board, 1935.

———. *The Five-Day Week in Manufacturing Industries.* New York: National Industrial Conference Board, 1929.

———. *The Thirty-Hour Work Week.* New York: National Industrial Conference Board, 1935.

———. *Wages and Hours in American Industry.* New York: National Industrial Conference Board, 1925.

Neufeld, Maurice F. *A Representative Bibliography of American Labor History.* Ithaca: Cornell University Press, 1964.

Nichols, Egbert R., and Joseph H. Baccus, eds. *Selected Articles on Minimum Wages and Maximum Hours.* New York: H. W. Wilson Co., 1937.

O'Brien, David J. *American Catholics and Social Reform.* New York, Oxford University Press, 1968.

Ohl, John Kennedy. *Hugh S. Johnson and the New Deal.* DeKalb: Northern Illinois University Press, 1985.

Ornati, Oscar A. *Poverty Amid Affluence: A Report on a Research Project carried out at the New School for Social Research.* New York. The Twentieth Century Fund, 1966.

Parrish, Michael E. *Felix Frankfurter and His Times.* New York: Free Press, 1982.

Parsons, Donald O. *Poverty and the Minimum Wage.* Washington, D.C.: American Enterprise Institute for Public Policy Research, 1980.

Paster, Irving I. "National Minimum Wage Regulation in the United States." Ph.D. diss.,University of Michigan, 1948.

Patterson, James R. *Congressional Conservatism and the New Deal.* Lexington: University of Kentucky Press, 1967.

Perkins, Frances. *People at Work.* New York: John Day Co., 1934.

———. *Reminiscences of Frances Perkins.* Columbia University Oral History Collection. Columbia University N.Y., 1975.

———. *The Roosevelt I Knew.* New York: Viking Press, 1946.

Rescher, Nicholas. *Distributive Justice, A Constructive Critique of the Utilitarian Theory of Distribution.* Indianapolis: Bobbs-Merrill Co., 1966.

Richberg, Donald R. *My Hero.* New York: G. P. Putnam's Sons, 1954.

Riesenfeld, Stefan A., and Richard C. Maxwell. *Modern Social Legislation.* Brooklyn: Foundation Press, 1950.

Rohlfing, Charles C., Edward W. Carter, Bradford W. West, and John G. Hervey. *Business and Government.* Chicago: Foundation Press, 1941.

Romasco, Albert U. *The Politics of Recovery, Roosevelt's New Deal*. New York: Oxford University Press, 1983.

———. *The Poverty of Abundance*. New York: Oxford University Press, 1965.

Roos, Charles F. *NRA Economic Planning*. New York: DeCapo Press, 1971.

Roosevelt, Elliott, ed. *F.D.R.: His Personal Letters, 1928–1945*. vol. 3. New York: Duell, Sloan and Pearce, 1950.

Roosevelt, Franklin D. *Looking Forward*. New York: John Day Co., 1933.

Roper, Elmo. *You and Your Leaders*. New York: William Morrow & Co., 1957.

Rosenman, Samuel I., ed. *The Public Papers and Addresses of Franklin D. Roosevelt*. vol. 1, *The Genesis of the New Deal, 1928–1932*. New York: Random House, 1938.

———. Vol. 2, *The Year of Crisis, 1933*.

———. Vol. 3, *The Advance of Recovery and Reform, 1934*.

———. Vol. 4, *The Court Disapproves, 1935*.

———. Vol. 5, *The People Approve, 1936*.

———. Vol. 6, *The Constitution Prevails, 1937*.

———. Vol. 7, *The Continuing Struggle for Liberalism, 1938*.

Rosenoff, Theodore. *Dogma, Depression, and the New Deal*. Port Washington, N.Y.: Kennikat Press, 1975.

Rosenthal, Benjamin J. *Reconstructing America Sociologically and Economically*. Chicago: Arcadia Book Co., 1919.

Ryan, John A. *A Better Economic Order*. New York: Harper & Bros., 1935.

———. *A Living Wage, Its Ethical and Economic Aspects*. New York: Arno Press, 1971.

———. *Distributive Justice*. New York: Macmillan Co., 1916.

Schlesinger, Arthur M. *The Crisis of the Old Order*. Boston: Houghton Mifflin Co., 1957.

———. *The Politics of Upheaval*. Boston: Houghton Mifflin Co., 1960.

Schwarz, Jordan S. *The Interregnum of Despair*. Urbana: University of Illinois Press, 1970.

Sells, Dorothy. *British Wage Boards, A Study in Industrial Democracy*. Washington, D.C.: Brookings Institution, 1939.

Snowden, Philip. *The Living Wage*. London: Hodder and Stoughton, 1912.

Soule, George. *Sidney Hillman, Labor Statesman*. New York: Macmillan Co., 1939.

Steinberg, Ronnie. *Wages and Hours: Labor and Reform in Twentieth-Century America*. New Brunswick, N.J.: Rutgers University Press, 1982.

Sternsher, Bernard. *Rexford Tugwell and the New Deal*. New Brunswick: Rutgers University Press, 1964.

———, ed. *The New Deal, Doctrines and Democracy*. Boston: Allyn & Bacon, 1966.

Stokes, Thomas L. *Chip Off My Shoulder*. Princeton: Princeton University Press, 1940.

Streightoff, Frank H. *The Standard of Living Among the Industrial People of America*. Boston: Houghton Mifflin Co., 1911.

Swisher, Carl B., ed. *Selected Papers of Homer Cummings*. New York: Charles Scribner's Sons, 1939.

Taft, Philip. *The A.F. of L., From the Death of Gompers to the Merger*. New York: Harper and Bros., 1959.

Trattner, Walter I. *Crusade for the Children, A History of the National Child Labor Committee and Child Labor Reform in America*. Chicago: Quadrangle Books, 1970.

Tugwell, Rexford G. *In Search of Roosevelt*. Cambridge, Mass.: Harvard University Press, 1972.

————. *The Brain Trust*. New York: Viking Press, 1968.

————. *The Democratic Roosevelt*. Garden City, N.Y., Doubleday & Co., 1957.

United Mine Workers of America. *Proceedings of the Thirty-Fifth Constitutional Convention of the United Mine Workers of America, 1938*. Washington, D.C., 1938.

Voorhis, Jerry. *Confessions of a Congressman*. Garden City, N.Y.: Doubleday & Co., 1948.

Ware, Susan. *Beyond Suffrage: Women in the New Deal*. Cambridge, Mass.: Harvard University Press, 1981.

Welch, Finis. *Minimum Wages: Issues and Evidence*. Washington, D.C., Enterprise Institute, 1987.

Wilcox, Clair et al. *America's Recovery Program*. Freeport, N.Y.: Books for Libraries Press, 1970.

Wolfskill, George. *The Revolt of the Conservatives*. Boston: Houghton Mifflin Co., 1962.

Woll, Matthew. *Labor, Industry and Government*. New York: Appleton-Century Co., 1935.

Woytinsky, W. S. and associates. *Employment and Wages in the United States*. New York: Twentieth Century Fund, 1953.

Youtsler, James S. *Labor's Wage Policies in the Twentieth Century*. Saratoga Springs, N.Y.: Twayne Publishers, Skidmore College, 1956.

Zucker, Norman L. *George W. Norris*. Urbana: University of Illinois Press, 1966.

ARTICLES

Achinstein, Asher. "Can Budget and Cost of Living Studies Be Used as Aids in Determining a Differential Wage?" *Journal of the American Statistical Association*, 24 (March 1929).

Altman, O. R. "First Session of the Seventy-Fifth Congress, January 5, 1937, to August 21, 1937." *American Political Science Review*, 31 (December 1937).

————. "Second and Third Sessions of the Seventh-Fifth Congress, 1937–38." *American Political Science Review* 32 (December 1938).

————. "Second Session of the Seventh-Fourth Congress, January 3, 1936, to June 20, 1936." *American Political Science Review* 30 (December 1936).

"American Industry and the Five-Day Week." *Congressional Digest* 11, no. 10. (1932).

Andrews, Elmer F. "Making the Wage-Hour Law Work." *The American Labor Legislation Review*, 29 (June 1939).

————. "The Administration of the Fair Labor Standards Act in the United States." *International Labor Review* 40 (November 1939).

Andrews, Irene O. "Minimum Wage Comes Back!" *The American Labor Legislation Review* 23 (1933).

Andrews, John B. "A Southern State Pioneer in Federal Cooperation, Labor Law

Administration in North Carolina." *The American Labor Legislation Review* 30 (September 1940).

"Are the Provisions of the National Recovery Act Constitutional?" *Congressional Digest* 12 (1933).

Auerback, Jerald S. "Lawyers and Social Change in The Depression Decade." In John Braeman, Robert Bremner, and David Brody. eds. *The New Deal, I. The National Level.* Columbus, Ohio State University Press, 1975.

———. "The Influence of the New Deal." *Current History*, 48 (June 1965).

Bari, Valeska. "From Minimum Wage to Mass Production." *Yale Review* 16 (October 1926).

Barrett, Harrison J. "Is there a National Police Power; If So, What Is Its Relation to the Recent Federal Statutes Affecting Industry and Trade Generally, Particularly the 'National Industrial Recovery Act'?" *Boston University Law Review,* 14 (April 1934).

Barron, Paul R. "Constitutional Law-Commerce Clause-Constitutionality of the Fair Labor Standards Act." *Boston University Law Review* 21 (April 1941).

Beard, Charles A., ed. "A 'Five Year Plan' for America." *America Faces the Future.* Boston: Houghton Mifflin Co., 1932.

———. "Rendezvous With the Supreme Court." *New Republic* 88 (September 1936).

Berry, George L. "Voluntary Codes." *American Federationist* 42 (November 1935).

Beyer, Clara M. "Wage-Hour Inspection, A Federal Program." *The American Labor Legislation Review* 31 (June 1941).

Black, Andrew K. "Wages and Hour Laws in the Courts." *University of Pittsburgh Law Review* 5 (May 1939).

Borah, William E. "Our Supreme Judicial Tribunal." *Vital Speeches* 3 (February 1937).

Brandeis, Elizabeth. "Organized Labor and Protective Labor Legislation." In Milton Derber and Edwin Young, eds. *Labor and the New Deal.* Madison: University of Wisconsin Press, 1957.

Brooks, Evelyn C., and Lee M. Brooks. "A Decade of 'Planning' Literature." *Social Forces* 12 (March 1934).

Browder, Olin L. "Constitutional Law-Due Process Clause-Validity of Washington Minimum Wage Law." *Illinois Bar Journal* 25 (April 1937).

Brown, Douglas V. "Helping Labor." In Douglass V. Brown et al., eds. *The Economics of the Recovery Program.* New York: McGraw-Hill Book Co., 1934.

Brozen, Yale. "The Effect of Statutory Minimum Wage Increases on Teen-Age Employment." *Journal of Law and Economics* 12 (April 1969).

Burns, A. E. and P. Kerr. "Survey of Work Relief Wage Policies." *American Economic Review,* 27 (December 1937).

Caplin, M. M. "The Fair Labor Standards Act: Evils and Burdens in Interstate Commerce." *Virginia Law Review* 15 (January 1939).

Carver, T. N. "The Theory of the Shortened Working Week." *American Economic Review* 26 (September 1936).

Cates, Dudley. "A Current Appraisal of the National Recovery Administration." *Annals of the American Academy of Political and Social Science* 172 (March 1934).

Chamberlin, Edward. "Purchasing Power." In Douglas V. Brown et al. *The Economics of the Recovery Program.* New York, McGraw-Hill Co., 1934.

Cheadle, J. Kennard. "The Parrish Case: Minimum Wages for Women and, Perhaps, for Men." *University of Cincinnati Law Review* 11 (May 1937).

Cheyney, Alice S. "The Course of Minimum Wage Legislation in the United States." *International Labor Review* 38 (July 1938).

Cohen, Benjamin V. "Constitutional Aspects of the New Standard Minimum Wage Bill." *Proceedings of the National Conference of Social Work, 1933.* Chicago: University of Chicago Press, 1933.

Commons, John R. "Wage Theories and Wage Practices." *American Economic Review, Proceedings* 13 (1923).

Cook, Virginia G. "State Cooperation in Enforcement of the Federal Wage-Hour Law." *American Political Science Review* 48 (September 1954).

Cooper, Frank E. "The Coverage of the Fair Labor Standards Act and Other Problems in Its Interpretation." *Law and Contemporary Problems* 6 (summer 1939).

Corwin, Edward S. "Social Planning Under the Constitution." In Alpheus T. Mason and Gerald Garvey, eds. *American Constitutional History, Essays by Edward S. Corwin.* New York: Harper & Row, Publishers, 1964.

————. "The Schechter Case-Landmark Or What?" *New York University Law Quarterly Review* 13 (January 1936).

Cushman, Robert E. "Constitutional Law in 1934–1935." *American Political Science Review* 30 (February 1936).

————. "Constitutional Law in 1936–37." *American Political Science Review* 32 (April 1938).

Daugherty, Carroll R. "The Economic Coverage of the Fair Labor Standards Act: A Statistical Study." *Law and Contemporary Problems* 6 (summer 1939).

————. "Wage Policies." *American Economic Review,* 28 (March 1938).

Derber, Milton. "Wage and Hour Policies in Historical Perspective." *Current History* 36 (June 1959).

Despres, Leon. "Wage and Hour Act." *The John Marshall Law Quarterly* 4 (December 1938).

de Vyver, Frank T. "Regulation of Wages and Hours Prior to 1938." *Law and Contemporary Problems* 6 (summer 1939).

Dickinson, Frank G. "Public Construction and Cyclical Unemployment." *Annals of the American Academy of Political and Social Science* 139 (September 1928).

Dickinson, Z. Clark. "The Organization and Functioning of Industry Committees Under the Fair Labor Standards Act." *Law and Contemporary Problems* 6 (Summer 1939).

Dodd, E. Merrick. "From Maximum Wages to Minimum Wages: Six Centuries of Regulation of Employment Contracts." *Columbia Law Review* 43 (1943).

Douglas, Paul H. "Are There Laws of Production?" *American Economic Review* 38, no. 1 (March 1948).

————. "Factors in Wage Determination–Discussion." *American Economic Review,* 13 (1923).

————. "The Economic Theory of Wage Regulation." *University of Chicago Law Review* 5 (February 1938).

————, and Joseph Hackman. "Fair Labor Standards Act of 1938." *Political Science Quarterly,* 53 (December 1938), and 54 (March 1939).

"Economic Statistics, What Is a Living Wage?" *American Federationist* 37 (May 1930).

Edelman, Murray. "New Deal Sensitivity to Labor Interests." In Milton Derber and Edwin Young eds. *Labor and The New Deal*. Madison: University of Wisconsin Press, 1957.

Epstein, Abraham. "Have American Wages Permitted an American Standard of Living?" *Annals of the American Academy of Political and Social Science*, 97 (September 1921).

Epstein, Henry. "The 'Fair Labor Standards Act of 1938'." *American Bar Association Journal* 14 (December 1938).

Featherston, C. Moxley. "The Commerce Clause and the Fair Labor Standards Act." *George Washington Law Review* 8 (November 1939).

Felt, Jeremy P. "The Child Labor Provisions of the Fair Labor Standards Act." *Labor History* 11, no. 4 (fall 1970).

Fine, Sidney. "Government and Labor Relations During the New Deal." *Current History* 37 (September 1959).

Forsythe, John. "Legislative History of the Fair Labor Standards Act." *Law and Contemporary Problems* 6 (summer 1939).

Frankfurter, Felix, and Henry M. Hart. "The Business of the Supreme Court at October Term, 1934." *Harvard Law Review* 99 (November 1935).

————, and Adrian S. Fisher. "The Business of the Supreme Court at the October Terms, 1935 and 1936." *Harvard Law Review* 51 (February 1938).

Fraser, Steven. "Dress Rehearsal for the New Deal: Shop Floor Insurgents, Political Elites, and Industrial Democracy in the Amalgamated Clothing Workers." In Michael H. Frish and Daniel J. Walkowitz, eds. *Working Class America: Labor, Community, and American Society*. Urbana, University of Illinois Press, 1983.

"FTC Ready to Go." *Business Week* (July 13, 1935).

Gompers, Samuel. "Labor, Its Grievances, Protests, and Demands." *American Federationist* 27 (January 1920).

Gramlich, Edward M. "Impact of Minimum Wages on Other Wages, Employment, and Family Incomes." *Brookings Papers on Economic Activity, 1976*, no. 2. Washington, D.C.: Brookings Institution, 1976.

Grantham, Dewey W. "Government and Labor Before the New Deal." *Current History* 37 (September 1959).

Green, William. "Cut Hours and Maintain Wages." *American Federationist* 43 (May 1936).

————. "Fair Labor Standards." *American Federationist*. 44 (July 1937)

————. "Five-Day Week." *American Federationist* 39 (August 1932).

————. "Is It Stalemate?" *American Federationist* 43 (July 1936).

————. "Minimum Wages." *American Federationist* 43 (April 1936).

————. "Six-Hour Day." *American Federationist* 39 (July 1932).

————. "30-Hours." *American Federationist* 42 (January 1935).

————. "Thirty-Hour Week." *American Federationist* 45 (November 1938).

————. "Wages and Hours Act." *American Federationist* 45 (July 1938).

————. "Wages and Hours Law." *American Federationist* 45 (August 1938).

————. "What Labor Wants." *American Federationist* 42 (March 1935).

————. "Why Eight Hours?" *American Federationist* 39 (December 1932).

Grunfel, Judith. "Regulation of Child Labor." In W. S. Woytinsky and associates, eds. *Employment and Wages in the United States.* New York: Twentieth Century Fund, 1953.

———. "Regulation of Women's Work." In W. S. Woytinsky and associates, eds. *Employment and Wages in the United States.* New York: Twentieth Century Fund, 1953.

Hart, Vivian. "Minimum Wage Policy and Constitutional Inequality: The Paradox of the Fair Labor Standards Act of 1938." *Journal of Policy History* 1 (1989).

Hartley, Fred A. "Wages and Hours," radio address, December 3, 1937. *Vital Speeches,* vol. 4 (1938).

Hawley, Ellis W. "The Discovery and Study of 'Corporate Liberalism'." *Business History Review* 52 (autumn 1978).

"Helpless in No Man's Land." *Christian Century* 53 (June 1936).

Herman, Samuel. "The Administration and Enforcement of the Fair Labor Standards Act." *Law and Contemporary Problems* 6 (summer 1939).

Herring, E. Pendleton. "Second Session of the Seventy-Second Congress." *The American Political Science Review* 27 (June 1933).

Hester, John W. "How the Supreme Court Has Dealt With the 'New Deal'," *Congressional Digest* 14 (1935).

Hillman, Sidney. "A Shorter Working Day and a Minimum Wage." *Harvard Business Review.* 11 (July 1933).

———. "The NRA, Labor, and Recovery." *Annals of the American Academy of Political and Social Science* 172 (March 1934).

"Interstate Commerce-Federal Regulation of Tobacco Marketing Held Constitutional." *Harvard Law Review* 52 (June 1939).

Johnson, Ethel M. "Minimum Wage Legislation." *American Federationist* 43 (July 1936).

Johnson, James P. "Drafting the NRA Code of Fair Competition for the Bituminous Coal Industry." *Journal of American History* 53 (December 1966).

Johnston, Alva. "White House Tommy." *Saturday Evening Post* 210 (July 31, 1937).

Kaufman, Jacob J., and Terry G. Foran. "The Minimum Wage and Poverty." In Sar A. Levitan, Wilbur J. Cohen, and Robert J. Lampman, eds. *Towards Freedom From Want.* Madison, Wis.: Industrial Relations Research Association, 1968.

Kelley, Florence. "Thirty Years of the Consumers' League." *Survey* 68 (November 1929).

King, Allen G. "Minimum Wages and the Secondary Labor Market." *Southern Economic Journal* 41 (October 1974).

Kittredge, Dorothea D. "Determining a Living Wage." In Thomas D. Eliot, ed. *American Standards and Planes of Living.* Boston: Ginn & Co., 1931.

Kolehmainen, John I., and John C. Shinn. "Labor and Public Representation on Industry Committees," *The American Labor Legislation Review* 31 (December 1941).

"Labor's Ultimatum to Industry." *Literary Digest* 114 (December 10, 1932).

Lauck, W. Jett. "Coal Labor Legislation: A Case." *Annals of the American Academy of Political and Social Science.* 184 (March 1936).

Levy, Irving J. "A Year of Wage-Hours Litigation." *The Law Society Journal* 8 (November 1939).

Lewis, John L. "Labor and the National Recovery Administration." *Annals of the American Academy of Political and Social Science* 172 (March 1934).

Lewisohn, Samuel A. "Factors in Wage Determination-Discussion." *American Economic Review* 13 (1923).

Lively, Robert A. "The South and Freight Rates: Political Settlement of an Economic Argument." *The Journal of Southern History* 14, no. 3 (August 1948).

Lorwin, Lewis L. "A Federal Economic Council." *New Republic* 66 (April 19, 1931).

Lucey, Robert E. "Industrial Life: Gains and Losses." *Proceedings of the National Conference of Social Work, 1929.* Chicago: University of Chicago Press, 1930.

Lumpkin, Katharine D. "The Child Labor Provisions of the Fair Labor Standards Act." *Law and Contemporary Problems* 6 (summer 1939).

Madison, Charles. "Boss of the 'Fighting Carpenters', William L. Hutcheson." *American Scholar* 18 (spring 1949).

Magruder, Calvert. "Administrative Procedures Under the Fair Labor Standards Act." *American Bar Association Journal* 25 (August 1939).

Mason, Lucy Randolph. "Progress and Administration of Minimum Wage Laws in 1933." *Proceedings of the National Conference of Social Work, 1933.* Chicago: University of Chicago Press, 1933.

McCabe, David A. "The American Federation of Labor and the NIRA." *Annals of the American Academy of Political and Social Science* 179 (May 1935).

Miller, Arthur S. "An Affirmative Thrust to Due Process of Law?" In Arthur S. Miller, ed. *Social Change and Fundamental Law. America's Evolving Constitution.* Westport, Conn.: Greenwood Press, 1979.

———. "Technology, Social Change, and the Constitution." In Arthur S. Miller, ed. *Social Change and Fundamental Law, America's Evolving Constitution.* Westport, Conn. Greenwood Press, 1979.

———. "Toward a Concept of Constitutional Duty." In Arthur S. Miller, ed. *Social Change and Fundamental Law, America's Evolving Constitution.* Westport, Conn., Greenwood Press, 1979.

Mitchell, Wesley C. "The Economic Basis for Social Progress." *Proceedings of the National Conference of Social Work, 1930.* Chicago: University of Chicago Press, 1931.

Moore, John R. "Senator Josiah W. Bailey and the 'Conservative Manifesto' of 1937." *Journal of Southern History* 31 (February 1965).

Moulton, Harold G. "In Defense of the Longer Work Week." *Annals of the American Academy of Political and Social Science,* 184 (March 1936).

Mund, Vernon A. "Prosperity Reserves of Public Works." *Annals of the American Academy of Political and Social Science* 149, part 2 (May 1930).

Murphy, Walter D. "The Fair Labor Standards Act of 1938." *Georgetown Law Journal* 27 (February 1939).

Murtha, Donald. "Wage-Hour and Child Labor Legislation in the Roosevelt Administration." *Lawyers Guild Review* 5, no. 3 (May-June 1945).

Myer, J. E. "The Present Economic Situation and the 5-Day Week." *American Federationist* 39 (November 1932).

Nash, Gerald D. "Franklin D. Roosevelt and Labor: The World War I Origins of Early New Deal Policy." *Labor History* 1 (winter 1960).

Nathan, Otto. "Favorable Economic Implications of the Fair Labor Standards Act." *Law and Contemporary Problems* 6 (summer 1939).

"National Minimum for Labor." *New Republic* 93 (December 1, 1937).

"Necks In: Irishman and Jew Keep Quiet Behind Today's Rooseveltian Brain Trust." *Literary Digest* 123 (May 22, 1937).

"New Jersey and the Ribnik Case." *The American Labor Legislation Review* 17 (September 1928).

Norton, Mary. "Wage and Hour Legislation, The Object of the Law." *Vital Speeches* 4 (June 1938).

November, Harold. "Enforcement of the Wage and Hour Law." *American Federationist* 47 (February 1940).

———. "Industry Committees Under the Fair Labor Standards Act." *American Federationist* 47 (March 1940).

"NRA in No Man's Land." *Business Week* (November 23, 1935).

Ogburn, William F. "The Standard-of-Living Factor in Wages." *American Economic Review, Proceedings* 13 (1923).

Patterson, James T. "Mary Dewson and the American Minimum Wage Movement." *Labor History* 5 (spring 1964).

———. "The Failure of Party Realignment in the South, 1937–1939." *Journal of Politics* 27 (August 1965).

———. "The New Deal and the States," *American Historical Review.* 73, no. 1 (October 1967).

Paulsen, George E. "Ghost of the NRA: Drafting National Wage and Hour Legislation in 1937." *Social Science Quarterly* 67, no. 2 (June 1986).

———. "The Federal Trade Commission versus the National Recovery Administration: Fair Trade Practices and Voluntary Codes, 1935." *Social Science Quarterly* 70, no. 1 (March 1989).

Pegues, William T., and Benjamin B. Taylor. "The Wage and Hour Law in the Supreme Court." *Louisiana Law Review* 3 (March 1941).

Peterson, John M. "Employment Effects of Minimum Wages, 1938–1950." *Journal of Political Economy* 65 (October 1957).

Phelps, Orme W. "The Legislative Background of the Fair Labor Standards Act." *Journal of Business* 12 (April 1939).

Plesur, Milton. "The Republican Congressional Comeback of 1938." *Review of Politics* 24 (October 1962).

Polenburg, Richard. "The National Committee to Uphold Constitutional Government, 1937–1941." *Journal of American History* 52 (December 1965).

Poole, Rufus G. "Relationship of State and Federal Wage and Hour Legislation." *American Labor Legislation Review* 31 (March 1941).

Powell, Thomas Reed. "Commerce, Pensions, and Codes, II." *Harvard Law Review* 49, no. 2 (December 1935).

Radosh, Ronald. "The Corporate Ideology of American Labor Leaders From Gompers to Hillman." *Studies on the Left* 6 (November-December 1966).

Rankin, J. Lee. "Federal Wages and Hours Act." *Nebraska Law Bulletin* 18 (December 1939).

Reynolds, Lloyd G. "Cutthroat Competition." *American Economic Review* 30, no. 4 no. 4 (December 1940).

Rollins, Alfred B. "Franklin Roosevelt's Introduction to Labor." *Labor History* 3 (winter 1962).

Rudolph, Frederick. "The American Liberty League, 1934–1940." *American Historical Review* 56 (October 1950).

Ryan. John A. Fr. "The Catholic Church and Social Questions." *Annals of the American Academy of Political and Social Science* 165 (January 1933).

Sargent, Noel. "Economic Hazards in the Fair Labor Standards Act." *Law and Contemporary Problems* 6 (summer 1939).

Schumpeter, Joseph A. "The American Economy in the Interwar Period, The Decade of the Twenties." *American Economic Review* 36 (May 1946).

Shefelman, S. Harold. "Fair Labor Standards Act of 1938." *Washington Law Review* 14 (January 1939).

Shishkin, Boris. "Wage-Hour Law Administration From Labor's Viewpoint." *American Labor Legislation Review* 29 (June 1939).

"Should Congress Be Empowered to Override Supreme Court Decisions?" *Congressional Digest* 14 (1935).

Slichter, Sumner H. "Should We Deflate Labor?" *New Republic* 74 (May 3, 1933).

———. "The Immediate Unemployment Problem." *Annals of the American Academy of Political and Social Science* 165 (January 1933).

Smethurst, R. S. "How the Supreme Court May View the Fair Labor Standards Act, An Opinion Holding the Act Unconstitutional." *Law and Contemporary Problems* 6 (summer 1939).

"Social Justice," *The American Labor Legislation Review* 22 (December 1932).

Soule, George H. "National Planning, The Problem of Creating a Brain for Our Economy." *New Republic* 66 (March 4, 1931).

———. "The Productivity Factor in Wage Determinations." *American Economic Review, Proceedings* 13 (1923).

———. "What Planning Might Do." *New Republic* 66 (March 11, 1931).

"State Wage and Hour Legislation." *American Federationist* 46 (January 1939).

Stern, Robert L. "How the Supreme Court May View the Fair Labor Standards Act, An Opinion Holding the Act Constitutional." *Law and Contemporary Problems* 6 (summer 1939).

———. "That Commerce Which Concerns More States than One." *Harvard Law Review* 47 (June 1934).

———. "The Commerce Clause and the National Economy, 1933–1946." *Harvard Law Review,* 59 (May 1946).

Sternsher, Bernard. "The New Deal 'Revolution'." *Social Studies* 57 (April 1966).

———. "Tugwell's Appraisal of F.D.R." *Western Political Quarterly* 15 (March 1962).

Stigler, George T. "The Economics of Minimum Wage Legislation." *American Economic Review* 36 (June 1946).

Stitt, Louise. "State Fair Labor Standards Legislation." *Law and Contemporary Problems* 6 (summer 1939).

Swenson, Rinehart J. "The Chamber of Commerce and the New Deal." *Annals of the American Academy of Political and Social Science* 179 (May 1935).

Taylor, Overton H. "Economics Versus Politics," in Douglas V. Brown, et al. eds., *The Economics of the Recovery Program.* New York: McGraw-Hill Book Co., 1934.

"The Fair Labor Standards Act." *New York University Law Quarterly* 16 (March 1939).

"The Fair Labor Standards Act of 1938." *Columbia Law Review* 39 (May 1939).

"The Federal Wages and Hours Act." *Harvard Law Review* 52 (February 1939).

"The Industrial Recovery Bill and the Antitrust Laws." *Congressional Digest* 12 (1933).

"The Question of Fixing a Minimum Wage for American Industry." *Congressional Digest* 15 (November 1936).

"The Wage and Hour Law." *American Federationist* 45 (October 1938).

"The Week." *New Republic* 83 (June 5, 1935).

Tugwell, Rexford. "The Compromising Roosevelt." *Western Political Quarterly* 6 (June 1953).

———. "The Progressive Orthodoxy of Franklin D. Roosevelt." In Bernard Sternsher, ed. *The New Deal, Doctrines and Democracy.* Boston: Allyn & Bacon, 1966.

Tyson, William S. "The Fair Labor Standards Act of 1938: A Survey and Evaluation of the First Eleven Years." *Labor Law Journal* 1 (January 1950).

"Wage and Hour Administration, Area of Production." *American Federationist* 46 (April 1939).

"Wages and Hours." *Commonweal* 29 (June 10, November 4, 1938).

"Wages, Hours, and the Constitution." *Illinois Law Review* 33 (December 1938).

"Washington Notes." *New Republic* 83 (May 22, June 5, 1935).

Webbink, Paul. "Unemployment in the United States, 1930–1940." *American Economic Review* 30, no. 1 (February 1941).

Weingast, David E. "Walter Lippmann: A Content Analysis." *Public Opinion Quarterly* 14 (summer 1950).

Weiss, Harry. "Administering 'Fair Labor Standards'." *The American Labor Legislation Review* 28 (September 1938).

———. "The Enforcement of Federal Wage and Hour Regulations." *American Federationist* 43 (September 1936).

Wikersham, Cornelius W. "The NIRA From the Employers' Viewpoint." *Harvard Law Review* 48 (April 1935).

Williams, Nathan B. "Advisory Councils to Government." *Annals of the American Academy of Political and Social Science* 147 (January 1930).

Wolfe, Allis Rosenberg. "Women, Consumerism and the National Consumers' League in the Progressive Era, 1900–1923." *Labor History* 16, no. 3 (summer 1975).

Wolman, Leo. "Accomplishments of the NRA in Labor Legislation." *American Labor Legislation Review* 25 (March 1935).

———. "Wage Rates." *American Economic Review* 28 (March 1938).

Worchester, Daisey Lee Worthington. "The Standard of Living." *Proceedings of the National Conference of Social Work, 1929.* Chicago: University of Chicago Press, 1930.

Woytinsky, W. S. "The Institutional Setting of the Labor Market." In W. S. Woytinsky et al., eds. *Employment and Wages in the United States.* New York: Twentieth Century Fund, 1953.

———. "Wage Theories." In W. S. Woytinsky et al., eds. *Employment and Wages in the United States.* New York: Twentieth Century Fund, 1953.

Wright, Esmond. "The Roosevelt Revolution of 1933–1938." *History Today* 12 (December 1962).

Wright, John A. "Fair Labor Standards Act." *John Marshall Law Quarterly* 6 (March 1941).

Yarros, Victor S. "Progress and the Supreme Court." *American Federationist* 43 (June 1936).

Zellers, John A. "Wage and Hour Legislation." *Vital Speeches* 3 (October 1937).

NEWSPAPERS

American Federation of Labor Weekly News Service. 1933–38.

CIO News. 1938.

New York Herald Tribune. 1937.

New York Times. 1931–38.

Washington Evening Star. 1937.

Washington Post. 1936.

Index

205